Equality in the City

Equality in the City

Imaginaries of the Smart Future

EDITED BY

Susan Flynn

intellect

Bristol, UK / Chicago, USA

First published in the UK in 2022 by
Intellect, The Mill, Parnall Road, Fishponds, Bristol, BS16 3JG, UK

First published in the USA in 2022 by
Intellect, The University of Chicago Press, 1427 E. 60th Street,
Chicago, IL 60637, USA

A catalogue record for this book is available from
the British Library.

Cover designer: Aleksandra Szumlas
Copy editor: Newgen
Production manager: Georgia Earl
Typesetting: Newgen

Hardback ISBN 978-1-78938-464-2
Paperback ISBN 978-1-78938-761-2
ePDF ISBN 978-1-78938-465-9
ePub ISBN 978-1-78938-466-6

To find out about all our publications, please visit
www.intellectbooks.com

There you can subscribe to our e-newsletter,
browse or download our current catalogue,
and buy any titles that are in print.

This is a peer-reviewed publication.

As a remedy to life in society I would suggest the big city. Nowadays, it is the only desert within our means.

– Albert Camus

What strange phenomena we find in a great city, all we need do is stroll about with our eyes open. Life swarms with innocent monsters.

– Charles Baudelaire

Contents

Figures

Acknowledgements

Where cities once had gatekeepers, academic territories are now often disputed, controlled and guarded. This collection is an attempt to bridge the often-disparate fields of equality and digital studies; to bring together dissenting voices, to look at the future of cities from alternative viewpoints and to celebrate different perspectives and multidisciplinarity. This would not have been possible without the encouragement of my friends and colleagues. Special thanks to Damien Raftery, Irene McCormick and Cathy Fennelly at IT Carlow, and to Emmett Cullinane at WIT, for their friendship and humour. Thanks to Richard Hayes at WIT for his insight and enthusiasm for this project. Thanks to Professor Kathleen Lynch, UCD, for generously sharing her work, time and encouragement.

Thanks, as always, to Jarek. Finally, to Alex, Jeffrey, Amy, Juliette and Tristan, thank you for inspiring me every day to try to make the world a better place.

Introduction

Susan Flynn

Equality in the city is an aspiration. Cities have never been equal, equitable or fair. Now, optimum efficiency is celebrated as progress, and reconfigurations of urban spaces are focused on the clean lines of punctual service delivery. Smart cites are controlled cities, where data is the fuel that pumps through the heart. The common denominator in smart city rhetoric is the assumption that organization, planning and programmability will provide optimum conditions for comfortable urban life. Yet some aspects of our cities and our lives within them will never be machine-readable (Mattern 2014) and there may be a growing disparity between the natural and the constructed; the vagaries and messiness versus the program-mable and measurable life in cities. Giddens's theory of social structure suggested that spaces and buildings are what people do with them – spaces themselves struc-ture social relations and practices, and therefore 'relations of power and discipline are inscribed into the apparently innocent spatiality of social life' (Soja 1989: 6). If urban life is to be smart, digital and codified, then what becomes of the varied human experiences and how can we consider their relation to power? How can this be married to digital futures?

The smart city emerges from networked urbanism, propagated by the promises of efficiency, using technologies to deliver and manage services to city dwellers; embedded sensors, drone surveillance and real-time monitoring to give us more effective transportation, waste, security and energy systems. Within this discourse, people are sources of data that are fed into algorithms; their experience of the city is muted in favour of the foregrounding of digital efficiency. Much great work on the neo-liberal ideals that underpin smart discourse has already been done (Kitchin 2014; Mattern 2017; Cardullo et al. 2018; Kitchin et al. 2018; Cardullo and Kitchin 2019). The various essays in this collection consider the promises of the smart future and provide some new discussions and provocations, moving beyond the field of human geography and urban planning to a social, personal and egalitarian approach.

By theorizing and interrogating various theoretical approaches to the promises of the smart city, we question how humans can feasibly have fair and equal access to those smart technologies that promise a better future. How can cities better support human life? What makes cities liveable in an era of growing urban inequality? While housing, service provision, health care, education and other important social needs are critical issues in imagining future cities, this collection looks more broadly at how we conceive of the city of the future and what sorts of steps can be taken to 'take back the city' in the digital future.

Smart futures and smart urbanism are situated in a paternalistic ethos rather than focused on human rights, citizenship and fair access to digital technologies that ostensibly improve human life. Such technologies are changing the places in which we live and the way we live in them. They also impact on our ideas about how and where we might live in the future. There is a reverence for what is called 'disruptive technologies' and the way in which disruption is deemed not just ok, but excellent, when it comes to how we live, work and exist in spaces. Disparate fields such as human geography, information and communications technology (ICT), engineering and social sciences have addressed many of the debates around the forms of (digitized) governance that smart cities propose. Here, we bring together scholars from across disciplines to consider ideas of active participation in the imagined smart cities of the future. The essays consider the ruptures in smart discourse, the spaces where we might envisage a more user-friendly and bottom-up version of the smart future and imagine participation in novel ways.

Equality

The aim of this book is to consider ways in which we can foreground and prioritize meaningful and impactful participation; vital in the unequal society we find ourselves in. Contemporary society, in which smart city discourses nestle, is wildly unequal, with gross inequalities of wealth, access to health care, digital skills, education and political power, as well as inequalities in people's access to and experience of respect, care and solidarity. Digital inequality, of particular importance here, has the potential to shape life chances in multiple ways. People's digital engagements and digital capital are critical to a wide range of outcomes: academic performance, employment, health services uptake and political engagement (Robinson et al. 2015). Social structures have maintained and buttressed inequalities and divisions, regularly failing to address the lived realities of huge swathes of people and thus a structural approach is critical. This collection uses an equality studies lens to assess how we might conceive of a future smart city and what fissures need to be addressed to ensure the smart future is equitable. Equality studies as a field of enquiry seeks not just to describe patterns of inequality but to also develop principles of equality, design egalitarian institutions, form egalitarian policies and devise political strategies to bring these aims to fruition (Baker et al. 2006). A fairer, more equal future smart city would involve the participation of people in the stewardship and decision-making of the service control and provision, a democratic governance that would extend throughout the gamut of social systems and foster an inclusive and dynamic ethos that will deeply affect civil liberties for the better. In the project of envisaging this, we consider here various approaches and arguments for equality in the imagined future city, putting people at the forefront of our discussions, rather than technologies. In the smart discourse, hard data, technological solutions, global and national policy and macro issues tend to dominate. Here, we include ethnographic evidence, rather than rely on the perspectives of smart technologies experts, so that the arena for meaningful social development of the smart future can develop.

The work within this collection is broadly concerned with how the urban fabric of the future could provide the capacity to live equitably, and with the potential for inclusiveness that technologies and smart design could provide. While our work here acknowledges that true social citizenship will demand large-scale intervention, and the creation of non-market forms of production and ownership, we suggest that in our social citizenship perspective, technologies could be employed to mediate, to intervene or to reconcile the promises of the smart future with real and equal participation so that all citizens have 'the right to share to the full in the social heritage and to live the life of a civilized being according to the standards prevailing in the society' (Marshall 1992: 8).

There is an assumption, often held in academia, that equality is a generic, self-explanatory term, however approaches to equality vary. What *sort* of equality do we aspire to? Equality of opportunity, where everyone has equal access to goods and services, is the main approach endorsed by state and society today. An 'equality of condition' approach goes beyond equality of opportunity and sets out to eliminate major inequalities altogether, or at least to massively reduce the current scale of inequality. It calls for members of different social groups to engage in critical dialogue from which everyone can learn, and therefore it envisages a world in which people's prospects for a good life are roughly similar. It aims for social conditions under which people would have ample prospects for caring relationships and access to forms of learning that contribute to their self-development (Baker et al. 2006). Invariably, this approach invokes a critique of neo-liberalism, which itself can be said to 'promote a strategic and reciprocal mistrust of others, due to the fear of being exploited for someone else's benefit' (Lynch and Kalaitzake

2020: 16), a concern that is rife in smart city debates. For the imagined smart city of the future, adaptability to new technologies will invariably be a concern. Within this paradigm, it is hard to imagine the technologically illiterate and the marginalized having equal access to services and supports. Neo-liberal approaches and the marketization of life itself has led to smart city agendas prioritizing corporations and the needs of the wealthy over the majority of inhabitants (Kempin Reuter 2020; Wastl-Walter et al. 2005). This collection and the case studies within it form an attempt to bridge the gap between normative and empirical enquiry, taking into account and critically addressing people's real lives, the social systems and institutions in which they live and the manner in which these operate together to form present society vis-à-vis the imagined future.

Much of the research in this collection foregrounds people and lived experiences, specific design approaches and ideas, voices and places that are more than urban spaces. As such, we move away from the alienating discourse of the smart city that houses our 'data doubles', the smart logic of abstracting human bodies from their territorial settings and separating them into a series of discrete flows (Hagerty and Ericson 2000). We take an empirical approach to living in the city and the assorted interactions, emotions and needs therein. As Giddens (1979: 207) notes, 'a setting is not just a spatial parameter, and physical environment, in which interaction occurs: it is these elements mobilized in interaction'. Cities are and have always been repositories of knowledge and experience. When Mumford wrote of the city, perhaps he rightly surmised that our present electronic mechanisms for storing and transmitting information are crude and limited compared to the complex human order of the city (Mumford 1961).

> (Mumford) would remind us that the processes of city-making are more complicated than writing parameters for rapid spatial optimization. He would inject history and happenstance. *The city is not a computer.* This seems an obvious truth, but it is being challenged now (again) by technologists (and political actors) who speak as if they could reduce urban planning to algorithms.
>
> (Mattern 2017: n.pag., original emphasis)

Deleuze (1992) foresaw the societies of control where there is no individual, only 'dividuals', masses for whom the language of control is made of codes that mark access to information. The society of control's unique machines are computers, with the passive danger of the threat of viruses, of jamming and of piracy. In this regime we are all coded figures, deformable and transformable, in a society where control is continuous. Deleuze references Felix Guattari's vision of a city where we would each be able to leave home thanks to our electronic card that raises a barrier in certain agreed hours. Now, however, Deleuze insists, what counts is not

4

the barrier but the computer that tracks us and 'effects a universal modulation'. Such considerations of surveillance, latent control and lack of autonomy haunt smart discourse and smart city planning.

Technological solutionism

In the smart city discourse, consumerism and the needs of citizens merge to form 'the market'. 'Beyond making the city a market in and of itself, the neoliberal smart city is an explicitly economic project, aiming to attract foreign direct investment, fostering innovative indigenous start-up sectors or digital hubs, and attracting mobile creative elites' (Kitchin et al. 2018: n.pag.). The privatization of city services has emerged in part due to austerity, and some of the work in this book examines the critical link between austerity, neo-liberal governmentality and the imagined smart spaces of the future. During the 2000s the smart city has gained traction

> driven by companies rapidly seeking new markets for their technologies in the wake of the global financial crash, and in part, by city administrations simultaneously seeking ways to do more with less through technical solutions given austerity cuts, and to attract investment and boost local economies. This was aided by an already well-established neoliberal political economy that promoted the marketisation and privatisation of city services.
>
> (Kitchin et al. 2018: n.pag.)

As Karvonen (2020) observes, there is palpable enthusiasm to increase our knowledge of cities through the application of big data, ubiquitous sensing, geospatial and social network analyses, algorithms, machine learning and artificial intelligence. Here, though, is a space for different approaches, for other fields and perspectives to address smart city debates, such as considerations of citizens' own notions of the future city, design for inclusivity, how the internet may facilitate or challenge belonging, how education will deal with the city of the future, the power of walking the city, the concerns of austerity and various projects that address place, space and citizenship – deeply person-centred questions. As Mattern (2014: n.pag., original emphasis) writes:

> assuming that greater populations will find themselves residing in networked, intelligent megalopolises, we need to give more serious consideration to designing urban interfaces for urban *citizens*, who have a right to know what's going on inside those black boxes – a right to engage with the operating system as more than mere reporters-of-potholes-and-power-outages.

Of course, detractors of smart technologies have often discussed smart technologies as gargantuan, eternally battling with their nemesis, civil liberty. The term 'digital' offers the illusion of information extracted from reason, of competence and fairness, just as the 'smart' moniker dares us to question the innate wisdom of these technologies. The smart city, then, is the imagined future where data is extracted and used for insurantial, predictive modelling, where patterns facilitate management and impose a system of rational control on to the chaotic reality of everyday life. The urban space, as such, would be modelled on precision. In the smart city, then, urban life would be transformed; no longer messy but programmable and subject to order (Mattern 2017). The actions and movement of people within the city space, would be codified and ordered; it would be known.

> Spaces, and the masses which pass through them, are the subject of surveillance, and both are animated and given form by remaking the city, through the addition of sensorial capacities, into a data extraction machine. Surveillance is not interested in uncovering personal secrets, but in the ability to track movements in space en masse – like soldiers and enemy combatants in a theater of war – and then to turn that collective activity into decipherable patterns.
>
> (Rogan 2020; n.pag.)

Such changes would raise multiple ethical issues such as the erosion of privacy through mass surveillance, lack of consent, lack of clarity concerning ownership, use, repurposing and privatization of data, the marketization of infrastructure and services, and differential access to services and biases in data, resulting in differential treatment, governmentality and stewardship of data. Of course some cities are already being built from the ground up in Asian and Middle Eastern countries, where Cisco, Siemens and IBM have partnered with real-estate developers and governments; these cities are projects in the making, always 'versioning' toward an ideal future model (Mattern 2017).

This collection acknowledges that knowledge silos do not and cannot attend to the questions that smart futures bring to cites and spaces. The contributors, who work across a variety of disciplines, purposefully respond to the smart imperative, to the disruptive potential of smart technologies in our cities; issues of change, design, austerity, ownership, citizenship and equality. The collection is heavily focused on methods attuned to the pull between equality and engagement in smart futures. Conversations about method are crucial in this area as empirical realities are shifting so much. We seek here to open new discussions about what a smart future could do to bridge divides, to look at governmentality in the context of (in)equality in the city. The chapters here seek to imagine a truly egalitarian city of the future and to ponder on how that might come about.

Citizens

Smart city discourses are glamorized by notions of technological urban revitalization, community well-being and active citizens. However, this rhetoric is haunted by the acknowledgement that corporate interests are imperative to smart urban governance; traditional neo-liberal top-down management. Future smart cities can thus be seen to reinscribe urban social and spatial inequalities by privileging free-market, technology-centric governance, where data is commodified and citizens consequently disempowered. Citizens' data is already widely used to drive social policy (termed 'data-driven social policy') without their knowledge, consent or involvement. As such, the so-called digital welfare state takes place out of political and social view, and escapes democratic decision-making (van Zoonan 2020).

While I mention citizens of (future) cities, I refer to the persons who do or would live within cities and urban areas. I acknowledge that the word is an often-contested term and am acutely aware of the resonances of citizenship in this unequal and often unfair world. One of the criticisms of smart cities is the framing of the city as a set of systems rather than a lived-in and living entity, layered with history, cultures and rituals. The technological solutionist approach that smart technologies offer does not allow for the vagaries of human difference and indeed many studies show that digital solutions serve to further exclude the already marginalized. For example, Eubanks (2018) has discussed the 'careless automation and datafication' in US social policy, which saw millions of people wrongly accused of fraud and consequently denied benefits. Her work concludes that data technologies have created a 'digital poorhouse' in which already marginalized and disadvantaged groups are subject to more control and surveillance than ever. Furthermore, many other studies have shown that software-based and computational forms of participation do not have the same implications on quality of life, community-building and belonging as face-to-face interactions (Lee and Kim 2011). In terms of digital communication, virtual interaction is limiting, as it establishes communication in a specific path that does not allow for flexible reactions or changing circumstances. Online interactions cannot replace face-to-face community building (Kempin Reuter 2020).

The right to the city, of which Lefebvre spoke, is a right 'to urban life, to renewed centrality, to places of encounter and exchange, to life rhythms and time uses, enabling the full and complete usage of these moments and places' (Lefebvre [1967] 1996: 179). In a very real sense, the digital future is a contested terrain. This collection seeks to claw back some of the discussions of the smart future from the realm of ICT, digital media and urban studies, and call for methodological innovations and new discourses of the digital divide. We seek here to make discussions accessible to all people; we cannot claim to enable or to be inclusive if citizens of potential smart cities are not informed, consulted or involved in smart city developments. We wish to move away from the traditional and dominant tropes of stewardship. Instead, consideration should be given to what Harvey (2008) termed 'a genuinely humanizing urbanism'. Addressing the ideals of the public good and the shared ownership or right to the city inevitably means addressing neo-liberal governmentality and the sometimes-oversimplified policy responses to changing social and physical landscapes. There is a need for more sustained enquiry using exploratory methodologies, in order to tease out the many ways in which smart futures might impact wider society, to examine the needs and wants of the general populace in terms of digital technologies and to gain a deeper understanding of spatiality. As Richardson and Bissell (2019) point out, digital skills are discretely located in particular bodies and in particular geographical locations. Going digital or going smart is not an act that is or will be open to everyone. Lefebvre (1991: 34) suggested that our rights should include

> the right to information, the rights to use of multiple services, the right of users to make known their ideas on the space and time of their activities in urban areas; it would also cover the right to the use of the center.

What possibilities remain for citizens to defy or resist the 'necessary' upskill to be part of a smart city? The compulsory drive toward digital citizenship is mired in social, cultural and material difficulties. The digital citizen is one who belongs in the smart city, thus asking the citizen to be colonized in yet another regime of power. The social construction of future smart cities therefore is spattered with controversies over the products, services and (unintended) consequences these smart technologies introduce to society. As such, smart technologies, when used for city governance, are more complex than technological, disembodied and dematerialized accounts.

Lefebvre's work was often concerned with such a 'colonization of everyday life' by the market and by the state. In his three volumes of *Critique of Everyday Life* ([1947, 1961, 1981] 2014) he maintains that everyday life is a key domain of alienation and is simultaneously the locus of developing resistance against the forces of organized capitalism and the state.

> The right to the city is like a cry and a demand. This right slowly meanders through the surprising detours of nostalgia and tourism, the return to the heart of the traditional city, and the call of existent or recently developed centralities.
>
> (Lefebvre [1967] 1996: 158)

Following Lefebvre, Harvey (2008: n.pag.) points out that

The right to the city is an active right to make the city different, to shape it more in accord with our collective needs and desires and so re-make our desires and to re-shape our architectural practices (as it were), and to define an alternative way of simply being human.

Harvey is clear that this effort will require social mobilization and collective political/social struggle and must be about conflict. Such a conflict may be a contestation of spatial administration, which seeks to erase the layers of history in any given place. We could say that the drive to smart cities is an act of what Bauman and Donskis (2013) called 'soft totalitarianism', stripping us of our most personal and intimate information, from banking to travel, education to health, as the individual is invaded by the state and deprived of privacy.

In our age of technocracy walking in the guise of democracy, liberals betray a human being every time they treat him or her just in terms of the workforce, as a statistical unit, or merely as part of a majority and 'the electorate'.

(Bauman and Donskis 2013: 76)

As Rouvroy (2012: 11) has written, algorithmic governance no longer addresses the subject as a moral agent. Instead, the individual becomes a bundle of data, needed for the production of profiles – what we term 'data behaviourism' – which is evocative of Deleuze's society of control.

Many of the chapters included here work against such a disappearance of the individual into the algorithm and into the smart city of the future. The multidimensionality of the city calls for a multidisciplinary approach, so the chapters take a variety of approaches to articulate the ways in which the algorithm cannot facilitate the nuance of history, place and the lived realities of disparate people. Though the contributors come from a variety of scholarly traditions, they are united in the goal of providing fair representations of our situated historical location. There are three sections that address three dimensions of equality in the city of the future: Section 1 considers the urban crisis that is symptomatic of the smart city's promise; Section 2 examines the design of cities and some of the mediated solutions trialled in various cities; and Section 3 offers a more humanistic approach to the spatial, and a reconsideration of terms.

Urban crisis

Chapters 1 to 4 employ various modes of theorization and challenge methodologies, investigating some of the failings of smart technology and its lack of accountability. In Chapter 1, 'Locked Down in the Neo-Liberal Smart City: A-Systemic Technologies in Crisis', Eleanor Dare analyses the failure of the neo-liberal smart city during the 2020–21 COVID-19 pandemic. Examining the COVID-19 crisis in the city of London and beyond, the chapter considers the failings of smart ideology, asking how might we formulate alternative imaginaries for technology and its relationship to wealth and resource distribution to support a lasting reimagination of cities and of 'smartness'. Dare considers the More-cambe Bay Poverty Truth Commission, the Design Justice Network, Data for Black Lives and Our Data Bodies, highlighting alternative constructions of smartness and smart subjectivity. She asks whether we can trust the smart city concept that is driven by free-market ideologies and imperatives, downgrading the value of human lives, since the optimization at the heart of the smart city concept is above all financial, premised on the laissez-faire rhetoric of free-market capitalism.

This seeming impartiality of smartness is further considered by Delfina Fantini van Ditmar in Chapter 2, 'If (Equality)', examining power asymmetry and lack of accountability in smart city rhetoric. Considering 'surveillance capitalism' and the collection of data, this chapter exposes smart incongruences and the passive acceptance of 'smartness'. Through an examination of Toronto (Google urbanism), Xinjiang ('smart' prison) and Amaravati (the concrete on halt farm), this work illustrates how 'smartness' can perpetuate or increase inequality and therefore calls for global ethical oversight.

Further considering citizens within cities, Chapter 3, 'Reading Lefebvre's Right to the City in the Age of the Internet', by Alan Reeve, utilizes a Lefebvrian lens to examine the nature of citizens in the internet age. The proliferation of the internet as a medium has transformed distinctions between public and private, between the space of representation and representational space, the symbolic and the lived. The internet may now be seen to occupy a 'third space' where private and public are brought together and public rights are privately negotiated. Considering Mouffe's view of the potential of the internet as a site of agonistic pluralism, Reeve draws parallels with Lefebvre's city as a space of 'practice'. Reeve here challenges the simplified view of the internet as a neutral medium; the despatialized nature of the web is exposed as failing to provide an exit from spatial discrimination. Reeve's discussion of the attempts to regulate the internet exposes how smart rhetoric posits the individual as a consumer and a service user, contrary to the Lefebvrian notion of the 'citaden' as a creative agent.

Following on from the Lefebvrian lens, in Chapter 4 Richard Hayes considers Harvey's notion of the right to the city in terms of the strategic development of universities in his chapter 'Universities, Equality and the Neo-Liberal City'. Exam-ining how policy and strategy have co-opted the term 'equality' in tandem with the neo-liberal drive to 'efficient' smart cities, this chapter investigates the threads that bind the concepts of the university of the future, its locale and the rights of its people, asking if as well as 'the right to the city' there is a 'right to the university city'. The university, as a landmark and an anchor, can be seen as a neo-liberal tool, implicated in the creation of 'human capital' and this chapter questions how such a tool can be further implicated in potential inequalities.

City design

Chapters 5 to 8 examine interventions (and disruptions) at the design level, considering some of the ways in which design in the city can mitigate alienation and exclusion of citizens. An ethical approach to design for future cities is explored by Eoghan Conor O'Shea in Chapter 5, 'Universal Smart City Design'. This chapter considers how design has always been a negotiation between past and present and how smart technologies can have a tangible effect on how built spaces are produced, and the consequences for end users/citizens. Critical of technocratic approaches to smart city design, this chapter offers a nuanced understanding of universal design principles.

Continuing the discussion on design, in Chapter 6, 'The Design and Public Imaginaries of Smart Street Furniture', Justine Humphry, Sophia Maalsen, Justine Gangneux, Chris Chesher et al. query the inclusivity of smart futures as they investigate the design of smart street furniture and its end users. Examining the smart kiosk and smart bench projects in Glasgow and London, this chapter considers the differences and similarities between the imaginaries and realities of smart technologies. Considering the needs of citizens and non-citizens, the authors address unequal levels of access to resources and capital, and the perceived needs and uses of smart technologies.

In Chapter 7, 'Co-Creating Place and Creativity Through Media Architecture: The InstaBooth', Glenda Caldwell considers how the need for connection to information and devices is affecting how we experience urban environments and interact with local communities. Examining a design intervention, the InstaBooth, deployed in 2015 in Queensland, Australia, Caldwell looks at the possibility of creating citizen agency. Interviews with InstaBooth users indicated that engaging with the InstaBooth provided an opportunity for reflection and learning, which in turn helped to foster better understanding of diverse perspectives and people in the community. The chapter illustrates the possibility of providing new communication channels for citizen engagement, fostering expression, openness and empowerment and facilitating the co-creation of place.

In Chapter 8, 'Narratives, Inequalities and Civic Participation: A Case for "More-Than-Technological" Approaches to Smart City Development', Carla Maria

Kayanan, Niamh Moore-Cherry and Alma Clavin investigate three site-specific incidences of disinvestment and urban regeneration projects: Smart Docklands, 'A Playful City' and 'Mapping Green Dublin'. Examining the remit and challenges of these projects in the context of the neo-liberal forces that shaped them, this chapter illustrates the exclusionary nature of smart initiatives and exposes the manner in which they can ignore the complexity of urban living. This chapter establishes the need for a broader conceptualization of the smart city that recognizes the value of multiple and diverse intelligences, privilege lived experience and place-based knowledges and that becomes comfortable with slower, more iterative and longer-run approaches to urban development in order for different imaginaries to evolve and be inscribed.

Spatial humanism

'Life stories' have a geography too; they have milieux, immediate locales, provocative emplacements that affect thought and action (Soja 1989: 14). Chapters 9 and 10 consider spatiality and offer a renegotiation of spatial disciplinary approaches, considering new modes of theorization. Citizen initiatives and participation are critical for Carl Smith, Fred Garnet and Manuel Laranja in Chapter 9, 'Building Participatory City 2.0: Folksonomy, Taxonomy, Hyperhumanism'. Here the authors acknowledge some of the many authors who suggest that the twentieth-century city was shaped by the rise of popular culture and its impact on identity, social behaviour and neighbourhood developments. The authors have worked on a number of projects where citizen initiatives have created original ways of thinking about and designing for the city. Such participatory behaviours offer an alternative 'playbook' of new popular culture, which the authors here term a 'Folksonomy of the Participatory City'. The authors argue for an alternative taxonomy for the emerging networked city that arises from citizen behaviours rather than smart city protocols. Finally, this chapter argues for a values-based approach to 'rights to the city' based on hyperhumanism, a design approach that enables the human to emerge from developing technology platforms.

Finally, placing humanism as a possible intervention into 'smart' rhetoric, in Chapter 10, 'Psychogeography: Reimagining and Re-Enchanting the Smart City', Adrian Sledmere gives a psychogeographic account of 'his' London. Acknowledging the assumptions and imperatives upon which our ideas of the modern city are based, Sledmere argues for an alternative geography, suggesting that psychogeography can be used to critique the smart city and the philosophical assumptions that underpin it. Offering a reimagining of what a city might look like, Sledmere offers a personalized version of one particular locale: Burgess Park in London. Such an approach may be an act of resistance in the smart future, working against the power structures of future cities. This chapter explores how our relationship with the space in which we live is contingent, organic and mutually constitutive, in ways that are neither recognized nor valued by smart discourses.

In the afterword, Rob Kitchin acknowledges that in the smart city discourse, citizens are often cast as consumers, data points, or subjects to be steered or controlled. The chapters in this book critique this imagined future, seeking instead to imagine alternatives, radical ideas that might intervene in more humanistic ways. Together, the authors in this collection provocate for an alternative future, one which is centred on fairness, equity and inclusion.

REFERENCES

Baker, J., Lynch, K., Cantillon, S. and Walsh, J. (2006), 'Equality: Putting the theory into action', *Res Publica*, 12, pp. 411–33.

Bauman, Z. and Donskis, L. (2013), *Moral Blindness: The Loss of Sensitivity in Liquid Modernity*, Cambridge, UK: Polity.

Cardullo, P. and Kitchin, R. (2019), 'Being a "citizen" in the smart city: Up and down the scaffold of smart citizen participation in Dublin, Ireland', GeoJournal, 84: 1, pp. 1–13.

Cardullo, P., Kitchin, R. and Di Feliciantonio, C. (2018), 'Living labs, vacancy, and gentrification', Cities, 73, pp. 44–50.

Deleuze, G. (1992), 'Postscript on the societies of control', *October*, 59, pp. 3–7.

Eubanks, V. (2018), *Automating Inequality: How High-Tech Tools Profile, Police, and Punish the Poor*, New York: St Martin's Press.

Giddens, A. (1979), *Central Problems in Social Theory*, Berkeley: University of California Press.

Hagerty, K. D. and Ericson, R. V. (2000), 'The surveillant assemblage', *British Journal of Sociology*, 51:4, pp. 605–22

Harvey, D. (2008), 'The right to the city', *New Left Review*, 53, n.pag.

Karvonen, A. (2020), 'Urban techno-politics: Knowing, governing, and imagining the city', *Science as Culture*, 29:3, pp. 417–24. https://doi.org/10.1080/09505431.2020.1766011. Accessed 1 June 2020.

Kempin Reuter, T. (2020), 'Smart city visions and human rights: Do they go Together?' *Carr Center Discussion Paper Series: Understanding the Impact of Technology on Urban Life, 2020(006)*. Cambridge, MA: Carr Center, Harvard University, https://carrcenter.hks.harvard.edu/publications/smart-city-visions-and-human-rights-do-they-go-together. Accessed 7 December 2020.

Kitchin, R. (2014), 'The real-time city? Big data and smart urbanism', Geojournal, 79, pp. 1–14.

Kitchin, R., Cardullo, P. and Di Feliciantonio, C. (2018), 'Citizenship, justice and the right to the smart city', *Programmable City Working Paper 41*, Maynooth: Maynooth University, http://progcity.maynoothuniversity.ie/. Accessed 7 December 2020.

Lee, S. J. and Kim, Y. (2011), *Community Wellbeing and Community Development*, Cham: Springer.

Lefebvre, H. (1991), 'Les illusions de la modernite', in I. Ramoney, J. Decornoy and C. Brie (eds), *La ville partout et partout en crise, Manière de voir, no. 13*, Paris: Le Monde diplomatique.

Lefebvre, H. ([1967] 1996), *Writings on Cities* (trans. E. Kofman and E. Lebas), Oxford: Wiley-Blackwell.

Lefebvre, H. ([1947, 1961, 1981] 2014), *Critique of Everyday Life*, vols I–III (trans. J. Moore and G. Elliott, preface M. Trebitsch), London: Verso.

Lynch, K. and Kalaitzake, M. (2020), 'Affective and calculative solidarity: The impact of individualism and neoliberal capitalism', *European Journal of Social Theory*, 23:2, pp. 238–57. https://doi.org/10.1177/1368431018786379. Accessed 10 January 2021.

Marshall, T. H. (1992), *Citizenship and Social Class*, London: Pluto Press.

Mattern, S. (2014), 'Interfacing urban intelligence', *Places Journal*, https://placesjournal.org/article/interfacing-urban-intelligence/. Accessed 7 December 2020.

Mattern, S. (2017), 'A city is not a computer', *Places Journal*, https://placesjournal.org/article/a-city-is-not-a-computer/. Accessed 7 December 2020.

Mumford, L. (1961), *The City in History: Its Origins, Its Transformations, and Its Prospects*, New York: Harcourt.

Richardson, L. and Bissell, J. (2019), 'Geographies of digital skill', *Geoforum*, 99, pp. 278–86.

Robinson, L., Cotten, S. R., Ono, H., Quan-Haase, A., Mesch, G., Chen, W., Schulz, J., Hale, T. M. and Stern, M. J. (2015), 'Digital inequalities and why they matter', *Information, Communication & Society*, 18:5, pp. 569–82.

Rogan, K. (2020), 'Digital contact tracing is the new "smart" frontier of urban surveillance', Failed Architecture, https://failedarchitecture.com/digital-contact-tracing-is-the-new-smart-frontier-of-urban-surveillance/. Accessed 7 December 2020.

Rouvroy, A. (2012), 'The end(s) of critique: Data-behaviourism vs. due process', in M. Hildebrandt and E. De Vries (eds), *Privacy, Due Process and the Computational Turn: Philosophers of Law Meet Philosophers of Technology*, London: Routledge, pp. 143–68.

Soja, E. W. (1989), *Postmodern Geographies*, London: Verso.

van Zoonan, L. (2020), 'Data governance and citizen participation in the digital welfare state', *Data & Policy*, 2, p. e10. https://doi.org/10.1017/dap.2020.10. Accessed 30 October 2020.

Wastl-Walter, D., Staeheli, L. and Dowler, L. (eds) (2005), *Rights to the City*, vol. 3, Home of Geography Publication Series, Rome: Società Geografica Italiana.

SECTION 1

URBAN CRISIS

1

Locked Down in the Neo-Liberal Smart City
A-Systemic Technologies in Crisis

Eleanor Dare, University of Cambridge

Pre the start of the COVID-19 pandemic in 2020, the intended premise of this chapter was that it would analyse the relationship between the overdetermination of virtual reality (VR) and neo-liberal smart city rhetoric, outlining the limitations and potential of these spatial ideologies and their supporting epistemic foundations; in particular, critiquing the entrepreneurial solutionism enmeshed with technocratic rationality, namely the abstracted information-processing paradigms of both a priori and machine-learnt modelling, which are present in both the overdetermination of VR technology and the neo-liberal smart city. These paradigms are irreconcilable with equality or social justice, they are entangled with a narrow, normative, a-systemic, uncritically entrepreneurial construct of subjectivity and agency. The COVID-19 pandemic has made the connection between information-processing paradigms, technological overdetermination and smart city rhetoric increasingly clear, not least, in the failure of the smart city and its mechanisms (a-systemic modelling, the internet of things, pervasive surveillance and a bedrock of entrepreneurial hackathon culture) to provide equality of access to health care and key resources within (and without) the pandemic. In light of these failings, how might we formulate alternative imaginaries for technology and its relationship to wealth and resource distribution, to support a lasting reimagination of cities and of 'smartness'? Taking the example of the Morecambe Bay Poverty Truth Commission, the Design Justice Network, Data for Black Lives and Our Data Bodies (ODB), the chapter explores both the failings of the smart city project while highlighting alternative constructions of smartness and smart subjectivity.

Introduction

This chapter was written before and during the COVID-19 pandemic of 2020. It was largely written while 'locked down' in London, between 24 March and May 2020. A lockdown or mass quarantine, in this context and at this point (late April 2020) means that the state has enforced an emergency protocol to prevent the spread of disease, in which citizens cannot leave their homes except to exercise once a day, shop for essentials or travel to seek urgent medical treatment. Universities, schools (except for key workers), non-essential shops, pubs, restaurants and other spaces have closed or moved their services and communities online. How then do the technologies and ideological constructs that form the smart city play out in the day-to-day lived experience of a pandemic and UK (and indeed worldwide) lockdown?

While it is also important to write and research significant events with a 'long view' and with the benefit of hindsight, there is an urgency to this situation that has surfaced many key aspects and failings of the smart city concept, as well as surfacing different forms of 'smartness', which this chapter will discuss. It is arguably both contrived and impossible for me to focus on anything else whilst in the midst of such a crisis, in which a-systemic technologies have largely failed to support equality of access to key resources.

This chapter analyses the failure of the neo-liberal smart city, which, under the crisis of a pandemic, has become viscerally prescient. However, as Tyler (2020: 2704) reminds us, since 2010, the austerity state has been characterized by

> the inability of increasingly large swathes of people to access the basic resources of shelter, food, heating and healthcare which they require to adequately sustain the lives of themselves, their children, and disabled and elderly relatives. What this state-crafted, government-planned and-managed programme of 'disaster capitalism' has left in its wake is an immense crisis of social reproduction.

The COVID-19 crisis is exacerbated by both austerity and the privatization of infrastructure that was tethered to it. The rise of hackathons and competitions to address the pandemic, in the midst of the crisis, as well as the escalation of virtual spatiality and an upturn in the VR hype cycle, are analysed and connected here, while alternative ideas and practices of 'smartness' are proposed. The chapter evaluates the hyperbole and abstracted framings of what constitutes a city by the likes of Intel, Cisco, IBM, Siemens, Amazon and Google, who have benefited from the privatization of services that was key to the austerity agenda. The urbanism modelled by the smart city as supported by big-tech corporations and neo-liberal states, is contrasted here with the city as it is lived, the city of AbdouMaliq Simone,

Sun Ra, Design Justice, Data for Black Lives, ODB and the Morecambe Bay Poverty Truth Commission; in other words, the city from the ground up, far from the neo-platonic idealizations of technocratic ideology. The data science that underpins the smart city can be understood

> as an echo of the neo-platonism that informed early modern science in the work of Copernicus and Galileo. That is, it resonates with a belief in a hidden mathematical order that is ontologically superior to the one available to our everyday senses.
> (McQuillan 2017: 4)

Given this 'view from nowhere', how can the redaction of situated, lived experience implicit in neo-platonic data science hope to deliver equality in the city? Furthermore, it is appropriate to question whether that was ever the intention of the smart city initiative.

Unprecedented efficiency, connectivity and social harmony?

Back in 2017, in the paper 'A City Is Not a Computer', Mattern (2017: n.pag.) wrote that if we believe in the marketing hype,

> we're on the cusp of an urban future in which embedded sensors, ubiquitous cameras and beacons, networked smartphones, and the operating systems that link them all together, will produce unprecedented efficiency, connectivity, and social harmony. We're transforming the idealized topology of the open web and internet of things into urban form.

At the time of writing in 2020, in lockdown because of the COVID-19 pandemic, millions of us are living in circumstances in which infrastructure becomes visible because it is broken (Star and Bowker 2000: 35); equality, or rather, inequality in the city, becomes, if not more important than ever before, more exposed. In lockdown, a series of systemic interdependencies, from food access, to employment conditions, health care, childcare and transport are now highly visible; likewise, wealth distribution, in terms of access to basic care and services, even to open space and sunlight, make the issue of resource and access inequality salient in more minds and bodies than ever before. Some of us with elderly parents find them making connections between the scarcity of the pandemic and their childhood memories of war-time rationing and disruption, while others, such as Roy (2020: n.pag.), point out that the impact of the pandemic on the affluent is the norm for millions of poor people, that the pandemic 'is the wreckage of a train that has been careening down the track for years'.

19

Tufecki (2020: n.pag.), has highlighted the 'inability to think about complex systems and their dynamics' as a key failing of neo-liberal policies during the COVID-19 pandemic, the failure to 'understand that complex systems defy simplistic reductionism'. The accusation that smart cities are simplistic and abstracted, or rather, idealized, is one of Greenfield's (2013) main criticisms. According to Greenfield (2013: 273), developers of smart cities 'think of the urban environment primarily as an abstract terrain for business operations'. Greenfield (2013: 281) uses the term 'pure background' to describe the abstracted way 'designers of informatic systems have historically treated the environment in which their products and services are used'. Mattern (2017: n.pag.) points out the long historical trajectory of the city as an informational site, but also highlights how 'the idea of the city as an information-processing machine has in recent years manifested as a cultural obsession with urban sites of data storage and transmission'.

There are a number of competing definitions of the smart city, ranging from Deakin and Al Waer (2011) to Caragliu et al. (2009), with varying degrees of emphasis for human and cultural factors, but as Shelton et al. (2014: 14) state, the smart city is 'a somewhat nebulous idea which seeks to apply the massive amounts of digital data collected about society as a means to rationalise the planning and management of cities'. The concept is not new. Jeremy Bentham's early nineteenth-century vision of technologically mediated colonies or 'industry houses', inspired by slavery, envisaged the 'enserfment of the entirety of England's poor in a system which would combine the panoptical prison factory with the colonial plantation system' to form what Bentham termed 'a domestic colony' (Tyler 2020: 1113). The connection to the smart city of today is evident in his plans for 'introducing a system of what he termed "identity washing" (using chemical dyes to mark the faces of inmates) as a surveillance technology for managing the pauper labour force in his proposed domestic colony of industry houses' (Tyler 2020: 1128).

Today's smart cities are essentially sites of computational and ideological optimization, premised on the idea that its locations, flows and subjects can be understood via the information-processing paradigm that underpins big data and artificial intelligence, 'as if they could reduce urban planning to algorithms' (Mattern 2017: n.pag.). The COVID-19 pandemic viscerally reveals the wilfully 'unseeing' smart city imperatives of Western, industrialized nations. 'Unseeing' (Roy 2014: 33) is Roy's term for what dominant discourse chooses to omit; for example, the systematic erasure of cast and racist determinism from Indian textbooks. Tyler (2020) uses Roy's construct of unseeing to articulate the normalization of austerity in the United Kingdom, which is systematically disavowed by a government committed to austerity, to tax breaks and privatization of the welfare state.

States and corporations that have financed smart city initiatives are, above all, free-market states, keen to deploy an array of technologies within an entrepreneurial teleology that has benefited from austerity and the decimation of the welfare state, from the privatization of services and infrastructure. Kitchin et al. (2018: 1) identify a strong relationship between the smart city and hackathons, manifest in the 'belief that urban issues are solvable through technological fixes, with hackathons leveraging the innovation capacity of a crowd of talented, technically literate citizens to practice what Morozov (2013) terms "solutionism" '. The COVID-19 pandemic, far from being a time for revaluation and reflection on the failings of technology to provide actionable insights and functioning supply chains for citizens in the United States and the United Kingdom, is instead another business or promotion opportunity, evidenced by the myriad hackathons, such as the COVID-19 global hackathon, advertised as follows:

> Facebook CEO Mark Zuckerberg said yesterday that his company, Microsoft and other tech companies, including Slack, Pinterest and Twitter, are lending their support to the COVID-19 global hackathon. The hackathon invites software engineers to build software solutions that drive social impact, with the aim of tackling some of the challenges related to the current coronavirus (COVID-19) pandemic.
> (Mott 2020: n.pag.)

The very corporations that have actively supported climate change denial lobbies (such as Google; see Cuthbertson 2019), and have been slow to act on the dissemination of neo-Nazi hate (Facebook, Google, Twitter), while also supporting Cambridge Analytica to subvert democratic processes in favour of far-right populist politics (Facebook; see Cadwalladr 2018), are at the same time positioning themselves as the providers of 'solutions' that will bring positive social impact. The expectation is that the putative 'solutions' produced via such hackathons are then 'commercialised and scaled up into marketable products and implemented through the sale/licensing to, or public-private partnerships (PPPs) with, city administrations' (Kitchin et al. 2018: 1). But smart cities, as conceived of by big-tech firms, above all, optimize individuals to 'reproduce neoliberal and entrepreneurial labour' (Kitchin et al. 2018: 1) and technocratic rationality, characterized by employment precarity and deregulation. This chimes with Irani's (2015: 3) analysis of hackathons as sites of rehearsal for 'an entrepreneurial citizenship celebrated in transnational cultures that orient toward Silicon Valley for models of social change'. But, as Irani also points out, the prototypes developed during hackathons rarely go beyond the hackathon, they are also the product of homogeneity: 'To get to the demo in five days, the people coming together had to be sufficiently similar, sufficiently flexible, and sufficiently few' (Irani 2015: 13). Which begs the question, what is the function of a smart city hackathon? Kitchin et al. (2018: 1), as well as Irani, are clear that the purpose of the hackathon is ideological:

> We argue that hackathons interpellate by attracting participants to desire and believe in entrepreneurial life and technocratic rationality to the effect of furthering the precarity of work and life and intensifying the corporatisation of cities. As such, hackathons reinforce the neoliberal underpinnings and ethos of entrepreneurial and smart urbanism.

As Irani (2015) states, while hackathons sometimes produce technologies, they always produce subjects. Costanza-Chock (2020: 138) also critiques the neo-liberal hackathon as part of 'start-up culture and a neoliberal discourse of individual technical mastery and entrepreneurial citizenship'. However, Costanza-Chock (2020: 144) cites studies that frame the first hackathon participants as

> explicitly antiauthoritarian and opposed both capitalism and authoritarian communism. They also rejected bourgeois norms, culture, values, and lifestyles. Often physically located within squats, these hackerspaces served as models for an alternative spatial organization of life because they were mixed environments for work, play, and sleep.

Such 'hacklabs' were a counter to the rise of capitalist globalization, 'in the wake of the collapse of the vague utopics of late 1960s counterculture' (Costanza-Chock 2020: 144). The subjectivity of the neo-liberal hackathon, however, is closely aligned to the humanist, a-systemic subject of the smart city. Both the neo-liberal hackathon and the neo-liberal smart city are subject generating, but the subjectivity they model is narrow and determinist, enmeshed in competition, laissez-faire free-market ideology and the neo-platonic idealizations of data scientism. This data-driven system is what D'Ignazio and Klein (2020: 2925–26) provocatively call 'big dick data': 'a formal, academic term that we, the authors, have coined to denote big data projects that are characterized by masculinist, totalizing fantasies of world domination as enacted through data capture and analysis'.

Nowhere are the ideological imperatives and contradictions of a neo-liberal business ontology (that which defines our own needs and priorities as aligned to those of business and a profit motive) more nakedly exposed then in the domain of VR, in which the rhetoric of empathy cynically coexists with profitable military rehearsal, trauma treatment for exposure to the side effects of military activity and a clear thrust towards virtual reality therapy (VRT) as a privatized replacement for in-person health care.

Virtual and algorithmic smart cities

VR is often used to visualize smart city futures and their supporting information structures. As the pandemic spreads, and the death toll rises, many VR firms are rushing to push the idea that their services are essential in the midst of a pandemic. Far from exercising ethical restraint and tentativeness, some VR firms are promoting spurious 'solutions' to an array of issues, from online schooling to conferences, tourism and entertainment (let us remember the age and time restrictions associated with VR headset use that make some of these claims absurd). What these 'solutions' reveal is the profit-at-all-costs individualism of big-tech entrepreneurism. Similarly, a rush of competitions to find pandemic 'solutions' via hackathons of a few days or weeks, does not arise from the ground up and does not engage significantly with the ground truth of complex lives, but superimposes bogus a-systemic 'solutions'. Nor do these solution-seeking hackathons embrace an examination of their own ideologies, as Irani's (2015) research clearly shows; reflexive criticality is rarely welcomed in the neo-liberal hackathon. As in the hackathon, all of us exposed to VR are subject to a form of 'smart' ideology, but they are also exposed to neo-liberal subject formation, which seeks to individualize systemic processes, often in the name of empathy (Dare 2019; Rose 2018). Examining VR hype cycles, and the phenomena of VR hackathons, smart virtual spaces must be critically connected to the notion and problematic of the smart city and the implied smart subject. The irony of VR as part of the smart city is manifest in its limitations, in which, as one study noted, a blind participant found that 'VR was not compatible with the assistive technology that person used, and that the audio information conveyed by most VR content was not enough to fill in for the visual cues that seeing users experienced' (Philips 2020: n.pag.). Furthermore, 'several explained that anything that required the use of more than one controller – as many room-scale experiences do – was out of the question because of challenges with motor skills or lack of two typically functioning hands or arms' (Philips 2020: n.pag.). This is not to imply that accessible VR or an accessible city is impossible, or that technology might not have the potential to support equality in the city; rather, the techno-determinism and control of these technologies is problematic, and likewise the model of rationality that underpins them. We cannot trust any claims to create a politically neutral digital infrastructure. There is now more than ample evidence to support a critical view of algorithmic processes, despite advances in machine learning, there is worry that an array of processes including speech-recognition systems, 'suffer from racial bias, a problem that has recently come to light in several other advancing applications of machine learning, such as face recognition, natural language processing, online advertising, and risk prediction in criminal justice, healthcare, and child services' (Koenecke et al. 2020: 1).

Error rates for African American speakers were dramatically worse, double the error rate for White Americans. The issues are well known in facial recognition systems, health care and financial systems, as all algorithmic systems are subject to systematic biases (see Caliskan et al. 2017). Constructs of transparency and building new data sets do not remove the underlying problematics of scientism and the reductionism of data science. Not least, competition 'based on mono-technology is devastating the earth's resources for the sake of competition and profit, and also prevents any player from taking different paths and directions' (Yuk Hui 2020: n.pag.).

Evidence for the failure of the smart city to deliver an adequate response to the COVID-19 pandemic within the United Kingdom and the United States is clear. Statistics currently suggest the United Kingdom has the highest death rate in Europe, that even countries with densely packed populations (such as Hong Kong and Japan) have responded more effectively and have significantly lower death rates, as well as more effective means for supplying key resources to their populations. Deaths in the United States are currently higher than any other country in the world (as of 19 April 2020), though of course, these figures are not stable or final and there are a range of different calculation methods (e.g. deaths per head of population, death per density of population or age). While statistics can always be challenged or denied, what is harder to refute are the assertions by leaders in the United Kingdom and the United States that point to an underlying ideology of profit at all costs, deeply implicated in the rhetoric of the smart city and its complex, systemic inequalities and broken infrastructures. In the words of Tufecki (2020: n.pag.): 'As it turns out, the reality-based, science-friendly communities and information sources many of us depend on also largely failed.'

Broken infrastructures

Stories of inequitable access to key services and resources during the pandemic were initially prominent in the British (and other) media, with myriad news stories, at least from late March to early April 2020, covering the hoarding of food and other supplies, such as toilet rolls and handwash, at the expense of those deemed vulnerable by the press, in particular elderly people and people with a disability. As *The Sun* and the *Daily Mail* respectively reported on 21 March 2020: 'Yesterday, an elderly woman was pictured walking through an empty supermarket after panic buyers stripped its shelves bare' (Zeltman 2020: n.pag.) and 'Hundreds of shoppers queue all around Tesco car park before 6 am waiting for it to open as police step in and supermarkets hire security guards to stop selfish stockpilers amid coronavirus panic' (Nikolic and Elsom 2020: n.pag.). Access to health care, medicine and protective clothing in Europe and America were also themes pervasive within the British press, such as the *Daily Mirror* that reported on 24 March 2020: 'Man, 74, dies after being refused coronavirus test because he "wasn't sick enough"' (Murphy 2020: n.pag.). Stories of health workers who had made homemade protection from bin bags becoming ill also made the headlines (Press 2020), as well as coverage to date at the time of writing (April 2020) of at least 26 London bus drivers who died from COVID-19 due to lack of protective measures (Brown 2020; Reynolds 2020). These news headlines and their accompanying texts imply being left out of equal access to health care and subsistence items due to poverty, ethnicity, age or disability, and is a shocking occurrence. At the same time, the failure of supermarket 'just-in-time' (JIT) algorithms or control systems (Miltenburg and Sinnamon 1992) to provide a sufficient and consistent supply of food and other key resources in a crisis reveals the entrepreneurial underpinnings of the smart city construct, one that is defined and limited by a neo-liberal business ontology that is not always (or ever) compatible with imperatives of access and equality. Indeed, personal health and economic health have been overtly framed as irreconcilable:

> As Donald Trump pushed to re-open the US economy in weeks, rather than months, the lieutenant governor of Texas went on Fox News to argue that he would rather die than see public health measures damage the US economy, and that he believed 'lots of grandparents' across the country would agree with him.
>
> (Beckett 2020: n.pag.)

These blunt assertions from free-market politicians reveal their imperatives and thus the priorities of the smart city projects that they have enthusiastically funded. Companies that bankroll the neo-liberal business agenda, we must assume, like President Trump, approach the free-market economy as more important than the lives of working people, a fact confirmed by the Amazon warehouse worker strike of late March 2020, in which workers in an Amazon Staten Island distribution facility went on strike in protest at their lack of protective clothing. They were joined by Amazon workers in Chicago and Detroit, who wanted their workplaces closed for cleaning (Marx 2020). Despite the investment in automated infrastructures for optimized manufacture and delivery, it would seem basic safety for workers is absent from the smart spaces of Amazon, a corporation that is deeply involved in the smart city agenda. Judging by the lack of provision for worker safety, however, it would seem the smart city has a very narrow set of imperatives, almost exclusively focused on optimizing profit. Amazon's 'City on a Cloud Innovation Challenge 2019' clearly did not address the basic rights of its own workers, despite the claim that Amazon Web Services (AWS) hosts 'impactful solutions that specifically address issues for constituents through justice and public safety, elections, transportation, health and human services, digital government, and K12 education' (AWS 2019: n.pag.).

In the context of raw capitalism, assertions that bring fear to many of us are apparently reassuring for those with a neo-liberal, profit-at-all-cost agenda, whether they are big-tech corporations or neo-liberal politicians. On 24 March 2020, the White House coronavirus response coordinator, Dr Deborah Birx, announced that 'the data on the spread of coronavirus in the New York City region was concerning, but data from Europe, which showed that 99% of the deaths from coronavirus were in people over 50, was reassuring' (Beckett 2020: n.pag.). This begs the question, how can we trust the smart city concept if it is driven by free-market ideologies and imperatives that downgrade the value of human lives? The optimization at the heart of the smart city concept is above all financial, premised on the laissez-faire rhetoric of free-market capitalism. Its connection to hackathon and smart city culture is overtly linked (see Kitchin et al. 2018) by the entangled ideological network that connects government-funded think tanks, innovation 'social purpose' organizations such as Nesta and initiatives such as Digital Catapult, the Knowledge Transfer Network or Immerse UK. In the case of Nesta, the relationship with laissez-faire neo-liberalism is overt: 'The Behavioural Insights Team – also known as the Nudge Unit – is now a social purpose company. It is partly owned by the Cabinet Office, employees and Nesta' (Gov.UK 2020). The relationship to neo-liberal states is also overt. Big-tech corporations that promote the smart city construct, such as Microsoft, Google, Twitter and Facebook, all have

> partisan teams, often made up of practitioners with backgrounds in Democratic and Republican politics, which work with campaigns and parties of the same political affiliation. One universally stated reason is that campaigns and party operatives are more likely to trust, and therefore work with, people who share their political ideology and identity.
>
> (Kreiss and McGregor 2018: 8)

The cynical support for both Republican and Democrat candidates (such as Bush, Romney, Trump and Clinton) reveals a flattened political landscape in which all major parties share near identically neo-liberal, free-market ideologies and a willingness to influence those in power, regardless of their track record, so that 'Trump was able to make up for his competitive staffing disadvantage against Clinton through leveraging the talent and expertise of firms such as Facebook, Twitter, and Google' (Kreiss and McGregor 2018: 14). The same politicians who see the death of the over fifties as part of 'herd immunity' align themselves with an imperative to protect the economy, and, as allegedly stated by UK prime minister Boris Johnson's chief adviser, Dominic Cummings, 'if that means some pensioners die, too bad' (Walker 2020: n.pag.). These are the same politicians who some suggest have overtly supported eugenics, as Walker writes: 'It later emerged that in his own prior writings, Cummings had suggested that the NHS should cover the cost of selecting babies to have higher IQs' (Walker 2020: n.pag.). President Trump has publicly mocked disabled people while boasting about his own genetic superiority. Activists such as Sara Ryan have observed: 'It's been extraordinary to see the speed and spread of soft eugenic practices', adding 'there are clearly systems being put in place to judge who is and isn't worthy of treatment' (Quarmby 2020: n.pag.). In relation to the COVID-19 pandemic, academic and disability rights campaigner Tom Shakespeare states that

> the Germans are doing better because they are systems-oriented. Social care and the NHS have been historically underfunded and so we have come up with what looks like Heath Robinson solutions and things and people get overlooked. We are not seen as priority, we are out of sight, out of mind.
>
> (Quarmby 2020: n.pag.)

The invisible orderings implicit in constructs of smartness and mobility are not so easy to obfuscate in the midst of a pandemic, while many of us struggle to obtain food and a significant minority face a struggle for health care. Under these conditions, the 'taken-for-grantedness of artefacts and organisational arrangements' (Star and Bowker 2000: 35) is arguably denaturalized, conventions of practice broken down and surfaced, even for those who are part of the communities of practice of which Star and Bowker (2000) identify as the very definition of infrastructure. This is not to assert that the COVID-19 crisis will lead to a linear trajectory of 'improvement' in access or disability rights, or an equitable city infrastructure for those of us considered 'elderly' or 'non-normative', quite the opposite. The UK government's Coronavirus Action Plan, published on 3 March 2020, has been critiqued by, among others, Butler and Walker (2020: n.pag.), who write:

> Emergency measures to tackle the coronavirus will put disabled and older people at risk, charities and human rights experts are warning. Campaigners say measures being introduced in the government's coronavirus bill will temporarily remove the legal duty on councils to provide social care to all who are eligible.

The powers exerted by the British state in crisis diminish equality. The charity Disability Rights UK has articulated their concerns that the bill will exacerbate an already inadequate social care system, leaving thousands of disabled people lacking essential support and rights to request support, and risking their lives.

> Rather than removing disabled people's right to social care support the government must treat our essential social care service as key infrastructure, alongside the NHS, and as such it must immediately provide the necessary funding to keep this vital service running.
>
> (Butler et al. 2020: n.pag.)

How does the smart city construct support equality as it currently stands? The reality, despite all the hype of smart city rhetoric, is that

> lack of care and support will have a significant impact on disabled people's well-being, but may not be considered to reach the threshold for their human rights to have been breached – they will NOT have a right to care and support.
>
> (Inclusion London 2020: n.pag.).

Figures so far suggest that Black, Asian and minority ethnic (BAME) people have experienced far greater loss of life in the COVID-19 pandemic (Barr and Siddique 2020). Reports also point to the burden of care placed on women around the world, who make up a majority of health care workers,

> almost 70 percent according to some estimates, and most of them occupy nursing roles – on the front lines of efforts to combat and contain outbreaks of disease. In China's Hubei Province, where the current coronavirus outbreak originated, about 90 percent of health care workers are women. In the United States, that number is around 78 percent.
>
> (Gupta 2020: n.pag.)

Women are also more likely to be carers at home as well as casual workers:

> Economically speaking, outbreaks could have a disproportionately negative impact on women, who make up a large chunk of part-time and informal workers around the world. Those kinds of jobs are also usually the first to get sliced in periods of economic uncertainty. And during outbreaks, when women have to give up work and income to stay home, they often find it harder to spring back after the crisis.
>
> (Gupta 2020: n.pag.)

A number of studies worldwide (Graham-Harrison et al. 2020) and in the United Kingdom, as well as the Metropolitan Police, have highlighted the dramatic rise in domestic violence during COVID-19 lockdowns, factors that were not, it seems, calculated into the construct of the smart city, and were not represented in the a priori models that underpin it. Gupta (2020: n.pag.) asks, 'What might be a gender-sensitive response to the coronavirus? Policies like paid sick leave and accessible, affordable health care would be a start – both of which are notably absent for many in the US', adding that governments should distribute 'protective gear and even basic needs like pads and tampons' (Gupta 2020: n.pag.).

As lockdown has progressed in the United Kingdom, the question of access to open space and exercise becomes infused with moral judgement, so that those of us with no access to a garden, who wish to have access to urban open spaces, are presumed to be risky. The discourse has shifted rapidly from that of hoarding and lack of food access for elderly and disabled people, to one of transgression and out-of-control communities. Brockwell Park, in south-east London, which is close to Brixton (historically an area with a large percentage of people of Afro-Caribbean descent), is characterized as a locus of 'undeserving recreation', leading to calls for more surveillance, 'smart' apps and compulsory monitoring of 'way-ward' individuals. Unlike the super-rich and government ministers who (with the exception of the Scottish minister who resigned for visiting a second home) can dodge the question of whether they visited their out-of-London homes at the weekends. The park was closed to the public over the Easter 2020 weekend, as a precaution against overcrowding, while ultra-rich celebrities flaunted their escape to spacious second homes on social media (Matthews and Veljanovski 2020: n.pag.).

Who gets to be monitored, ignored or protected in the smart city is always and inevitably political. The fast pace of the pandemic 'is prompting govern-ments to put in place a patchwork of digital surveillance measures in the name of their own interests, with little international coordination on how appropriate or effective they are' (Singer and Sang-Hun 2020: n.pag.). The UK press have widely covered the extent of surveillance in South Korea, particularly through phone data, but have not so closely followed the retraction from that in the wake of attacks on people who test positive for COVID-19. As other countries increase surveillance, South Korea had an unusual reaction. Concerned that privacy inva-sions might discourage citizens from getting tested for the virus, health officials announced that they would refine their data-sharing guidelines to 'minimize patient risk' (Singer and Sang-Hun 2020: n.pag.). Mattern (2017: n.pag.) asks what exactly is being optimized in the smart city? The answer, it seems, is not only our urban sites but our subjectivity. Hackathons and, as this chapter asserts, VR empathy hype, are part of the nexus of subject formulation and optimization within the smart city construct, in which the 'city as computer model likewise conditions urban design, planning, policy, and administration – even residents' everyday experience – in ways that hinder the development of healthy, just, and resilient cities' (Mattern 2017: n.pag.). Given the limitations and failings of the neo-liberal smart city project, what hope, if any, is there for the idea of data, sensors and communication networks to improve the lives and processes that unfold in cities and, furthermore, to make those cities more accessible and equitable places?

Just smart cities

Dominant smart city constructs have let us down because they are a-systemic, idealized, top down and unsituated. Bastani's (2019) futurist left luxury communism, Bentham's ([1789] 1907) felicific calculus and Aristotle's *Organon* (1933), while centred on ideals of utopian logic, are still top-down, determinist 'views from above', and, as Tyler (2020: 1151) reminds us:

> Bentham's panoptical workfare scheme has continued to cast a long shadow over welfare policy making in Britain (and further afield). Indeed, Bentham's legacy weighs heavily on the ongoing austerity enclosures of the twentieth-century welfare commons, and the rise of what Virginia Eubanks has described as 'digital poor houses', namely the development of high-tech tools to mark out, survey, profile, police and govern the poor.

What is missing from neo-liberal smart city rhetoric is the voice and agency of those with lived expertise, voiced not for purposes of neo-liberal tokenism or individualism, but to effect systemic change and systemic wealth redistribution. Tyler (2020) highlights the Poverty Truth movement, specifically the Morecambe Bay Poverty Truth Commission, in which participants who have experienced the impact of austerity as well as key workers within that location, testify about the impact of austerity on their lives, not in the interests of neo-liberal storytelling projects with individualizing de-stigma goals, but to surface that which is systematically *unseen*, with the premise that

> those with lived experiences of poverty need to have voice and agency in social and political decision making; that people in poverty are not the problem; that poverty is everybody's problem; and that effecting change begins with attitudinal change. At the core of the Poverty Truth movement is an understanding that stigmatising public beliefs about the causes of poverty are a block to social change, and that the sharing of lived experience is the first step in devising collective solutions.
>
> (Tyler 2020: 2860–66)

We might also look to ODB and the Design Justice Network, to locate constructs of smartness that are taken out of the service of extractive forms of capitalism, and instead seek to emulate Sun Ra's commitment to a visionary urban knowledge, a 'technical capacity for going into the future' (Simone 2019: 5); in Sun Ra's case to effect a Black knowledge society, a counter to dominant epistemic regimes. Likewise, ODB arises from an urgent concern with

> the ways our communities' digital information is collected, stored, and shared by government and corporations. Based in marginalized neighborhoods in Charlotte, North Carolina, Detroit, Michigan, and Los Angeles, California, we look at digital data collection and our human rights, work with local communities, community organizations, and social support networks, and show how different data systems impact re-entry, fair housing, public assistance, and community development.
>
> (ODB 2020: n.pag.)

ODB organizes community workshops and publications including the Digital Defence Playbook (Lewis et al. 2018). Likewise, Data for Black Lives (n.d.: n.pag.) identifies big data as 'part of a long and pervasive historical legacy of scientific oppression, aggressive public policy, and the most influential political and economic institution that has and continues to shape this country's economy: chattel slavery'. Data for Black Lives (n.d.: n.pag.) calls for the abolition of big data, while 'exploring alternative models of data governance'. Their policy working group brings together 'data scientists, public interest technologists, legal scholars, and people whose lives are directly impacted by technological bias to collaborate and identify approaches/risks to data governance frameworks' (Data for Black Lives n.d.: n.pag.).

The Design Justice Network (n.d.) also emphasizes the knowledge and skill of local communities, but it does not idealize their approach to socio-technological knowledge and skills, instead, it acknowledges a complexity in which

> neither subaltern design sites nor privileged design sites are utopias. Many, or most, of the power dynamics that we would like to critique and transform in the latter also often operate within the former. For example, an auto workshop may be a site for the development, expression, and sharing of socio-technological knowledge and skills between working-class men while simultaneously reproducing heteropatriarchal norms of gendered technical knowledge and skills that exclude women and femmes. Or it may be a site where those norms are challenged or transformed.
>
> (Costanza-Chock 2020: 142)

The premise of the Design Justice Network (n.d.) is to collaboratively rethink design processes, centring on people who are normally marginalized by design. Its dynamic formulation of principals from within communities runs counter to the neo-liberal technocratic logic of the smart city, providing, as the other activist groups cited here do, a useful counter to the top-down rhetoric and hyperbole of the neo-liberal smart city.

Conclusion

Moody (2020: n.pag.) reminds us that a 'pandemic travels along the circuits of capital'. Within the smart cities of the West these are sites of extractive entrepreneurship. The subjects inhabiting the smart city, as modelled by big data constructs, mirror a corporate notion of a-systemic, normative subjectivity, 'unseeing' poverty and homelessness as well as the wider impact of austerity. The subjects the smart city models are narrow and essentialized; the COVID-19 pandemic has further revealed the inadequacy of the smart city, manifest in the shock that resources are finite, that key workers are skilled, that previously invisible and still undervalued workers are essential to its function. The fact that systemic racism has led to greater death rates for BAME people and that precarity and poverty underpin the profits of an ultra-rich minority is another apparent shock to the smart city. One that it has been useless to anticipate, adapt to or mitigate, because the neo-liberal smart city is as limited as its initiators. The neo-liberal smart city is a-systemic, unsituated and idealizing, yet so often presented as democratizing and improving of all our lives. In a less cynical era, the idea of a smart city, much like self-quantification for smart health and monitors for energy efficient smart homes, might have seemed benign and credibly pro-social, but, to quote Zuboff (2019: 247), 'surveillance capitalism overwhelms the digital milieu' making 'that vision ridiculous'. With obscure privacy settings and the prevalence of platform capitalism (Uber, Amazon, Facebook, Google, etc.), few of us can hope to understand the extent to which our data is shared and commodified. Human and environmental data is passively and proactively monitored on an unimaginable scale, converged to create what Zuboff (2019: 247) has described as 'the fusion of "smart cities"; and what is now called "m-health" to produce "smart health"'. Likewise, the ideology of VR hackathons, science, technology, engineering and mathematics (STEM) and science, technology, engineering, the arts and mathematics (STEAM) learning 'agendas' (supported, of course, by digital learning platforms) have enabled a tranche of ideologies and educational imperatives to be defined and deployed as reinforcement for the urgency of corporate agendas. In this opaque milieu, what gets to count as knowledge is now almost seamlessly blurred with the needs of big business. And yet, do we, as individuals have the same needs as Google or Amazon or any of the other vast tech businesses that increasingly get to define what knowledge or 'smartness' can be? As Tufecki (2020: n.pag.) reminds us:

> We faltered because of our failure to consider risk in its full context, especially when dealing with coupled risk – when multiple things can go wrong together. We were hampered by our inability to think about second- and third-order effects and by our susceptibility to scientism – the false comfort of assuming that numbers and percentages give us a solid empirical basis. We failed to understand that complex systems defy simplistic reductionism.

The premise of this chapter is that the smart city as it currently stands, and as originally conceived, is fundamentally irreconcilable with equality and social justice. Instead, we must look to other forms of smartness, in particular activism, for forms of smartness that do not emanate from the extractive rhetoric of neo-liberal capitalism and reductive scientism. In lockdown in London reading these words evokes both anger and sadness:

> London has the ambitious goal to be the smartest city in the world by 2020. To achieve this, the mayor of London is encouraging participation from both the public and private sectors. The city is launching over 20 initiatives that will tackle urban challenges and change the face of London.
>
> (Here Mobility 2020: n.pag.)

The truth is that (at the time of writing in April 2020) London has the highest death rate in the United Kingdom for the COVID-19 pandemic and Londoners are currently dying of the virus at a rate of dozens per day (on 18 April 2020, 160 people died in London, though exact figures are currently hard to obtain and not now prominent on the BBC news site). Key workers, BAME, disabled and elderly people appear to be dying at a higher rate than wealthier White people (again, at the time of writing in April 2020 specific figures are not yet available). Emergency law has diminished care for disabled people, access to food and basic resources is extremely challenging for many people, with huge queues outside food shops and delivery services booked up weeks in advance. The impact of job losses and economic depression makes the smart city project as envisaged by a neo-liberal mindset an inadequate and cruel initiative that has neglected the reality and complexity of our lives while creating profits of unimaginable proportion for corporations such as Amazon (and its chief executive officer Jeff Bezos), but not for the workers who struggle to remain safe from the virus while working within Amazon's smart buildings.

A ground-up, anti-neo-liberal smart city, focused on the imperative of wealth distribution and social justice, may not expose itself to surveillance, reduction, essentialism or scientism of big data (the same scientism and data classification that has supported the prison industrial complex, articulated by Costanza-Chock [2020] and Tyler [2020]). A socially just smart city might even choose invisibility from data acquisition:

> Invisibility may be strategic: subaltern communities sometimes shield their practices and innovations from mainstream visibility to avoid incorporation and appropriation. In addition, innovations in many fields often operate in legal grey zones, and systematically unequal policing may expose subaltern innovators to harm from the various arms of the prison industrial complex.
>
> (Costanza-Chock 2020: 142)

Indeed, a truly smart city needs to be one in which the technologies deployed, as the Design Justice Network (n.d.) principals state, centre the voices of those who are directly impacted by the outcomes of the design process and draw upon the knowledge and skill of the community, focusing not on the imperatives of the designer or of corporations, but on community knowledge, needs and practices. Whether these needs and practices are reconcilable with the organizing ideas and abstracting reductionism of data science is the key question. Above all, whether we value our own and others' lived experience less than the technocratic 'view from nowhere' implicit in the neo-liberal smart city.

REFERENCES

Aristotle (1933), *Metaphysics* (vol. 1, bks 1–9), trans. Hugh Tredennick, Loeb Classical Library 271, Cambridge, MA: Harvard University Press.

AWS (2019), 'City on a cloud, innovation challenge', https://aws.amazon.com/stateandlocal/cityonacloud/. Accessed 17 April 2020.

Barr, C. and Siddique, H. (2020), 'Failure to publish data on BAME deaths could put more lives at risk, MPs warn', *The Guardian*, 16 April, https://www.theguardian.com/world/2020/apr/16/data-on-bame-deaths-from-covid-19-must-be-published-politicians-warn#maincontent. Accessed 17 April 2020.

Bastani, A. (2019), *Fully Automated Luxury Communism: A Manifesto*, London: Verso.

Beckett, L. (2020), 'Older people would rather die than let COVID-19 harm US economy – Texas official', *The Guardian*, 24 March, https://www.theguardian.com/world/2020/mar/24/older-people-would-rather-die-than-let-covid-19-lockdown-harm-us-economy-texas-official-dan-patrick. Accessed 20 April 2020.

Bentham, J. ([1789] 1907), *An Introduction to the Principles of Morals and Legislation*, Oxford: Clarendon Press.

Brown, F. (2020), '26 TFL workers have now died from coronavirus', *The Metro*, 15 April, https://metro.co.uk/2020/04/15/26-tfl-workers-died-testing-positive-coronavirus-12562009/. Accessed 17 April 2020.

Budds, D. (2020), 'Design in the age of pandemics', Curbed, https://www.curbed.com/2020/3/17/21178962/design-pandemics-coronavirus-quarantine. Accessed 12 April 2020.

Butler, P. and Walker, P. (2020), 'UK's emergency coronavirus bill "will put vulnerable at risk"', *The Guardian*, 23 March, https://www.theguardian.com/society/2020/mar/23/uks-emergency-coronavirus-bill-will-put-vulnerable-at-risk. Accessed 15 April 2020.

Cadwalladr, C. (2018), '"I made Steve Bannon's psychological warfare tool": Meet the data war whistleblower', *The Guardian*, 17 March, https://www.theguardian.com/news/2018/mar/17/data-war-whistleblower-christopher-wylie-faceook-nix-bannon-trump. Accessed 20 April 2020.

Caliskan, A., Bryson, J. J. and Narayanan A. (2017), 'Semantics derived automatically from language corpora contain human-like biases', *Science*, 356:6334, pp. 183–86.

Caragliu, A., Del Bo, C. and Nijkamp, P. (2009), *Smart Cities in Europe*, Serie Research Memoranda, No. 0048, Amsterdam: VU University Amsterdam.

Costanza-Chock, S. (2020), *Design Justice: Community-Led Practices to Build the Worlds We Need*, Cambridge, MA: MIT Press.

Cuthbertson, A. (2019), 'Google gave "substantial" amounts of money to climate change deniers', *The Independent*, 11 October, https://www.independent.co.uk/life-style/gadgets-and-tech/news/google-climate-change-denial-donation-contribution-a9151761.html. Accessed 20 April 2020.

Dare, E. (2019), 'Turpin's cave: Choice and deception in a virtual realm', *International Journal of Performance Arts and Digital Media*, 15:1, pp. 1–11.

Data for Black Lives (n.d.), 'Home page', http://d4bl.org. Accessed 18 April 2020.

Deakin, M. and Al Waer, H. (2011), 'From intelligent to smart cities', *Journal of Intelligent Buildings International: From Intelligent Cities to Smart Cities*, 3:3, pp. 140–52.

Design Justice Network (n.d.), 'Home page', https://designjustice.org/. Accessed 18 April 2020.

D'Ignazio, C. and Klein, L. F. (2020), *Data Feminism* (Kindle ed.), Cambridge MA: MIT Press.

Gov.UK (2020), 'Behavioural insights team', https://www.gov.uk/government/organisations/behavioural-insights-team/about. Accessed 17 April 2020.

Graham-Harrison, E., Giuffrida, A., Smith, H. and Ford, L. (2020), 'Lockdowns around the world bring rise in domestic violence', *The Guardian*, 28 March, https://www.theguardian.com/society/2020/mar/28/lockdowns-world-rise-domestic-violence. Accessed 17 April 2020.

Greenfield, A. (2013), *Against the Smart City* (Kindle ed.), New York: Do Projects.

Gupta, A. H. (2020), 'Why women may face a greater risk of catching coronavirus', *New York Times*, 12 March, https://www.nytimes.com/2020/03/12/us/women-coronavirus-greater-risk.html?auth=login-google. Accessed 17 April 2020.

Inclusion London (2020), 'Coronavirus bill could leave thousands of disabled people without support', 20 March, https://www.inclusionlondon.org.uk/campaigns-and-policy/act-now/coronavirus-bill-could-leave-thousands-of-disabled-people-without-support/. Accessed 17 April 2020.

Irani, L. (2015), 'Hackathons and the making of entrepreneurial citizenship', *Science, Technology and Human Values*, 40:5, pp. 799–824.

Kitchin, R., Donncha, D. M. and Perng, S.-Y. (2018), 'Hackathons, entrepreneurial life and the making of smart cities', *Geoforum*, 97, pp. 189–97.

Koenecke, A., Nam, A., Lake, E., Nudell, J., Quartey, M., Mengesha, Z., Toups, C., Rickford, J. R., Jurafsky, D. and Goel, S. (2020), 'Racial disparities in automated speech recognition', *Proceedings of the National Academy of Sciences*, 117:14, pp. 7684–89.

Kreiss, D. and McGregor, S. C. (2018), 'Technology firms shape political communication: The work of Microsoft, Facebook, Twitter, and Google with campaigns during the 2016 U.S. presidential cycle', *Political Communication*, 35:2, pp. 155–77.

Lewis, T., Gangadharan, S. P., Saba, M. and Petty, T. (2018), *Digital Defense Playbook: Community Tools for Reclaiming Data*, Detroit, IL: Our Data Bodies, https://www.odbproject.org/wp-content/uploads/2019/03/ODB_DDP_HighRes_Spreads.pdf. Accessed 17 April 2020.

McQuillan, D. (2017), 'Data science as machinic neoplatonism', *Philosophy & Technology*, 31, pp. 253–72.

Marx, P. (2020), 'Amazon and Instacart delivery is a coronavirus goldmine: Workers need to use that leverage', NBC News, 8 April, https://www.nbcnews.com/think/opinion/amazon-instacart-delivery-coronavirus-goldmine-workers-need-use-leverage-ncna1178546. Accessed 10 April 2020.

Mattern, S. (2017), 'A city is not a computer', *Places Journal*, February, https://doi.org/10.22269/170207. Accessed 18 April 2020.

Matthews, C. and Veljanovski, L. (2020), 'Inside Gordon Ramsay's luxury Cornish property as he isolates with family', Cornwall Live, 13 April, https://www.cornwalllive.com/news/cornwall-news/gallery/inside-gordon-ramsays-luxury-cornish-4043624. Accessed 17 April 2020.

Miltenburg, J. and Sinnamon, G. (1992), 'Algorithms for scheduling multi-level just-in-time production systems', *IIE Transactions*, 24:2, pp. 121–30.

Mobility Here (2020), 'London smart city: Tackling challenges with 20 initiatives', https://mobility.here.com/london-smart-city-tackling-challenges-20-initiatives. Accessed 18 April 2020.

Moody, K. (2020), 'How "just-in-time" capitalism spread COVID-19', *Spectre Journal*, https://spectrejournal.com/how-just-in-time-capitalism-spread-covid-19/. Accessed 11 April 2020.

Mott, N. (2020), 'COVID-19 global hackathon: Microsoft, WHO code against coronavirus', *Tom's Hardware*, https://www.tomshardware.com/uk/news/covid-19-global-hackathon-coronavirus-microsoft. Accessed 20 April 2020.

Murphy, N. (2020), 'Man, 74, dies after being refused coronavirus test because he "wasn't sick enough"', *Daily Mirror*, 24 March, https://www.mirror.co.uk/news/us-news/man-74-dies-after-being-21743152. Accessed 20 April 2020.

Nikolic, I. and Elsom, J. (2020), 'Hundreds of shoppers queue all around Tesco car park before 6 a.m. waiting for it to open as police step in and supermarkets hire security guards to stop selfish stockpilers amid coronavirus panic', *Daily Mail*, 21 March, https://www.dailymail.co.uk/news/article-8137409/Police-step-stop-selfish-stockpilers-barging-past-pensioners-supermarkets.html. Accessed 9 April 2020.

Our Data Bodies (ODB) (2020), 'Home page', https://www.odbproject.org/. Accessed 18 April 2020.

Philips, K. U. (2020), 'Virtual reality has an accessibility problem', *Scientific American*, 28 January, https://blogs.scientificamerican.com/voices/virtual-reality-has-an-accessibility-problem/. Accessed 17 April 2020.

Press, C. (2020), 'Coronavirus: The NHS workers wearing bin bags as protection', *The Guardian*, 5 April, https://www.bbc.co.uk/news/health-52145140. Accessed 9 April 2020.

Quarmby, K. (2020), 'Under pressure: Disabled people mobilise to defend their human rights', Liberty Investigates, 16 April, https://libertyinvestigates.org.uk/articles/under-pressure-disabled-people-mobilise-to-defend-their-human-rights/. Accessed 17 April 2020.

Reynolds, E. (2020), 'London bus drivers are dying from coronavirus. Demands to protect them better are growing', CNN, 8 April, https://edition.cnn.com/2020/04/08/uk/coronavirus-london-bus-driver-deaths-gbr-intl/index.html. Accessed 8 April 2020.

Rose, M. (2018), 'The immersive turn: Hype and hope in the emergence of virtual reality as a nonfiction platform', *Studies in Documentary Film*, 12:2, pp. 132–49.

Roy, A. (2014), *The Doctor and the Saint: Caste, Race, and Annihilation of Caste, the Debate Between B. R. Ambedkar and M. K. Gandhi*, London: Verso.

Roy, A. (2020), 'The pandemic is a portal', *Financial Times*, 3 April, https://www.ft.com/content/10d8f5e8-74eb-11ea-95fe-fcd274e920ca. Accessed 9 April 2020.

Shelton, T., Zook, M. and Wiig, A. (2014), 'The "actually existing smart city"', *Cambridge Journal of Regions, Economy and Society*, 8, pp. 13–25.

Simone, A. (2019), *Improvised Lives*, Cambridge, UK: Polity Press.

Singer, N. and Sang-Hun, C. (2020), 'As coronavirus surveillance escalates, personal privacy plummet', *New York Times*, 23 March, https://www.nytimes.com/2020/03/23/technology/coronavirus-surveillance-tracking-privacy.html#click=https://t.co/Vpnc6TVgIQ. Accessed 17 April 2020.

Star, S. L. and Bowker, G. (2000), *Sorting Things Out: Classification and Its Consequences*, Cambridge, MA: MIT Press.

Tufecki, Z. (2020), 'It wasn't just Trump who got it wrong', *The Atlantic*, 23 March, https://www.theatlantic.com/technology/archive/2020/03/what-really-doomed-americas-coronavirus-response/608596/. Accessed 11 April 2020.

Tyler, I. (2020), *Stigma: The Machinery of Inequality* (Kindle ed.), London: Zed Books.

Walker, P. (2020), 'No. 10 denies claim Dominic Cummings argued to "let old people die" ', *The Guardian*, 22 March, https://www.theguardian.com/politics/2020/mar/22/no-10-denies-claim-dominic-cummings-argued-to-let-old-people-die. Accessed 9 April 2020.

Yuk, H. (2020), 'One hundred years of crisis', *e-flux Journal*, 108, https://www.e-flux.com/journal/108/326411/one-hundred-years-of-crisis/. Accessed 10 April 2020.

Zeltmann, B. (2020), 'Every little yelp: Coronavirus crisis causes desperate shoppers to queue round the block from 5 a.m. to panic buy', *The Sun*, 21 March, https://www.thesun.co.uk/news/11223011/desperate-shoppers-panic-buy-5am/. Accessed 17 April 2020.

Zuboff, S. (2019), *The Age of Surveillance Capitalism: The Fight for a Human Future at the New Frontier of Power*, London: Profile Books.

2

Int 'smart':: cities (void) {

If (Equality){

Delfina Fantini van Ditmar,
Royal College of Art

Introduction

'Smartness' is a sociopolitical tool restructuring the interpretation, infrastructure and behaviour of the city. In the prevalent rhetoric of 'smart' cities, which is characterized by apparent impartiality, disinterest, neutrality and objectivity, equality is rarely mentioned, interrogated, discussed or assessed. As shown by a series of 'smart' cities – Toronto (Google urbanism), Xinjiang (the 'smart' prison) and Amaravati (the concrete on halt farm) – 'smartness' does not stop inequality correspondingly; rather, it can (often) perpetuate or increase it.

Under the sharp shadows of the imperceptible algorithmic 'smart' logic, this chapter will investigate power asymmetry, lack of accountability, transparency, the shortage of a civic debate and the lack of equality's weight in the 'smart' equation in prevalent 'smart' cities.

Foreseeing the algorithmic inclusion in the cities must come with an integrated debate and policies on equality. In an age where digital 'smartness' parameters seem to drive urban decisions, this chapter will question: Who are the people really benefiting? What is the value offered to society? How is it being discussed? Who is currently framing the urban 'smart' equality? In which instances is equality debated? By whom should it be discussed?

'Smartness', with its rhetoric of impartial progress, has evaded the scrutiny of its political governmentality and digital backbone biases. As Jacha Franklyn-Hodge notes in the preface of *The Smart Enough City*, 'for those on the front lines, words like "better" and "more efficient" are the tip of an iceberg, below which sit the competing interest and conflicting values of the city and the people who live in it' (Green 2019: x).

By promoting digital technology as the answer to a broad range of urban obstacles, in the contemporary neo-liberal system 'smart' cities have inevitably flourished since the early 2000s. Under the apparent neutrality of 'smartness', reliant on the assurance that 'smart' technology can eradicate analogue urban power regimes and hierarchies, 'smart' cities have been marketed and sold as a path to urban fairness, sustainability and convenience.

The speed at which the 'smart' city field is expanding has also led to neglect of its necessary ethical debate. Shielded by the prevailing uncritical enthusiasm for 'smart' innovations, its underlying algorithms have been marketed and accepted as fair and objective operational facts without much difficulty. However, in practice they have embedded human values and consequently potential biases. As Massimo Mazzotti insists in his article 'Algorithmic Life' (2017: n.pag.), 'algorithms can be carriers of shady interests and vehicles of corporate guile'. Mazzotti (2017: n.pag.) develops the discussion further by emphasizing the relevance of questioning and understanding algorithmic ecology and how it interacts with human logic:

> But what about the logic that shaped their design in the first place? Who decided the criteria to be adopted and their relative weight in the decision-making process? Why were the algorithms designed in one particular way and not another?

Digital technology is taken as the prevalent solution for most urban questions and problems. In a neo-liberal 'smart' city setting, another critical aspect to be aware of is how subjectivity, complexity and context is handled and manipulated. Optimization is described by Halpern et al. (2017: 119) as 'the technique by which smartness promulgates the belief that everything – every kind of relationship among human beings, their technologies, and the environments in which they live – can and should be algorithmically managed'. The term in the essence of the 'smart' city is conceptualized as collected data rather than generated by extrinsic entities such as political or commercial actors (Halpern et al. 2017: 115).

Under the vague conception of optimization the apolitically conceived 'smart' city is built on an urban landscape of simplistic inefficiencies. As Shannon Mattern (2013: n.pag.) describes,

> the default recourse to data-fication, the presumption that all meaningful flows and activity can be sensed and measured, is taking us toward a future in which the people shaping our cities and their policies rarely have the opportunity to consider the nature of our stickiest urban problems and the kind of questions they raise.

Placing technology first rather than people can create power imbalances resulting in critical repercussions of indiscriminate surveillance and social degeneration. Not every aspect of life can be solved by 'smart' technology. Evgeni Morozov (2020: n.pag.) points out the imminent danger of a 'solutionist toolkit as the default option for addressing all other existential problems – from inequality to climate change'. Naomi Klein (2020: n.pag.), addressing creators of the techno-solutionist approach, argues that

> the trouble with outsourcing key decisions about how to reimagine our states and cities to men such as Bill Gates and Eric Schmidt is that they have spent their lives demonstrating the belief that there is no problem that technology cannot fix.

As Cennydd Bowles (2018: 1) notes, 'technologists have learned how to build first and ask questions later'.

In addition to the intrinsic reductionism, 'smartness' does not inherently guarantee fairness, equality and inclusion. In 2018, Tim Berners Lee, founder of the World Wide Web, launched the campaign 'Magna Carta for the Web' in response to the devastating consequences of abuse discrimination, political manipulation and other threats to the internet (Sample 2018). As Berners Lee claims: 'Humanity connected by technology on the web is functioning in a dystopian way. We have online abuse, prejudice, bias, polarization, fake news, there are lots of ways in which it is broken' (Sample 2018: n.pag.). Berners Lee called on governments to provide free and safe internet for their citizens.

The issues addressed in the 'Magna Carta for the Web' are also apparent in the dangers of 'smart' cities; 'smart' decisions risk being unfair, having the potential to intensify ongoing societal issues. Within 'smart' city calculations are value judgements that have the potential to intensify pre-existing biases. As Virginia Eubanks argues in *Automated Inequality* (2018: 82), 'automated decision-making in our current welfare system acts a lot like older, atavistic forms of punishment and containment'.

Urban 'smartness' could lead to a system aiding the marginalized and the poor. However, if not designed ethically and with policies leading to benefit and support all of society there is a significant risk of deepening inequality. Eubanks (2018: 212–13) notes that 'digital technology has the potential to intensify the disadvantage created by historic patterns of racism, classism, sexism, homophobia, transphobia, religious intolerance and other forms of oppression'.

While environmental good, efficiency and luxury characterize images of 'smart' cities, the imperceptible integration of 'smart' algorithmic processes on the ground also comes with the danger of extensive behavioural data being extracted from urban practice. As Bria and Morozov (2018: 8) note, 'the current

41

wave of "smart" euphoria has resulted in many products traditionally classified as tools of surveillance and predictive policing being rebranded as essential components of the "smart city" package'. Central components of 'smart' cities such as internet of things technology (IoT), machine learning and artificial intelligence (AI) have the potential to lead to aggressive tracking, identification, detection and monitoring.

Ursula Pachl (deputy director general of the European Consumer Organisation [BEUC]) and Pamela Valenti (senior advocacy specialist at the Open Society) highlight the growing application of surveillance technology that is being justified as a necessary mechanism to deal with emerging societal threats in their report, *A Human-Centric Digital Manifesto for Europe: How the Digital Transformation Can Serve the Public Interest* (2019: 9). The authors describe the dangers of 'smart' city foundational technology:

> Such risks are exacerbated by the internet of things, since connected products and AI technology become a bigger part of consumers' lives. Monitoring and scrutinizing individual action for commercial purposes could influence the behaviour and decisions of consumers in ways beyond their knowledge, understanding or control, leaving them easily exposed to discrimination and manipulation [...] This is a problem that affects society at large, as it is becoming almost impossible to participate in the digital society and enjoy the benefits of digital technology without being subject to permanent surveillance.
>
> (Pachl and Valenti 2019: 16)

Under the illusion of eco-friendly, inclusive and optimized cities, the surveillance dimension is rarely addressed or contested. In her book *The Age of Surveillance Capitalism: The Fight for a Future at the New Frontier of Power*, Shoshana Zuboff (2019) defined 'surveillance capitalism' as the translation of human experience into raw material for behavioural extractive practice. Zuboff (2019: 21) address the unprecedented attributes of digital technology as the result of the current advanced state of capitalism: 'Surveillance capitalism and its rapidly accumulating instrumental power exceed historical norms of capitalist ambitions, claiming dominion over human, societal, and political territories that range far beyond conventional institutional terrain of the private firm or the market.'

By capturing behavioural data from the city and its population, 'smart' technologies undoubtedly risk facilitating profiling, surveillance, targeting (identification), classification, punishment, criminalization, stigmatization, control and regulation of citizens and marginal inhabitants. Zuboff (2019) shows how the aggressive and competitive dynamic of behavioural future markets leads to the acquisition of behavioural data from a broad range of sources to nudge and direct behaviour into profitable outcomes. Zuboff (2019) goes on to warn that surveillance capitalism not only knows our behaviour but also shapes our behaviour in real time, moving from knowledge to power. The academic and founder of AI Now Institute Kate Crawford (2021) identifies that profound logics of classification 'results in forms of discrimination, not just when systems are applied, but in how they are built and trained to see the world [...]. The idea that you can make these determinations based on appearance has a dark past and unfortunately the politics of classification has become baked into the substrates of AI'.

With no global conventions on ethical data governance, the resulting governmental and corporate (or the partnership of both) surveillant cities result in a power asymmetry potentially endangering equality. Eubanks (2018: 81–82) flags the risk new digital surveillant tools pose to targeted populations by enabling 'more precise measuring and tracking, better sharing of information, and increased visibility'. Based on extracted behavioural urban data, surveillance capitalist strategies have the potential to generate urban deterministic outputs, abusive policing and carry biased correlations that result in mechanisms for societal stratification.

Eubanks (2018: 9) argues that increased inequality in the world has developed alongside the use of digital technologies in public services (predictive algorithms, risk models and automated eligibility systems). Eubanks (2018: 199–200) analyses the danger of targeting and segregating specific groups under impenetrable 'smart' equations:

> Classifying and targeting marginalised groups for 'special attention' might offer helpful personalization. But it also leads to persecution [...] We must not dismiss or downplay this disgraceful history. When a very efficient technology is deployed against a despised outgroup in the absence of strong human rights protection, there is enormous potential for atrocity.

Discriminatory profiling is one of the most pressing risks of 'smartness'. In her studies, conducted in America, Eubanks (2018: 6–7) refers to the injustice of digital technologies and links it to its impact on social relegation:

> Marginalised groups face higher levels of data collection when they access public benefits, walk through highly policed neighbourhoods, enter the health care system, or cross national borders. The data acts to reinforce their marginality when it is used to target them for suspicion and extra scrutiny. Those groups seen as undeserving are singled out for punitive public policy and more intense data surveillance, and the cycle begins again. It is a kind of collective red-flagging, a feedback loop of injustice.

43

Regarding Europe, Pachl and Valenti (2019: 14) reported that in several European regions, based on assumptions, data is being used to feed the machine learning for surveillance and policing practices. This results in targeting colour and low-income communities as 'at risk of high crime', thereby reinforcing biases against groups that are already overpoliced.

In Asia, a concerning and significant illustration of the links between surveillance capitalism and social domination is the Chinese Social Credit System (SCS). The system, designed to socially engineer behaviour by punishments and reward, is based on rules set by the Chinese government marketed as 'a desirable way to measure and enhance trust nationwide and to build a culture of sincerity' (Botsman 2017: n.pag.).

The Chinese government gave the licence to design and implement the 'smart' algorithmic services to several tech companies that run all the social networks in China and therefore have access to an extensive amount of social behavioural data (Stanley 2015). The companies included China Rapid Finance, a developer of the messaging app *WeChat*, and Sesame Credit, an affiliate company of Alibaba (Botsman 2017).

Within the system, behaviours are rated as either positive or negative and result in a score linked to the subject's national identity card, which is not only affected by one's own behaviour, but is also dependent on the behaviour of one's friends (Stanley 2015). Professor of Law Frank Pasquale (2018: n.pag.) indicates that there is no appeal system and observes that 'this algorithmic contagion bears an uncomfortable resemblance to theories of collective punishment'.

As Stanley (2015: n.pag.) argues,

> In addition to measuring your ability to pay, the scores serve as a measure of political compliance. Among the things that will hurt a citizen's score are posting political opinions without prior permission, or posting information that the regime does not like.

Its restrictions are in accordance to a citizen's credibility and affect their daily life: 'people with low ratings will have slower internet speeds; restricted access to restaurants and the removal of the right to travel' (Botsman 2017: n.pag.).

'Smartness' is not only about optimization and convenience, it is also related to real estate, politics, business and control of the public domain. Using opaque 'smartness' is imposingly political: if it is not ethically assessed, it could lead to widening inequality. Because of this, if left unregulated, 'smartness' may lead to social compromises. Therefore, it is crucial to interrogate the ecology of both the actors and incentives behind 'smart' technology.

To expose further consequences of the prevalent ill-considered acceptance of 'smartness' and illustrate a spectrum of 'smart' city issues regarding social equality,

I have selected three critical 'smart' cities: Toronto, Xinjiang and Amaravati. Characterized by a unideological narrative of progress, through the implementation of digital technologies for 'fixing' urban issues such as sustainability, safety and traffic, they represent three case studies that neglected fundamental socio-ethical questions of 'smart' urbanism.

'Smart' incongruences

China: Kashgar, Xinjiang – the 'smart' prison

Xinjiang is an extreme surveillance capitalism example of the social adversity of 'smartness' urban applications. The segregation surveillance programme in Xinjiang was designed by the state defence manufacturer China Electronics Technology Corporation (CETC), which originated from the military research labs that developed China's first nuclear bomb, satellite and guided missile (Buckley and Mozur 2019).

Xinjiang's arguable 'smart' value system justified with the 'smart' rhetoric dictates the conditions of equality and citizenship. Buckley and Mozur (2019) went on to claim that Xinjiang's surveillance artillery was designed to monitor and repress ethnic minorities, specifically Uighurs and other Muslims, along with foreign tourists. This contention is supported by the fact that, in the name of 'quelling Islamic radicalism and strengthening Communist Party rules', the Chinese authorities have detained a million or more Uighurs and other Muslims. Moreover, it is important to note that not everyone has to undergo the surveillance procedure: while Uighurs and other Muslims are compelled to be monitored and surveilled, the system generally does not include the observation of privileged groups such as the majority of Han Chinese, 36 per cent of Xinjiang's population (Buckley and Mozur 2019)

This is an exemplary case of surveillance capitalism in which, according to CETC, its monitoring system 'taps into networks of neighbourhood informants; tracks individuals and analyses their behaviour; tries to anticipate potential crime, protest or violence; and then recommends which security forces to deploy' (Buckley and Mozur 2019: n.pag.). According to Graham-Harrison and Garside (2019 n.pag.),

the Integrated Joint Operations Platform (IJOP) combines all this information in a detailed database of everything from an individual's exact height and electricity use, to the colour of their car, whether they socialize with neighbours and even if they prefer to use the front or back door to their house.

As Buckley and Mozur (2019: n.pag.) note, at the level of urbanism at several points of the city one is required to swipe identity cards, moreover, 'identification cards are also needed to purchase knives, gasoline, phones, computers and even sugar'. This data is retrieved to a police database, which later is used to flag suspicious individuals and behaviours. Buckley and Mozur (2019) describe that in order to harvest information from the target groups, the government installed structures that looked like 'toll plazas' at the borders of towns and cities across Xinjiang. The city also monitors with smaller checkpoints at banks, parks, schools, gas stations and mosques. In addition, the police use the app at checkpoints that serve as virtual 'fences' across the city. If someone is tagged as a potential threat, the system can be set to trigger an alarm every time the person tries to leave the neighbourhood or enters a public place.

Furthermore, according to Zhong (2019: n.pag.), China's border authorities routinely install the app on smartphones belonging to travellers who enter Xinjiang by land from Central Asia, allowing police to flag suspicious people:

> The app collects personal data from phones, including text messages and contacts. It also checks whether devices are carrying pictures, videos, documents and audio files that match any of more than 73,000 items included on a list stored within the app's code.

Those items include Islamic State publications, recordings of jihadi anthems and images of executions [...] They also include material without any connection to Islamic terrorism. There are scanned pages from an Arabic dictionary, recorded recitations of Quran verses, a photo of the Dalai Lama and even a song by a Japanese band of the ear-splitting heavy metal style known as grindcore.

The biopolitics of repressive 'smart' urbanism has significant humanitarian consequences. Aimed to transform Uighurs and other Muslims into secular citizens who will not challenge the ruling Communist Party, its invasive urban surveillance programme helps identify target groups to be investigated or transferred to the indoctrination camps (Buckley and Mozur 2019). Furthermore, this behavioural extractive practice has been combined with biological sampling:

> Kashgar and other areas of Xinjiang have, in recent years, collected DNA and other biological data from residents, especially Muslims. Officials now collect blood, fingerprints, voice recordings, head portraits from multiple angles, and scans of irises, which can provide a unique identifier like fingerprints.
>
> (Buckley and Mozur 2019: n.pag.).

India: Amaravati, Andhra Pradesh – the concrete on halt farm

In Andhra Pradesh there is a greenfield project, called Amaravati, developed from scratch by Fosters + Partners and Singapore planners. It is described by Fosters + Partners (n.d.: n.pag.) as

> Inspired by Lutyen's New Delhi and New York's Central Park, a clearly defined green spine runs through its length, providing the foundation of the masterplan's environmental strategy, where at least 60% of the area is occupied by greenery or water. The city has been designed to the highest standards of sustainability, with the latest technologies that are currently being developed in India, such as photovoltaics. The transportation strategy includes electric vehicles, water taxis, and dedicated cycle routes, along with shaded streets and squares that will encourage people to walk through the city.

It is of note that both of these examples relied heavily on the destruction of pre-existing communities.

Despite a rhetoric of 'holistic integrated development' (Amaravati Official Website n.d.); Amaravati is a complex case where 'smartness' clashed with ancient spatial traditions and farmers union revolts. As an article in *The Guardian* (Ravishankar 2016) notes, in Amaravati the deep-rooted Hindu belief in the spatial tradition Vaasthu (science of architecture), in which the alignment of buildings correlates to good or bad luck, obstructed the master plan of developers and authorities. Another critical problem the Amaravati 'smart' city faces is land acquisition. Planners also encountered several instances where land records had not been updated for almost a hundred years and ambiguous land boundaries. In the same *The Guardian* article, Ravishankar (2016) claims that the government circumvented the fact that it has to purchase land from farmers for four times its market value by creating a land pooling policy.

According to Mohan (2017: n.pag.),

> the Land Pooling Scheme does not fall under the central government's land acquisition law – the Right to Fair Compensation and Transparency in Land Acquisition, Rehabilitation and Resettlement Act 2013 (LARR). Pooling emerges from a separate state law called the Andhra Pradesh Capital Region Development Authority Act passed by the Assembly on 22 December, 2014.

This caused several riots and lawsuits against the land pooling system, demanding to get fair compensations for the land (Ravishankar 2016).

The official website shows a very different version:

It is to give shape to this vision that the 'Bhumiputras' – the farmers – voluntarily donated their lands under the unique 'Land Pooling Scheme'. The citizens donated bricks as part of [the] 'My Bricks – My Amaravati' scheme, thereby laying the foundation and paving the path for progress. Amaravati is hence envisioned to be an important milestone in India's urbanization story promoting progress, welfare and happiness.

(Amaravati Official Website n.d.: n.pag.)

The way the system works is that

farmers contribute their land to a 'pool' for development of the new capital city; the state government develops the land as per the master plan; then it returns to the farmer roughly a quarter of the land that was originally contributed. The incentive for the farmer is the value conceivably added to his land by way of this development. An annuity of Rs 30,000–50,000 per year per acre will also be paid by the government to the farmer for a period of 10 years, to compensate loss of livelihood from agriculture.

(Ravishankar 2016: n.pag.).

Amaravati, known as the 'food bowl' of the region, is located along the Krishna River, standing on one of the most fertile lands in Andhra Pradesh. Despite this, the Sivaramakrishnan expert committee expressly recommended avoiding converting the fertile land in the Krishna delta into a concrete capital, by presenting objections to the diversion of already cultivated lands (55 per cent of the area). However, the government of the chief minister of Andhra Pradesh N. Chandrababu Naidu ignored the committee's petition (Mohan 2017).

Moreover, in addition to the questionable land pooling system, the urbanization of a fertile area and the pause on agriculture culture, is the fact that the planned city is nowhere in sight. As Venkata Reddy, a farmer who grows vegetables, paddy, Bengal gram, turmeric and bananas observed:

If there is no city, then what will I do with a tiny plot in it? [...] suppose I give my land and stop farming for 10–15 years, taking a Rs 50,000 monthly compensation from the government. What if Amaravati never comes up, or what if the land prices don't shoot up as they expect? I'll be left with no income, and a small piece of land that is unfertile and undeveloped'

(Mohan 2017: n.pag.).

According to Mohan (2017), despite the fact that the 'smart' city is far from being completed, farmers have reported that the Capital Region Development Authority (APCRDA) has been pushing them to stop cultivating in order to attract potential investors and start the 'smart' city construction. The 'smart' city plan is creating numerous concerns. One issue with the potential further inequality is the loss of regular income from farming. As Odur Srinivasa Rao, a farmer from the area, indicates:

> They are building a city with IT companies, banks and hospitals, and saying that our sons will get jobs there, that they will never have to farm. But how will my son become a doctor if his farmer father can't afford to educate him?
>
> (Mohan 2017; n.pag.)

Yamunan (2020) observed that Amaravati's riots reactivated in December 2019 when Chief Minister Jaganmohan Reddy announced that Andhra Pradesh would actually have three capitals sparking development across the state. Farmers from 29 villages in the area had been protesting, holding a green flag for almost two months against what they see as a betrayal of the development commitment given to them when they gave over 30,000 acres for the promised 'smart' city capital.

As Yamunan (2020) describes, farmers in Amaravati worry that the new plan will leave them 'short-changed'. Most of the infrastructure work has come to a halt and since only the state assembly will be located in their city (which opens only a few days each year), the government will not build all the infrastructure it has promised, resulting is no incentive for businesses to develop the region. The farmers worry that the government will try to give back the land to them without constructing the urban 'smart' proposition. This is critical, as the development is halfway complete, the land is no longer suitable for cultivation.

Canada: Quayside, Toronto – Google urbanism

Quayside is a partnership 'smart' city initiative between the city of Toronto and Alphabet (Google) Sidewalk Labs. This urban data capture test bed for Google was disseminated by a set of colourful renders offering a lively urban scene at a parcel of Toronto's waterfront along Ontario lake. The visual material provided by Alphabet is composed of terraces and organic exterior spaces. This includes renders from London-based Heatherwick Studio. The promise of Quayside is a city powered by a zero-emissions microgrid, modular buildings, adaptable common spaces, increased priority to pedestrians, cyclists and low-speed autonomous vehicles. It also proposes tiles capable of melting snow, absorbing storm water and directing traffic. The city also envisions robots delivering mail and transporting garbage through underground tunnels. As Eric Schmidt, Google's chief executive officer (CEO), expressed, 'all the things you could do if someone would just give us a city and put us in charge' (Digman 2017: n.pag.).

Another of Sidewalk's promises is inclusivity. Their website reads: 'Toronto's eastern waterfront presents an extraordinary opportunity to shape the city's future and provide a global model for inclusive urban growth.' However, their 'smart' inclusivity urban plan comes hand in hand with behavioural data extraction, 'with heightened ability to measure the neighbourhood comes better ways to manage it, Sidewalk expects Quayside to become the most measurable community in the world' (Sidewalk Labs n.d.: n.pag.).

Yet, these visions are not what make the 'smartness' case of Sidewalk noteworthy. Rather, the interest lies in the fact that residents revolted and questioned the societal benefits instead of accepting Alphabet's proposed 'smart' urbanism. A persistent and determined movement of citizens lead the campaign against Alphabet's Quayside #BlockSidewalk to stop the development of the project without the ethical clarity of its 'smartness'. By continuously raising concerns regarding safety, equality, democracy and freedom, #BlockSidewalk became a leading example of the crucial role of public analysis and resistance to corporate 'smart' city developments. The campaign included a letter of concern, 'Public Draft: Sidewalk Toronto Public Consultation Question List', protests, activities and group meetings.

Despite the proposed urban techno-solutions, a key civic question regarding 'smartness' is how data-gathering infrastructure is built into the city, how data would be gathered and how it could be owned and used. Critics questioned Sidewalk's use of behavioural data extracted from streets, washrooms and even garbage bins (Austen 2020). From the beginning of the project #BlockSidewalk stressed the importance of transparency, accountability, and democratic governance (Bliss 2019). As the founder of the Centre for International Governance Innovation, Jim Balsillie, argues, Sidewalk is 'a poorly disguised urban data front for Google' (Deschamps 2019: n.pag.). Balsillie added, 'your offline data is way more valuable than your online data – and your online data is really valuable' (Austen 2020: n.pag.).

The movement asked key societal questions regarding the proposed 'smartness' (Wylie 2017): What is the city's vision for 'smart' cities? How will people's movements be tracked in space and time? Especially marginalized community members, including homeless people? What do residents want to learn/build/pioneer with this opportunity? Who is the user that Sidewalks Labs is ultimately serving: companies that want to learn about how people interact with physical spaces? Real estate investors? Cities? Who will own/control/have access to the data captured by the sensors deployed in this project? Who controls the Sidewalk Labs platform: the residents? City Hall? Sidewalk Labs? What privacy protection process will be followed to ensure the data collected is anonymous? How will Waterfront Toronto engage the local community and who would they work for as a client? How will the internet protocol (IP) generated benefit Canada? Will there be a confidentially wall between Sidewalk and Google (and other related companies) on technology development? Will Google have access to Sidewalk's technology, IP, data stocks? Would Waterfront Toronto and Sidewalk be open to having a properly mediated Town Hall where citizens can do Q & A with senior leadership of both organizations and try to get these questions answered?

Yet in response to this criticism Sidewalk Labs CEO Dan Doctoroff responded, 'It isn't fully baked and people just naturally are afraid of new things' (Deschamps 2019: n.pag.). According to Austen (2020), Sidewalk proposed that Waterfront Toronto itself set the rules covering data use and that the information would be stored in an open 'data trust' managed by the agency. However, this didn't convince the opposition panel of technology experts assembled by Waterfront Toronto, including Professor Clement, who released a report on Sidewalk's proposal questioning 'whether sufficient benefits had been identified to justify the proposed collection or use of data' (Austen 2020: n.pag.).

In May 2020, Sidewalk Labs cancelled the 'smart' neighbourhood project in Toronto amid COVID-19. CEO Dan Doctoroff (2020: n.pag.), 'with great personal sadness and disappointment', described in a statement: 'As unprecedented economic uncertainty has set in around the world and in the Toronto real estate market, it has become too difficult to make the 12-acre project financially viable without sacrificing core parts of the plan we had developed.' The Canadian Civil Liberties Association framed Sidewalk Labs cancellation as

> a victory for privacy and democracy, clearing the way for that reset to take place [...] Waterfront Toronto never had the jurisdiction to sign off on a data surveillance testbed with a Google sibling. Serious harms to privacy would have been our future.
> (Carter and Rie 2020: n.pag.).

An imperative 'smart' comprehensive assessment

The depoliticization and blind acceptance of 'smartness' brings with it a critical threat to equality and human rights. Characterized by a biopolitical agenda based on an ignored and unscrutinized 'smart' value system, Toronto, Xinjiang and Amaravati expose how the implementation of preconceived digital 'smartness' shapes society, generating life-changing social repercussions not always favouring social justice. Guided with no consideration of those who are subordinated to the urban 'smart' systems, the uncontested apolitical logic of software applications in these 'smart' cities proves to be dangerous and insufficient.

Regardless of their selling point or if a corporation or government developed them, all evidence suggests potential automated, unfavourable sociopolitical repercussions for the society, raising concerns about possible 'smart' city futures based on undisclosed and unaccountable decision-making. In Xinjiang, the surveillance and suppression campaign is framed under the rhetoric of policing combating terrorism. Xinjiang's discriminatory targets are religious and anti-government groups leading to pre-emptive arrests directed at behaviour considered disloyal or threatening to the Communist Party (Clark and Mozur 2020).

Through AI, this 'smart' strategy is consolidated with genetic testing, allowing the police to identify 'religious extremism' specifically targeted for the minority group of Uighurs or opposition groups to the Communist Party. Out of the three cities, Xinjiang's 'smart' surveillance scheme exhibits the most violent and severe human rights outcome, resulting in targeted minorities taken into indoctrination camps. Xinjiang exemplifies 'smartness' servicing discrimination and digital injustice, resulting in racial segregation.

In Amaravati, under the discourse of a sustainable and holistic integrated development, the eradication of the farmer community is being accomplished by a debatable land-pooling system. Amaravati, the so-called food bowl region, illustrates an unfinished 'smart' city standing on fertile multicropping soil. The government left the new capital abruptly, leaving fertile land no longer suitable for cultivation while farmers are losing their regular income. While risking that the city never comes up, Amaravati's 'smart' outcome is resulting in an unfair compensation land system, devastating unemployment, loss of ancestral traditions, unfertile land and farmers left with a precarious and uncertain development plan.

Sidewalk Lab, characterized by opaque usage of behavioural data was founded on the promise of inclusivity and described by Alphabet as the most measurable community in the world to establish 'better ways to manage a city'. Until the project finally stopped it was never clear which are the advantages to justify its behavioural data collection: the question of the value system, data ownership and its usage remained. As Zuboff (2019: 11) observes, 'surveillance capitalists know everything about us whereas their operations are designed to be unknowable to us (they accumulate vast domains of new knowledge from us, but not for us)'.

What distinguishes Toronto from the previous cities is that it was a successful example of how citizens managed to revoke a big-tech company, demonstrating that 'smart' resistance is imperative. Considering that socio-cultural circumstances might be challenging, there is hope that the #BlockSidewalk movement will encourage stronger pushback around the world against the dubious gains that 'smart' cities promise society. Moreover, their success helps normalize the idea of citizens protesting against tech corporations and their opaque 'smart' propositions.

Society needs to rethink how 'smartness', with its augmented behavioural surveillance capacities and ambiguous 'smart' development plans, is embedding, perpetuating or intensifying previous inequalities. The three cases in this chapter evidence that it is crucial to approach 'smartness' carefully with disbelief and dubiousness; indisputably there is something fundamentally obscure in the way 'smartness' is being implemented – it is an error to accept 'smartness' passively.

A 'smart' city should be conceived in terms of privacy for equality rather than surveillance capitalism for the perpetuation of current societal injustice. 'Smart' technologies are being developed and implemented, but how is it applied to equality and how are they contributing to fair urbanism? 'Smart' city proposals should be scrutinized and discussed, questioning what they intend to do and are actually doing in regards to social gains, ethics and privacy. This includes adequately using policies and technology in place to battle discrimination and eradicate disparities.

As Eubanks (2018: 9) highlights, currently there is a lack of transparency and repercussions: 'the cheerleaders of the new data regime rarely acknowledge the impacts of digital decision-making on poor and working-class people'. 'Smart' city plans rarely provide a detailed description of the cities 'smartness' clarifying behavioural data collection policies and addressing the potential consequences of its usage in terms of inequality.

As most 'smart' city cases are governed by corporations, international consultancies and governments (and the partnerships between these entities), it is critical to analyse how key 'smart' city stakeholders incorporate and delineate equality. To have a 'smart' outcome requires data and a description of the achievement. What are the parameters? How will behaviours, demographics and background be used? How are choices and nudges being made with current machine-learning training and biases? In an age where the 'smart' parameters of convenience and efficiency seem to drive decision-making, it is important to ask: What are they improving? Who are the people really benefiting? What is the value offered to society? How is it being discussed?

As technology is not neutral, ethics and equality should be an integral aspect of 'smart' city design. With no control of the extrapolation, third-party destination or unforeseen outcomes of the extraction of urban behavioural data, it is important to have a critical debate about what happens after data is captured and who benefits from these data transactions. How could digital 'smartness' become transparent? How could it become accountable? 'Smart' devices can track and target, but what is the benefit for society?

Despite the sociopolitical relevance, there has been no discussions or protocols on who should compose the advisory boards for 'smart' cities to ensure ethics and equality. The perspective of minorities and endangered groups should be included in the debate. Who is going to participate in framing and regulating a fair 'smart' city? How? Which organization should regulate algorithmic decisions? How could algorithmic equality be guaranteed?

From the perspective of equality: Which entity should be responsible for evaluating it? Under which parameters is equality assessed? What is the benefit in terms of equality for the citizens and individuals living in the city? What will it mean to be a 'smart' citizen for marginal inhabitants? How will they be scrutinized? What are the sociopolitical risks of the urban 'smartification'? How is the urban data being collected? What is harvested? How is it aggregated, stored and used? Who will analyse it?

These critical interrogations have to be addressed when considering 'smart' urban outputs; a power balance between the entities behind 'smartness' (governments, consultancies, enterprises and the combination of them) and the communities living in the cities is critical. 'Smart' city design should incorporate in the equation inclusivity and the benefits for the whole society. As Pachl and Valenti (2019: 28) observe, 'such asymmetry may lead to a significant loss of trust, transparency and accountability, undermining people's privacy and autonomy as well as generating unfair competition and arbitrary discrimination'.

It is key to understand, rethink and reshape 'smartness', envisioning its fairness. Insufficient questioning of 'smart' technology in regards to equality will result in a discriminatory future. It is imperative that ethics and equality govern 'smartness' and that this is reflected in a revision of the legislation before it is operational. As Bowles (2018: 2) notes in his book *Data Ethics*, 'an ethical awakening is long overdue'. Each 'smart' city proposition should be accountable for bias and inequalities – they must be removed and the mechanisms under which they will be judged should be clarified before 'smart' city executions.

The creation of reliable and responsible 'smart' boards and propositions for the ethical and transparent use of urban data is a pressing need. Pachl and Valenti (2019: 4) describe in their report that to protect the citizen's rights from technological forces that often feel 'uncontrollable' and 'unaccountable', the European Commission has addressed a strong commitment to rights-based policies and regulation based on the principles of human dignity, freedom, democracy, equality, rule of law, human rights, solidarity, justice, inclusion and non-discrimination. Pachl and Valenti (2019: 5) suggest to the European Commission the need to 'adopt a comprehensive strategy to safeguard against the use of personal data and data systems in ways that perpetuate discrimination and exclusion, particularly when they affect vulnerable groups who already face high levels of inequality'.

With the support of the United Nations Human Settlements Program (UN-Habitat), the Cities Coalition for Digital Rights is committed to providing trustworthy and secure digital services and infrastructures that support communities. As the declaration states, attempts include privacy standards integrated into the design of technology implemented in public space and 'Ethical Digital Standards Policy Toolkits' (Cities for Digital Rights n.d.). While this is an encouraging starting point, 'smartness' requires a global ethical oversight coupled with revised legislation. The creators of such 'smart' systems will have to exercise responsibility in the transparency of data extraction and ethical 'smartness' accountable descriptors. A comprehensive ethical risk assessment providing justifications of the 'smart' urban decision-making is pressing.

REFERENCES

Amaravati Official Website (n.d.), 'Home page', https://amaravati.gov.in/EBricks/amaravati/index.aspx. Accessed 3 May 2020.

Austen, I. (2020) 'You can't fight City Hall but maybe you can fight Google', *New York Times*, 10 March, https://www.nytimes.com/2020/03/10/world/canada/toronto-sidewalk-labs-google.html. Accessed 3 May 2020.

Bliss, L. (2019), 'Critics vow to block Sidewalk Labs' controversial smart city in Toronto', *CityLab*, 25 February, https://www.citylab.com/equity/2019/02/block-sidewalk-labs-quayside-toronto-smart-city-resistance/583477/. Accessed 3 May 2020.

Botsman, R. (2017), 'Big data meets big brother as China moves to rate its citizens', *Wired Magazine*, 21 October, https://www.wired.co.uk/article/chinese-government-social-credit-score-privacy-invasion. Accessed 3 May 2020.

Bowles, C. (2018), *Future Ethics*, Hove: NowNext Press.

Bria, F. and Morozov, E. (2018), *Rethinking the Smart City: Democratizing Urban Technology*, New York: Rosa Luxemburg Siftung.

Buckley, C. and Mozur, P. (2019) 'How China uses high-tech surveillance to subdue minorities', *New York Times*, 22 May, https://www.nytimes.com/2019/05/22/world/asia/china-surveillance-xinjiang.html. Accessed 3 May 2020.

Carter, A. and Riet, J. (2020), 'Sidewalk labs cancels plan to build high-tech neighbourhood in Toronto amid COVID-19', CBC News, 7 May, https://www.cbc.ca/news/canada/toronto/sidewalk-labs-cancels-project-1.5559370. Accessed 19 May 2020.

Cities for Digital Rights (n.d.), 'Home page', https://citiesfordigitalrights.org/. Accessed 3 May 2020.

Clark, D. and Mozur, P. (2020), 'China's surveillance state sucks up data: U.S. tech is key to sorting it', *New York Times*, 22 November, https://www.nytimes.com/2020/11/22/technology/china-intel-nvidia-xinjiang.html. Accessed 20 November 2020.

Corbyn, Z. (2021), 'Microsoft's Kate Crawford: AI is neither artificial nor intelligent', *The Guardian*, 30 June, https://www.theguardian.com/technology/2021/jun/06/microsofts-kate-crawford-ai-is-neither-artificial-nor-intelligent. Accessed 14 June 2021.

Deschamps, T. (2019), 'Sidewalk Labs CEO responds to criticism around tax and transit plans', CTV News, 15 February, https://www.ctvnews.ca/canada/sidewalk-labs-ceo-responds-to-criticism-around-tax-and-transit-plans-1.4299648?cache=yes%3FclipId%3D89530. Accessed 3 May 2020.

Digman, S. (2017), 'With Toronto, Alphabet looks to revolutionize city-building', *Globe and Mail*, 17 October, https://beta.theglobeandmail.com/report-on-business/with-toronto-alphabet-looks-to-revolutionize-cit. Accessed 3 May 2020.

Doctoroff, D. (2020), 'Why we're no longer pursuing the Quayside project – and what's next for Sidewalk Labs', *Medium*, 7 May, https://medium.com/sidewalk-talk/why-were-no-longer-pursuing-the-quayside-project-and-what-s-next-for-sidewalk-labs-9a61de3fee3a. Accessed 9 May 2020.

Eubanks, V. (2018), *Automating Inequality: How High-Tech Tools Profile, Police, and Punish the Poor*, New York: Picador, St Martin's Press.

Fosters + Partners (n.d.), 'Amaravati masterplan', https://www.fosterandpartners.com/projects/amaravati-masterplan/. Accessed 3 May 2020.

Graham-Harrison, E. and Garside, J. (2019), 'Revealed: Power and reach of China's surveillance dragnet', *The Guardian*, 24 November, https://www.theguardian.com/world/2019/nov/24/china-cables-revealed-power-and-reach-of-chinas-surveillance-dragnet. Accessed 3 May 2020.

Green, B. (2019), *The Smart Enough City: Putting Technology in Its Place to Reclaim Our Urban Future*, Cambridge, MA: MIT Press.

Halpern, O., Robert, M. and Geoghegan, B. D. (2017), 'The smartness mandate: Notes toward a critique', *Grey Room*, 68, pp. 106–29.

Klein, N. (2020), 'The coronavirus crisis: Under cover of mass death, Andrew Cuomo calls in the billionaires to build a high-tech dystopia', *The Intercept*, 8 May, https://theintercept.com/2020/05/08/andrew-cuomo-eric-schmidt-coronavirus-tech-shock-doctrine/. Accessed 9 May 2020.

Mattern, S. (2013), 'Methodolatry and the art of measure', *Places Journal*, 13, November, https://doi.org/10.22269/131105. Accessed 3 May 2020.

Mazzotti, M. (2017), 'Algorithmic life', *Los Angeles Review of Books*, 22 January, https://lareviewofbooks.org/article/algorithmic-life/. Accessed 3 May 2020.

Mohan, R. (2017), 'Making of Amaravati: Andhra farmers pay the price for "dream city"', *The Quint*, 30 November, https://www.thequint.com/news/india/amaravati-farmers-in-doubt-rise-of-new-capital. Accessed 3 May 2020.

Morozov, E. (2020), 'The tech "solutions" for coronavirus take the surveillance state to the next level', *The Guardian*, 15 April, https://www.theguardian.com/commentisfree/2020/apr/15/tech-coronavirus-surveilance-state-digital-disrupt. Accessed 3 May 2020.

Pachl, U. and Valenti, P. (2019), *A Human-Centric Digital Manifesto for Europe: How the Digital Transformation Can Serve the Public Interest*, Brussels: Open Society European Policy Institute (OSEPI) and the European Consumer Organization (BEUC), https://www.opensocietyfoundations.org/publications/a-human-centric-digital-manifesto-for-europe. Accessed 3 May 2020.

Pasquale, F. (2018), 'Data nationalization in the shadow of social credit systems', *Political Economy of Technology*', 18 June, https://lpeblog.org/2018/06/18/data-nationalization-in-the-shadow-of-social-credit-systems/. Accessed 3 May 2020.

Ravishankar, S. (2016), 'From Singapore to Amaravati: The battle to build India's new state capital', *The Guardian*, 26 January, https://www.theguardian.com/cities/2016/jan/26/amaravati-andhra-pradesh-india-singapore-new-state-capital-city. Accessed 3 May 2020.

Sample, I. (2018), 'Tim Berners-Lee launches campaign to save the web from abuse', *The Guardian*, 5 November, https://www.theguardian.com/technology/2018/nov/05/tim-berners-lee-launches-campaign-to-save-the-web-from-abuse. Accessed 3 May 2020.

Sidewalk Labs (n.d.), 'Home page', https://www.sidewalktoronto.ca/. Accessed 3 May 2020.

Stanley, J. (2015), 'China's nightmarish citizen scores are a warning for Americans', *American Civil Liberties Union (ACLU)*, 5 October, https://www.aclu.org/blog/privacy-technology/consumer-privacy/chinas-nightmarish-citizen-scores-are-warning-americans?redirect=blog/free-future/chinas-nightmarish-citizen-scores-are-warning-americans. Accessed 3 May 2020.

Wylie, B. (2017), 'Civic tech: A list of questions we'd like Sidewalk Labs to answer', *Torontoist*, 30 October, https://torontoist.com/2017/10/civic-tech-list-questions-wed-like-sidewalk-labs-answer/. Accessed 3 May 2020.

Yamunan, S. (2020), 'In Amaravati, farmers protesting Andhra's new three-capital plan complain of brutal police action', *Scroll*, 28 January, https://scroll.in/article/951299/in-amaravati-farmers-protesting-andhras-new-three-capital-plan-complain-of-brutal-police-action. Accessed 3 May 2020.

Zhong, R. (2019), 'China snares tourists' phones in surveillance dragnet by adding secret app', *New York Times*, 2 July, https://www.nytimes.com/2019/07/02/technology/china-xinjiang-app.html. Accessed 3 May 2020.

Zuboff, S. (2019), *The Age of Surveillance Capitalism: The Fight for a Human Future at the New Frontier of Power*, New York: Public Affairs.

3

Reading Lefebvre's *Right to the City* in the Age of the Internet

Alan Reeve,
Oxford Brookes University

Introduction

Taking as its starting point Henri Lefebvre's apparently innocent concept of 'the right to the city' (Lefebvre 1968), this chapter speculates on how citizenship in relation to both access to and control over civic space is becoming nuanced and philosophically challenging with the insertion of the adjective 'smart', as a qualifier of the city. In particular, I am interested in the agency of individuals and communities as appropriators of the city when the space of the city moves online – how this may be both a threat to the historical autonomy of groups and individuals and also an opportunity for such autonomy. Central to the analysis offered here is Chantal Mouffe's (2000) notion of agonism, as a way of conceptualizing how agency may be negotiable both between communities of interest and with controlling authorities – either in the form of the state, or the market.

'Smartness' in the form of social media, big data, the technology of the virtual and the new technology is a double-edged phenomenon when set against the historically understood rights and powers of citizens. On the one hand, it is seen as a threat to the very notion of the individual (acting alone or collectively) in the invisibility, embeddedness and extensiveness of its reach; and, on the other hand, it is often regarded as an opportunity for a new sort of Habermasian communicative efficiency (i.e. merely a tool for better and more deliberatively democratic forms of dialogue). While the management and purpose of such technology (facilitating the interests of one state over another, or the promotion of commodified lifestyles) can be spatially, politically and temporally located, the technology exists in a sense outside of these dimensions. This means that while historically citizenship was citizenship of somewhere, it now occupies a global or non-locatable

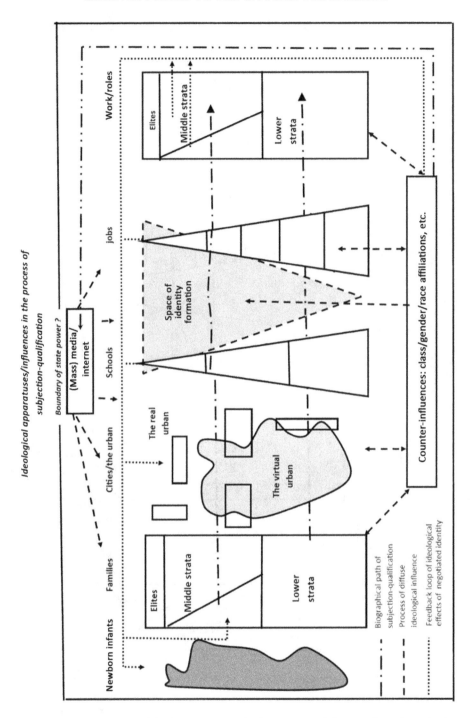

FIGURE 3.1: Modified modal of the process of subjection-qualification, based on Therborn (1980).

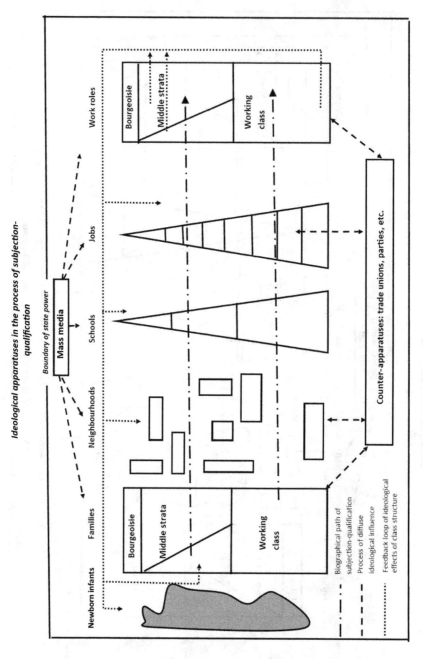

FIGURE 3.2: Ideological apparatuses in the process of subjection-qualification, from Therborn (1980).

space. The question arises, then, in what sense can citizenship have agency when detached from the contingent political and real conditions of the city or place, except through some sort of dialectical process of reflection or reaction, where global 'values' are translated into local and specific acts or perspectives – what Sassen (2007), has called 'glocalization'?

The internet as a new form of *dialogic* media also raises interesting questions about its role in both part of what Goran Therborn (1980) called the 'apparatus' of ideology, and of its counter-apparatus (see Figure 3.1). This model is revisited in the conclusions to the chapter as a possible way of conceptualizing the function of the web as a mechanism for articulating state power for spatialized/despatialized citizens, and countering that power, while at the same time informing and giving agency to identity formation and expression – identity as practice (Figure 3.4).

This chapter assumes that the reader has some familiarity with the basic concepts central to Lefebvre's work covered elsewhere in this text – including *lived* space, *spaces of representation* and *representations of space* and so on. They are diagrammatically summarized (in Figures 3.2 and 3.3), but also see Purcell's (2002) very helpful if committed explanation of the right to the city. He reminds us that Lefebvre uses the term 'citadens' in *Le Droit a la Ville* (instead of the term 'citizens'), in which he 'fuses the notion of citizen with that of denizen/inhabitant' (Purcell 2002: 102). Purcell (2002) goes on to argue that Lefebvre thereby implies that the 'right' to the city is more than simply an abstract legal entitlement, in the sense understood in terms of liberal democracy, but that it has to be *practised* (i.e. through the individual and collective actions of individuals in making use of, appropriating and occupying urban space):

> It would affirm, on the one hand, the right of users to make known their ideas on the space and time of their activities in the urban area; it would also cover the right to the use of the center, a privileged place, instead of being dispersed and stuck into ghettos (for workers, immigrants, the 'marginal' and even for the 'privileged').
>
> (Lefebvre cited in Purcell 2002: 102)

This core idea is also nicely captured in its essence by David Harvey (2008: 23):

> The right to the city is far more than the individual liberty to access urban resources: it is a right to change ourselves by changing the city. It is, moreover, a common rather than an individual right since this transformation inevitably depends upon the exercise of a collective power to reshape the processes of urbanization. The freedom to make and remake our cities and ourselves is, I want to argue, one of the most precious yet most neglected of our human rights.

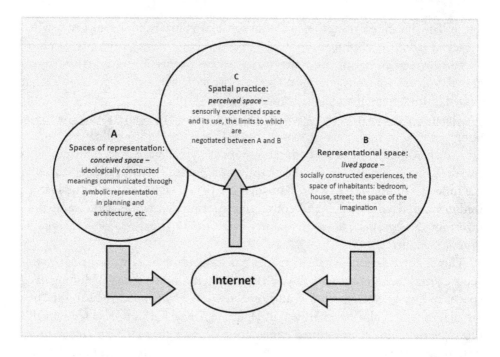

FIGURE 3.3: Diagrammatic representation of Lefebvre's triad of spatial practice, spaces of representation and representational space.

So, particularly through the lens of the notion of *agonism*, the chapter is concerned with how the agency of the citizen is empowered and constrained or limited through the technology of the internet – specifically in exercising power over the city. Finally, the chapter speculates on 'smartness' (i.e. the provision of the infrastructure of the internet) as an assumed good or necessity for the future of the city, and its implications for existing cities, future cities and embedded rights, equalities and inequalities of citizens.

Negotiating rights to the city in virtual space: The panopticon, agonism and the echo chamber

Lefebvre's notion of the city/the urban was first and foremost as real, sensorily apprehended, spatially and temporally located and experienced place. Exercise of the right to the city through acts of appropriation, and in terms of representational space for Lefebvre, in the pre-internet age, were always in the context of what real space, (the space of 'extension' in Descartes's terms; see Anscombe and Geach [1970]) in this sense, made possible: a distinction between the public and public culture and interests, and the private – specifically of the family and the home. The individual as an appropriator of the public or urban realm – as de Certeau has demonstrated in his seminal work *The Practice of Everyday Life* (1994), and in Lefebvre's *The Critique of Everyday Life* (1991a) – was always an actor/agent within a real setting, locatable in time and space and verifiable in its irreducible and specific qualities of place (whether as *flâneur* or terrorist, and everything in between).

When we consider the *real* as opposed to the *virtual* space of the city (see Figure 3.3), rights with (as *lived* space) or over it (as bureaucratically sanctioned) to the city has to be seen, therefore, in terms of the power and capacity, as well as the legitimacy of the exercise of that power in relation to a particular urban context and moment. The invention and then proliferation of the internet as a 'medium' has radically transformed and problematized conceptions of the urban and the city as real place, as it has problematized distinctions between the public and the private. We have to see the internet as providing a new and original interface between the *space of representation* and *representational space* – the symbolic and the lived in Lefebvre's sense (Lefebvre 1991b); and therefore something that opens up the possibility of the exercise of rights to the city both in the liberal sense (as challenging dominant interests in their own terms), and in the sense in which the individual has the right to *produce* space through their own actions and experiences – in the exercise of what might be called the micropolitics of appropriation.

The remainder of this section focuses on a number of themes related to the nature and powers of the internet as virtual urban and public realm, and the implications for citizenship/citadenship: the internet as a two way panopticon; popular culture as citizen agency and of dissensus; and it concludes with a brief discourse on agonism and the internet as a way of conceptualizing the negotiation of rights to the city through this evolving 'medium'.

The internet as two-way panopticon

There is an extensive literature on the panopticon, as a metaphor for surveillance culture, which there is not space to detail here (see Foucault 1973; Markus 1993; Reeve 1998). The term, of course, referred originally to the novel design by the eighteenth-century philosopher, Jeremy Bentham – for a prison organized around a central observation tower. Prisoners could be observed by their warders, but not themselves see who was observing them. In *Discipline and Punish* (1973) Foucault explores the nature of relations of power within bureaucratic institutions of the state by applying the panopticon as a symbol for the exercise of the power and therefore the violence of the state over the individual.

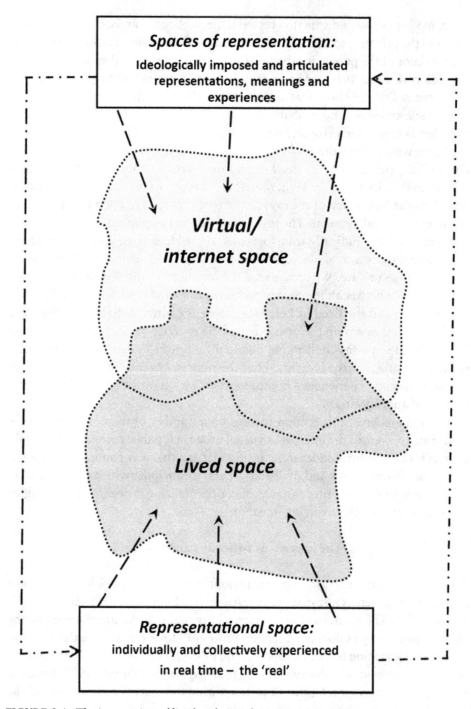

FIGURE 3.4: The intersection of lived and virtual space using Lefebvre's distinction between representational of representation.

However, Flyvbjerg and Richardson (2002) show the panopticon, as a real space and building of penal coercion, as a space of the oppositional culture of the incarcerated, who, despite the apparently omniscient surveillance of their warders, found ways of avoiding the controlling gaze and communicating between themselves – albeit in a setting of profound power inequality. Applied to the internet, the metaphor of the panopticon illustrates the fact that the technology is controlled and provided from the centre, institutionally and legally governed and organized and directed predominantly for the interests of the state and the market (thus a *space of representation*), but that it also provides opportunities for appropriation (a representational space) in which communities of interest as well as individual tastes can be fostered and communicated.

Popular culture, citizen power and the internet

Flyvbjerg (1998) is also critical of liberal notions in the work of Habermas and others, of rationality as a neutral competence, or facilitator of the negotiation of interests between otherwise unequal parties – for instance, the dominant class and the working class; or men over women. Instead, he sees rationality as a fundamentally weak tool for equal communication between unequal interests, because it is itself dominated by the powerful (although it could be argued that *irrationality* can also be exercised as a form of control by the powerful, as in the case of Donald Trump as president of the United States[1]). This being the case, Flyvbjerg (1998: 236) advocates 'forms of participation that are practical, committed and ready for conflict, over ones that are discursive, detached and consensus dependent – that is rational'. This is a view ultimately derived from Gramsci's political theory of *cultural hegemony*, a theory about the means through which power is gained by class groups that effectively control moral, political and cultural values in their own interest, represented and disseminated through the media as well as in everyday life, in Lefebvre's sense. Popular culture – the culture 'of the masses' according to Adorno (1991), can be both collaborative in the hegemonic interests of the dominant class, but also subversive of it. Rather like the panopticon, forms of popular culture colonizing the space of the internet can be both self-oppressing and progressive at the same time. As Bennett (1986: xv–xvi) put it,

> [popular culture is] an area of negotiation between an imposed mass culture that is coincident with dominant ideology, and spontaneously oppositional culture [...] within which [...] dominant, subordinate and oppositional cultural and ideological values and elements are 'mixed' in different permutations.

In cultural theory, the study of popular culture really only began in any seriousness in the 1970s and 1980s; and led, in Bennett's (1986: 14) view, to a 'new sense of the popular, as the site of critical and speculative intelligence'.[2] At the same time, it is well recognized that significant social and technological changes were occurring, both driving the claims of legitimacy of 'countercultures', as well as their medi- ated reach. According to Alex Niven (2011: 17), this period 'saw the popular take on an active role as a progressive force in political and societal change, largely independent of mainstream politics, "the voiceless finally finding a voice"'. So, for example, these decades saw the emergence of the gay liberation movement, feminism, environmentalism and other forerunners to identity-based political crusades, as a precursor to the expressions of both micro and collective positions, interests and narratives in part enabled by the internet over the last 25 years.

However, Fiske (1989) acknowledges that popular culture should not be reified into a fixed category in which there is a simple opposition between the/a dominant culture and a counterculture. He sees the history of western society as being characterized by 'constant conflict', in which cultural authority and voice is continuously being readjusted and negotiated; and in which popular culture needs to be understood as a shifting set of allegiances underpinned by both com- peting and complementary narratives of interest – some real (e.g. class based) and some illusionary. A key function of the popular – at least analogous to Lefebvre's notion of the appropriation of space for representation – in Fiske's terms is what he calls 'excorporation': 'a process by which the subordinate make their own culture out of the resources and commodities provided by the dominant system' (Fiske 1989: 15). Given or handed down and commodified components of consumer culture are reappropriated and imbued with new meanings and authen- ticity, and emerge transformed. This is a complex dynamic that at one level resembles the polysemous (and facile and merely decorative) plundering of styles for new effects, which was a characteristic of postmodernism in architecture in the 1980s and 1990s. In addition, and often in response, the excoroprated become reappropriated and recommodified – represented as a lifestyle 'choice' or brand. Perhaps the most often cited example of this being the punk move- ment, whose anti-style became itself merely a style, an emasculated surface referent. Likewise, excorporation resembles a much older concept developed by Levi Strauss, in relation particularly to artistic practice – that of *bricolage*. However, in the context of the internet and social media, and of popular access to a technology that allows instant appropriation and excorporation of images and identities, and their immediate reproduction and dissemination to mar- kets, audiences and constituencies, these practices range in their reach from the micropolitics of the everyday negotiations of individual identity, to something more collective in which a notion of the urban (albeit a virtual one) with its possibilities of engaged citizenship take on a much larger and collective political force. This is evident, for instance, in recent movements focused around the environment – in which Extinction Rebellion, without a hierarchy of leadership, has taken full advantage of the apparently unmediated power of the internet to organize the appropriation of urban space as a place of political protest. In Fiske's terms, such a movement might be seen to illustrate the 'guerrilla tactics' made possible through appropriation of the media of the internet, as well as the technological competencies of its users.

Agonism and the risk of the 'echo chamber'

The work of Chantal Mouffe, as a political theorist, is of significant value in thinking about the nature of democracy, citizenship and the internet as a medium for expressing and negotiating the political. Central to her contribution to theories of democracy and its practice is the concept of 'agonism'. *Deliberative Democracy or Agonistic Pluralism* (Mouffe 2000) provides a dense, and helpful, introduction to this concept. In it, she presents a critique of what has been termed 'deliberative democracy', which has underpinned liberal conceptualizations of the relationship between the public and the democratic state and political accountability, based on an assumption of normative rationality, and an equality of discourse between different interests. She argues that such conceptualizations assume that consensus between interests is both possible and desirable, and that such consensus is achieved through rational discourse in which 'participation in deliberation is grounded by norms of equality and symmetry and all have the same claims to initiate speech acts' (Mouffe 2000: 5). However, she also argues that there is a fundamental dichotomy buried within deliberative democracy and its expression in the conventionally understood political democracies. This dichotomy exists between 'the liberal emphasis on individual rights and liberties, and democratic emphasis on collective formation and will-formation' (Mouffe 2000: 4).

In addition, Mouffe (2000: 10) argues that

> the failure of democratic theory to tackle the question of citizenship is the consequence of their operating with a conception of the subject, which sees the individual as prior to society. As bearers of natural rights, and either as utility maximising agents or as rational subjects. In all cases they are abstracted from social and power relations, language, culture and a whole set of practices that make individuality possible.

She goes on to claim that the consequence of this is a rise in 'extreme forms of individualism', in which 'collective identification' threatens the civic, and even 'the possibility of identifying with citizenship' (Mouffe 2000: 11).

These are complex and highly nuanced arguments, but Mouffe presents a solution to this threat to the civic that foregrounds what she calls 'practices' (reminiscent of Lefebvre's use of the term, and the idea of the 'lived'), as against 'argumentation'. Our experience of the moment by moment, but reflexive practice of living within a political setting, provides the legitimacy for our values and justifies us as individual agents. In this, she posits a distinction between the *political* and *politics*:

> By 'the political' I refer to the dimension of antagonism that is inherent in human relations, antagonism that can take many different forms and emerge in different types of social relations; 'politics', on the other hand, indicates the ensemble of practices, discourses and institutions which seek to establish a certain order and organize human coexistence in conditions that are always potentially conflictual because they are affected by the dimension of 'the political'.
>
> (Mouffe 2000: 15)

Politics, as a situated and contingent experience of agency, is thus, in her view, necessarily pluralistic – as opposed to simply reducible to a defined set of oppositional interests or allegiances that require consensus for their legitimacy and power (see Ploger 2004). In addition, she argues that given this immense and immanent pluralism, rather than antagonism (where the other is the enemy to be overcome), we should think of relations between interests as *agonistic* (i.e. conflictual and characterized by dissensus) conflictual consensus. The term she uses for this is 'agonistic pluralism' – a state in which identities and interests, while grounded in collective experiences, traditions and histories, are also constantly negotiated and reformed through essentially conflictual practice *with*, rather than *against* others. She makes it clear, however, that such agonistic pluralism is a dynamic condition of the lived, and while the experience of the subject is at the heart of it, should not be taken as an argument in support of identity politics, which will always be antagonistic – because reifying – rather than agonistic.

Finally, Mouffe asserts that agonism is a struggle between adversaries that 'requires providing channels through which the collective passions will be given ways to express themselves over issues which, while allowing rough possibility for identification will not construct the opponent as an enemy but as an adversary' (Mouffe 2000: 16). The question here is in what ways might the internet and social media – particularly in relation to the expression of the citizen/citaden and rights to the city – be seen as such a channel?

In response to this, it is useful to consider Mouffe's own view of the potential of the internet as a site of agonistic pluralism. Citing an interview in Carpentier and Cammaerts (2006), Knight (2018: 59), suggests that she had particular doubts about the potential of the new media to realise 'direct democracy', on the basis that the definition of democracy as defined by proponents of new media as a site of political transformation is too restrictive, and for Mouffe too close to the expression of a vote [...] or to go beyond the individual and self-expressive.

The difficulty with respect to the power of the internet as a medium for agonism, is the anonymity and remoteness/virtuality of the adversary, and therefore their affective legitimacy and sincerity or authenticity, is always in doubt. The absence of the genuinely adversarial as a characteristic of much social media, has led to it being referred to as an 'echo chamber' (Ratto and Boler 2014): 'an environment in which somebody encounters only opinions and beliefs similar to their own, and does not have to consider alternatives' (Oxford Learner's Dictionary n.d.). That is, much social media, and particularly sites of political discourse, merely reinforce views already held rather than challenging these. This is, clearly, because unlike the public sphere of the city, the user exercises discretion and choice as an active participant – rarely seeking out opinions or experiences that run counter to their own assumptions, narratives and values. The real city, on the other hand, is a space in which encounters with the other are not always voluntary, but often incidental and in an important sense unmediated, except and ironically via the internet (see Reeve 2019). However, that cities themselves are organized along class and often ethnic and economic lines – with poor, often Black neighbourhoods, and more affluent and often generally White districts – territories or turfs, occupied through different forms of symbolic capital; and within city centres, spaces of spectacle – such as shopping centres and gated communities – are by their very nature exclusive enclaves. To this degree, the despatialized nature of the internet is seen by some as an opportunity for overcoming spatially based forms of discrimination.

However, the internet is not one monolithic entity and contains the possibility for public debate within a kind of third space – both and neither public nor private. According to Ratto and Boler (2014: 15), Rancier, for example, argues that the new media can build what he calls 'DIY citizenship combining "modalities of political participation" with "critical making"'. This latter phrase is crucial in understanding the potential of the internet as a mode of the lived and the real as much in public life as in other spheres. As Knight (2018: 43) suggests, such making 'carries with it critical-infused reflection', and can be seen as an aspect not just of the creation of new ideas, physical environments, cultural products, etc., but also of communities, via the established platforms such as Facebook, or emerging forms such as discussion forums. The internet exists both as a *space of representation* (reinforcing and imposing identities and values from outside) and *representational space* (a support for *agonism*), in which conflictual participation as critical making can flourish.

Finally, here, it is important to acknowledge that the internet is in some limited and highly qualified sense a neutral technology, and therefore capable of being both a form of the panopticon and a host for oppositional cultures and expression. Swartz and Driscoll (cited in Ratto and Boler 2014), articulate the obvious difference between message boards and online forums with their potential for voicing the particular, and the conformist, externally disciplined and centralized structures of corporate entities such as Facebook, with their algorithms designed to anticipate commodifiable interests and needs. They also see much forum discourse and DIY citizenship (as Knight [2018] puts it) as 'post-political' (Swartz and Driscoll cited in Ratto and Boler 2014: 298), where historically understood political organization – for example in political parties or other organized and state-sanctioned forms – has been displaced by 'social network markets'. The notion of the social network – exercised or expressed through the marketplace of the internet as a new kind of agora, illustrates Bauman's (2000) conception of what he has called 'liquid modernity'; an aspect of which is the overlaying of one type of interest and experience (e.g. economic struggle) with another (e.g. sexual identity), but where these interests and experiences while having some foundation (e.g. in terms of class and economic relations) are constantly renegotiated and practised in relation to the interests of others and the other, in real time.

The spatially independent or detached nature of the internet means that as a medium of citizenship it can be both local and global at the same time; as Miller (2016) argues, able to give voice to locally specific cultural and other practices and identities, at the scale of both the community and the nation, and even beyond. In this sense, the urban or the city as a real space of the exercise of rights and the practice of the lived is framed or qualified by its inherent lack of being in a specific urban or city setting, although its content may refer to real and local issues and concerns. Likewise, as a medium without a place, it blurs the distinction between the public and the private domains, and even makes them in themselves redundant or interchangeable categories, as discussed earlier.

At a very deep level, agonism as an experience of conflictual encounter with the world and with others, experienced within the moment, foregrounds the gaps and voids between different interests groups: in this sense it is at the heart of what Lefebvre terms 'lived space'. It parallels – as Gunder and Hillier (2009) have pointed out – Lacan's theory of the real, or the void, which exists beyond or prior to representation. The limits to the internet as a site of agonism lies in the fact that, as a medium, it requires acts of representation (assembling and giving content), although as in social media such as Tinder in a way that dangerously and/or joyously facilitates experiences that may go beyond mere representation.

The form and the management of the smart city: Justice and the right to the city

Turning from the internet as a medium for the expression of rights and identities; this chapter now considers how cities have been conceptualized by geographers and others in relation to the internet as techne – technology or instrument for political action and control.

Susan Fainstein (2014) asserts that Lefebvre's conceptualization of the right to the city had a profound influence on the way cities were thought about by urban geographers such as David Harvey and Manuel Castells, from the 1960s and in subsequent decades. Historically, Fainstein (2014) argues, urbanists saw cities (e.g. in terms of the distribution of land use and of class- and race-based or characterized neighbourhoods), as capable of analysis and explanation simply in terms of these objective characteristics; and, by implication, geography as a principally descriptive and empirical activity, in a positivist sense. If they were concerned with questions of justice and equality, this was through an analysis of 'spatial manipulation' (Fainstein 2014: 1), seeing space as a 'container of buildings, populations and production'. Injustice – and justice, as its corollary – were matters of how space was organized to the benefit of some groups and the detriment of others, measured against normative standards of access to resources, and, essentially, the means of production in Marxist terms.

Fainstein argues that, with Lefebvre, this way of understanding the relationship between cities as simple facts, and their relationship to the by-product of inequality, gave way to a more complex and politically committed understanding in which 'space [...] became a constituent of the relations of production and reproduction and a contributing source of inequality and by implication injustice' (Fainstein 2014: 1–2). Foregrounded here, and in line with Lefebvre's idea of the city as lived, is the city as composed of social relations rather than economic or class relations and class struggle based on competition for control over resources, including property and its location within the city.

Fainstein (2014) goes on to argue that this shift meant that the city could now be seen – in the work of Castells (1983), for example – as a site of social reproduction, in which the social situation of residents and urban space became central to understanding how social injustice and inequality might in some sense be rectified. For Castells, the exercise of control and influence over the city was conditioned or constrained by the relative power of different social interests. He advocated for a 'grass-roots', bottom-up struggle, from the very local and community led level, to articulate and express interests of hitherto disenfranchised groups, but groups whose interests he very much identified in terms of real and lived place, using their own experience of exclusion and inequality as the affective driver of change. The obvious question is what role might the internet and social media have in 'grass-roots', place-based struggle to achieve greater urban justice; and how, in practice, is this being facilitated or hindered through the provision of internet infrastructure and its regulation? In addition, Castells's (1989) notion of the city as a 'space of flows', in which interests are not permanently tied or fixed to spatial qualities (such as property), is at least metaphorically helpful in understanding the nature of the internet as a fluid medium that touches real places and the interrelations between people and place.

Fainstein's (2014) discussion of justice and the city in relation to Lefebvre speaks to the other component of the rights to the city, the question of *whose* rights? Using the work of Young (1990), Fainstein (2014) offers a critique of the inadequacy of liberalism in which individuals are seen atomistically (i.e. as separate, but equal agencies, abstracted from their lived realities). Instead, Fainstein, with Young,

> considers that a social group is defined by a sense of shared identity and that a liberal contract model of social relations only conceives of associations based on common interests and fails to take account of groups arising from shared identity [...] Liberal democratic theory [...] ignores the rootedness of people in class, gender, cultural and familial relations. In doing so, and by placing liberty at the top pf its pantheon of values, it fails to recognise the ties of obligation that necessarily bind people to each other and also the structurally based antagonisms that separate them.
>
> (Fainstein 2014: 9)

So, we can begin to say that the practice of the right to the city, in Lefebvre's terms, has necessarily to be exercised by individuals who are not political abstractions, but real people whose existential and therefore experiential and affective reality is inseparable from and dependent on their contingent (class, gender, race, ableist, place-based community and history, etc.) qualities and histories. We can also say that the practice of everyday life (and therefore the *practice* of identity), in so far as it takes place within the urban, is an exercise of citizenship, since it is always in relation to the other. In this sense, justice in the city may be about the capacity and limits to the exercise of the right to the city; and how it is agonistically negotiated moment by moment with the other. The question for this chapter, finally, is how does the internet connect with, add to or in some sense create a virtual urban space for representation of the citaden?

Reproducing inequalities: The real and the virtual city

The final section of this chapter considers the relationship between the real city and the virtual space of the internet, and the effects of the one on the other: first, in terms of how the city of bricks and mortar is changing and adapting and what this might mean for how it is experienced as a space of rights; and, second, in terms of the persistence of spatial inequalities and the reinforcing or reproduction of such inequalities as a characteristic of internet provision and access in the contemporary city.

The smart city is also the real city – not simply a virtual entity that has to be managed and regulated. The smart city as a real place, however, has distinct qualities produced by smartness, and on which its smartness depends, that sets it aside from cities prior to the proliferation of the web.

A considerable amount of academic writing has speculated on the new characteristics of smart cities – and there is not space to explore in detail much of it here (e.g. Castells 1989; Graham 2016; Mitchell 1996). However, central to the debates about the nature of the 'connected' city, is the question of whether, to what degree and in what ways the virtual is displacing the real – particularly in terms of face-to-face encounters and therefore the need for urban space for these. As William Mitchell, in his highly influential text, *City of Bits* (1996) put it:

> Indirect, anonymous, electronically enabled relationships are proliferating in our daily lives, while certain kinds of face-to-face transactions (and the secondary relationships with familiar intermediaries that these have fostered) are correspondingly being reduced. Society as a whole is becoming more dependent on a vast, complex web of automated, electronic intermediation.
>
> (Mitchell 1996: 120)

Others have argued that the shifting of some activities online – including work – in fact frees up (for some) time and opportunities for real-time and in-the-flesh encounters. There is also evidence that the digitalization of the city has increased rather than decreased the amount of time spent by people in public settings (see Haas 2008). The relationship between the social and the digital is complex, and not a matter of either/or: as Sassen (2007) has noted, there is a kind of 'imbrication' between the two in which the nature of social (the range of possible encounters with others, and how these are defined) is changed by the internet, but not displaced by it (see also Reeve 2019). There is also little evidence that activities such as work have moved to the home to the scale once anticipated.

In essence, the internet has not killed public space, or the urban, but has changed how it is experienced and has influenced how planners and the state in the interest (largely) of investment and local, regional and national competitiveness conceive of it. This has had consequences both for the form of the contemporary city, as well as for the nature of inequality within it.

The growing range of terms in use over the last twenty years, to define or describe cities with (enhanced) digital characteristics or ambitions speaks to the complexity of the nature of the contemporary city and its incorporation of the web. But, in a sense, this complexity can be simplified by thinking about the centrality of digitization as a variable within the vision that states and regions have for the future city. This is also and again bound up with questions of whose city? And of social and economic equality and justice.

Under the smart city umbrella term, then, a plethora of types exist, defined by the scale and reach of the investment intention and vision. So, as adjuncts, but spatially discrete districts or neighbourhoods, are science parks, or digital hubs and incubators, as well as identifiable quarters within existing cities where, say, creative industries cluster. At the other extreme, whole new cities are constructed and designed around digital competence – digital media cities. And, finally, technopoles and the 'intelligent city', where the technology is dispersed across a city or even subregion, where the virtual network is overlaid on to an already existing physical network.

Smart cities are not smart simply because they have the digital infrastructure of smartness, of course. As Castells and Hall (1994: 237) noted two decades ago:

> All technopoles, in order to deserve that title at all, must articulate certain key features; some form of generation of – or access to – new, valuable technological information; a highly skilled labour force; and (a production factor that cannot be taken for granted) capital ready to take the risk of investing in innovation.

Clearly there are implications here for understanding the differences between smart and not so smart cities, particularly in terms of future prospects, but also in relation to their citizen composition. It is therefore possible to postulate a scale of 'smartness', and to begin to interrogate different cities on the basis of the characteristics of the urban, in Purcell's (2002) terms, that follow. At the one end, would be the truly smart city, where investment has been aimed at digitalization, marketing or branding the city to encourage technological and entrepreneurial investment; and, at the other, the digitally poor or left-behind cities, with little investment in digital dependent industries or service sectors; and, in the middle, 'normal' or ordinary cities where digital investment is seen as necessary for ongoing competitiveness, but not the core function.

Under certain political circumstances, there is at least an association between the smartness of a city and its civic qualities – at least in the public sphere. The theory includes a possibility that smart cities express their privilege through a more commodified public realm, which becomes part of their brand. At the same time, they exhibit highly polarized communities: on the one hand, an elite of well-paid workers with secure employment, directly or indirectly supporting digital industries; and, on the other – and generally at the periphery – the digital and economic poor, with precarious employment, servicing the interests and needs of the elite. These inequalities are not, of course, a product of smart cities – any city under

74

neo-liberal forms of government will exhibit this tendency, but smart cities may exhibit it to its full extent.

There is research evidence that there is a correlation between digital poverty and spatial inequality; and that because of reasons of cost, primarily, but also because of unequal infrastructure investments across the city, internet poverty can be mapped alongside other forms of disadvantage. That is, poor neighbourhoods are poor in terms of web access and provision in addition to everything else (see Wilson et al. 2019).

As Mitchell (1996: 81) put it,

> Urban areas could well continue to congeal into introverted, affluent, gated communities intermixed with 'black holes' of disinvestment, neglect and poverty – particularly if, as the unrestrained logic of the market seems to suggest, low-income communities turn out to be the last to get digital telecommunications infrastructure and the skills to use it effectively.

Conclusion

This chapter has taken as its focus Henri Lefebvre's theory of the right to the city as a starting point for a consideration of the effect of the internet and the smart city as an influence or modifier of citizenship. The chapter began with a diagrammatic review of some basic, if complex, concepts in Lefebvre's work, specifically the triad of spaces of representation, representational space and spatial practice; as well as the fundamental position that the right to the city is not primarily for him about liberal rights (although he did not dismiss these as irrelevant), but the rights of the subjective individual to appropriate the city as a lived space with which the practice of identity/interest could be negotiated. This was based on the other fundamental proposition in Lefebvre's work that urban space is both manufactured and created. The citizen is seen here as both a political entity, with legal rights, but also as a personal project in relation to the other.

The chapter then examined Chantel Mouffe's concept of agonism, as a way of seeing – in line with Lefebvre – the city as a space of 'practice', in which everyday life provides the context for the negotiation of identities and interests through conflictual consensus, or dissensus.

Underpinning this discussion, we have been concerned with the internet as both a medium through which ideological constructs of representation are communicated, but also as a reflexive medium that can appropriated in real time by individuals to articulate, express and negotiate with other interests and identities, and with the powers that be – whether the state or the market through the excorporation of images and meanings.

To conclude, I want to propose a revised version of Goran Therborn's model (Figure 3.1) of social and class reproduction, where I have attempted to set out a possible conceptualization of the place of the internet as a medium for both replicating existing and historic class/social structures and hegemonic interests and provide a mechanism (Therborn's 'apparatus') to challenge these (Figure 3.4).

If citizenship exists in a political reality, part of which is the maintenance of economic interests, part of it is also, and increasingly, the affordance provided by the internet as a means of giving voice to counter-interests through creative engagement with place and others. However, while the expression of such citizenship, and its experience by individuals as *citadens*, can be given greater agility and reach, as a function of the World Wide Web and therefore affordance to individuals as an end for themselves, it can equally be used to treat citizens as a means in the ideological, institutional and commercial ends of other interests and powers. It is a contested space, but one without physical walls.

NOTES

1. As I write, in early November 2020, Donald Trump is deploying his access to Twitter to challenge the legitimacy of the ballot in the presidential elections in the United States – a prime example of how the very personal medium of the internet is used to challenge the most obvious instance of civic and public rights in a democratic society.
2. Having said this, the work of Richard Hoggart should not be forgotten, particularly his seminal study *The Uses of Literacy* (2009), first published in the 1950s.

REFERENCES

Adorno, T. (1991), *The Culture Industry: Selected Essays* (ed. J. M. Bernstein), London: Routledge.

Anscombe, E. and Geach, P. T. (1970), *Descartes: Philosophical Writings*, London: Open University Press.

Bauman, Z. (2000), *Liquid Modernity*, Cambridge, UK: Polity Press.

Bennett, T. (1986), 'The politics of the popular', in T. Bennett, C. Mercer and J. Woolacott (eds), *Popular Culture and Social Relations*, Milton Keynes: Open University Press, pp. 6–21.

Carpentier, N. and Cammaerts, B. (2006), 'Bringing hegemony, agonism and the political into journalism and media studies: An interview with Chantal Mouffe', *Journalism Studies*, 7:6, pp. 964–67.

Castells, M. (1983), *The City and the Grassroots*, Berkeley: University of California Press.

Castells, M. (1989), *The Informational City: Information Technology, Economic Restructuring, and the Urban Regional Process*, Oxford: Blackwell.

Castells, M. and Hall, P. (1994), *Technopoles of the World: The Making of 21st-Century Industrial Complexes*, London: Routledge.

Certeau, M. de (1994), *The Practice of Everyday Life*, Berkeley: University of California Press.

Fainstein, S. S. (2014), 'The just city', *International Journal of Urban Sciences*, 18:1, pp. 1–18.

Fiske, J. (1989), *Understanding Popular Culture*, London: Routledge.

Flyvbjerg, B. (1998), *Rationality and Power*, Chicago: University of Chicago Press.

Flyvbjerg, B. and Richardson, T. (2002), 'Planning and Foucault: In search of the dark side of planning theory', in P. Allmendger and M. Tewdr-Jones (eds), *Planning Futures: New Directions for Planning Theory*, London: Routledge, pp. 44–63.

Foucault, M. (1973), *Discipline and Punish*, London: Pantheon Books.

Graham S. (2016), *Vertical: The City from Satellites to Bunkers*, London: Verso.

Gunder, M. and Hillier, J. (2009), *Planning in Ten Words or Less: A Lacanian Entanglement with Spatial Planning*, London: Routledge.

Haas, T. (2008), *New Urbanism: Designing Cities for the Future*, New York: Random House.

Harvey, D. (2008), 'The right to the city', *New Left Review*, Sept./Oct., pp. 23–40.

Hoggart, R. (2009), *The Uses of Literacy*, London: Penguin Classics.

Knight, D. (2018), *Making Planning Popular*, unpublished Ph.D., London: Royal College of Art.

Lefebvre, H. (1968), *Le droit à la ville*, Paris: Anthopos.

Lefebvre, H. (1991a), *The Critique of Everyday Life*, London: Verso.

Lefebvre, H. (1991b), *The Production of Space*, Oxford: Blackwell.

Markus, T. A. (1993), *The Power of Buildings*, London: Routledge.

Miller, D. (2016), *Social Media in an English Village*, London: UCL Press.

Mitchell, W. (1996), *City of Bits: Space, Place, and the Infobahn*, Cambridge, MA: MIT Press.

Mouffe, C. (2000), *Deliberative Democracy or Agonistic Pluralism*, Reihe Politikwissenschaft/Institut fur Hohere Studien, Abt.Politikwissenschaft,72, Wien: Institut fur Hohere Studien (HIS), https://nbn-rsolving.org/urn:nbn:de:0168-ssoar-246548. Accessed 12 June 2020.

Niven, A. (2011), *Folk Opposition*, Winchester: Zero.

Oxford Learner's Dictionary (n.d.), 'Echo chamber', https://www.oxfordlearnersdictionaries.com/definition/english/echo-chamber?q=echo+chamber. Accessed 12 June 2020.

Ploger, J. (2004), 'Strife: Urban planning and agonism', *Planning Theory*, 3:1, pp. 71–92.

Purcell, M. (2002), 'Excavating Lefebvre: The right to the city and its urban politics of the inhabitant', *GeoJournal*, 58, pp. 99–108.

Ratto, M. and Boler, M. (eds) (2014), *DIY Citizenship: Critical Making and Social Media*, Cambridge, MA: MIT Press.

Reeve, A. R. (1998), 'The panopticisation of shopping', in C. Norris and J. Moran (eds), *Surveillance, Closed Circuit Television and Social Control*, Ashgate: Aldershot, pp. 69–88.

Reeve, A. R. (2019), 'Exercising control at the urban scale: Towards a theory of spatial organisation and surveillance', in S. Flynn and A. Mackay (eds), *Surveillance, Architecture and Control*, London: Palgrave, pp. 19–56.

Sassen, S. (2007), *A Sociology of Globalization*, New York: W. W. Norton & Co.

Therborn, G. (1980), *The Ideology of Power and the Power of Ideology*, London: Verso.

Wilson, C. K., Thomas, J. and Barraket, J. (2019), 'Measuring digital inequality in Australia: The Australian digital inclusion index', *Journal of Telecommunications and the Digital Economy*, 7:2, pp. 102–20.

Young, I. M. (1990), *Justice and the Politics of Difference*, Oxford: Oxford University Press.

4

Universities, Equality and the Neo-Liberal City

Richard Hayes, Waterford Institute of Technology

Introduction

This chapter offers some remarks on equality and (in?) the smart city through a consideration of the modern urban university. These remarks are occasioned by a convergence in Ireland of significant developments in national higher-education strategy that will see the creation of new universities in Ireland, technological universities (plans are set out in the *National Strategy for Higher Education to 2030*), coupled with the publication and implementation of a new national spatial strategy with cities strongly emphasized as the loci for future growth (*Project Ireland 2040: National Planning Framework*). Some of the terms in which the former has been presented – 'We now have a generational opportunity to transform the Irish higher education *landscape*' (Department of Education and Skills 2011: 4, emphasis added) – positively invite a consideration of the co-relatedness of spatial and educational strategy and suggest that an examination of these new universities might be of some interest to any analysis of the form and function of Ireland's cities. The specification of the new universities to be created under the national plan as 'digitally enhanced' organizations that can 'facilitate systemic engagement and data-informed decision-making', using digital technology to 'modernise business systems and reduce inefficiencies, [thus] freeing up time for higher-value work', suggests a consideration of this policy convergence and these new entities in connection with smart cities is also worthwhile (Department of Education and Skills 2020: 30). Moreover, that the national strategies highlight 'equality' as an important goal, with both suggesting that Ireland will be a more equal place when these strategies have been implemented, makes this case further relevant for the purposes of this book.

The two national strategies that form the backdrop to these remarks frame their plans as responses to particular challenges, and the deployment of a crisis narrative to which these plans form the solution is an interesting rhetorical strategy in itself (see Hart and Tindall 2009; Hay 1999; Kuipers 2006). The crises framing the strategies are quite different. The *National Strategy for Higher Education to 2030* presents itself as a response to the 2008 financial crisis and organizes its plans around the imperative of 'economic recovery': 'Higher education is the key to economic recovery in the short term and to longer-term prosperity', with the new universities being a critical instrument of the plan (Department of Education and Skills 2011: 29). The challenge to which *Project 2040* responds is that presented by growth, understood initially in the strategy as population growth (the plan projects an extra million people living in Ireland in the coming decades), though elsewhere in the plan there are references to 'economic growth', 'enterprise growth' and 'employment growth'. The strategy sees Irish cities (Dublin, the capital, and the four regional cities of Cork, Galway, Limerick and Waterford) as central both to creating and absorbing that 'growth' and the strategy is particularly insistent on the need for regionally balanced growth to mitigate an overconcentration of growth in Dublin and its environs (Government of Ireland 2018: 11). Though the crises to which these strategies are responses are different, and notwithstanding that the strategies were published some time apart (the higher-education strategy in 2011, the spatial strategy in 2018), I contend that both strategies are entirely consistent ideologically and I make the case in what follows for both as expressions of a deeper, neo-liberal project. Their interrelationship is realized primarily through the proposed creation of a number of new universities in Ireland that are place-defined and, as we will see, are presented as one means by which future growth is to be managed.

The remarks that follow seek at once to examine the positioning of the university as an institution within broader discursive strategies through an examination of some of the figurative devices frequently now deployed to speak of universities in connection with cities – centred on the idea of the university as a city 'anchor' – and at the same time to examine the positioning of the university in policy and practice. These discursive and operational strategies mirror one another and are mutually supportive. I endeavour to relate these strategies to smart city strategies and more broadly to ways of understanding urbanization. The ambition of this chapter is to clarify the various elements in the relationship between a public institution, its locale (specifically insofar as that place is 'smart') and the rights it upholds or otherwise through its multiple activities – indeed through its very existence. While the chapter is limited in drawing largely on Irish higher education and Irish spatial strategy, and while it is acknowledged that it is dangerous to generalize from this, it is hoped that, while necessarily oversimplifying, these notes can offer some useful starting points for more systematic analysis and sustained investigation in more general terms.

Universities: 'anchors' or 'ivory towers'?

The notion of the university as an 'anchor' institution in a city is one that has gained currency in recent literature (for a comprehensive review of the literature, see Taylor and Luter 2013). Anchor institutions are 'entities having a large stake in a city, usually through a combination of internal missions and landownership' – a large stake and, it must be emphasized, a permanent stake, having little incentive or reason to relocate (Penn Institute for Urban Research 2010: 1). They offer, in this sense, 'stability to local economies', for they are 'assumed to be immune to institutional failure or sudden contractions in size' (Goddard et al. 2014: 307). Anchor institutions have 'important economic impacts due to their employment, revenue-garnering and spending patterns' and, 'as entities consuming sizable amounts of land, they have an important [physical] presence in cities and their neighbourhoods' (Penn Institute for Urban Research 2010: 1). Typical examples of anchor institutions that display many if not all of the above characteristics are cultural institutions (such as museums, theatres, art galleries), sports facilities, prisons, military installations, churches – and hospitals and universities (that is, 'eds and meds'). In many cases, as the list suggests, anchor institutions are not market-facing; they manifest, insofar as they are directed away from profit, some manner of public profile. It is this sense of the anchor institution as a civic institution, giving expression to a particular way of being 'public', that is particularly interesting in any consideration of the role of an anchor institution in advancing equality in the smart city.

An examination of the role of a single 'anchor' institution – in this case a university – within what Lefevbre calls 'the urban phenomenon' (Lefevbre 2003: 53) is attractive methodologically, it should be said. 'The greatest single fact about cities,' Jane Jacobs declares in *The Death and Life of Great American Cities*, is 'the immense numbers of parts that make up a city, and the immense diversity of those parts' (Jacobs 1992: 144). Marshall Berman, after Baudelaire, refers to cities as being characterized by 'moving chaos' (Berman 1982: 171); the sheer number and diversity of those parts creates a complexity that, for Lefevbre (2003: 45), 'surpasses the tools of our understanding and the instruments of practical activity'. 'The urban phenomenon, taken as a whole, cannot be grasped by any specialized science,' Lefevbre says, and

> even if we assume as a methodological principle that no science can turn its back
> on itself but that each specialization must maximize the use of its own resources to

81

comprehend the global phenomenon, none of these sciences can claim to exhaust it. Or control it.

'In confusion', Lefevbre adds, 'urban is conceived, perceived, and revealed' (Lefevbre 2003: 53, 117). Now, for Jacobs, some buildings and other structures in cities have a critical role in 'clarifying the order of cities' (Jacobs 1992: 384). Jacobs calls these 'landmarks' that 'emphasize (and also dignify) the diversity of cities,' she says, 'by calling attention to the fact that they are different from their neighbours, and important because they are different' (Jacobs 1992: 384). Elsewhere in *The Death and Life of American Cities*, in writing about what she calls 'primary uses', she makes reference to organizations and buildings that function as 'anchorages', a notion that overlaps with 'landmarks' (Jacobs 1992: 161). An examination of the 'anchorage' role of the university as well as – and overlapping with – the role of the university as 'landmark' is attractive methodologically, at least as a means by which 'the whole equation' of the diverse city can be contemplated and negotiated; that is, crudely, a consideration of the singular part will allow for a consideration of the plurality of the whole.[1]

Though one hesitates to press too much on this figurative device, it must also be said that the metaphor of the anchor holds out considerable promise politically. The image of the anchor, with its implications of stability and security, offers a compelling metaphorical framework to place against the 'constant revolutionising of production, uninterrupted disturbance of all social conditions, everlasting uncertainty and agitation' that 'distinguish[es] the bourgeois epoch from all earlier ones', as Marx declares in *The Communist Manifesto*. If, for Marx, 'all fixed, fast-frozen relations, with their train of ancient and venerable prejudices and opinions, are swept away, all new-formed ones become antiquated before they can ossify. All that is solid melts into air', then surely the 'anchor' promises stability, even refuge from this ever-moving tide (Marx 1977: 224)? Anchor institutions – if the metaphor holds – can be an important force for cohesion, a guarantee that the social fabric of the city will to some extent be preserved against either decay or assault. Moreover, anchors, as keys to 'clarifying the order' of cities, have a role – surely – in promoting, even guaranteeing, the 'right to the city', which is in turn, as Harvey memorably says, 'the freedom to make and remake ourselves' (Harvey 2013: 4). In other words, the potential exists for the anchor – stable and inviolate – to act as the means by which the right to the city is exercised.

As Harvey is keen to point out, however, the notion of a 'fix' is double-edged. He writes of a 'spatiotemporal fix' as 'a metaphor for solutions to capitalist crises through temporal deferment and geographical expansion'; we must consider a 'fix' *as solution* as well as a 'fix' *as a spatial grounding* (Harvey 2017: 248). The 'anchor' metaphor declares itself a 'fix' perhaps in both these senses, a solution to a particular form of (capitalist?) crisis and a 'grounding' of that solution in space and time – in the shape of buildings in particular locations. The 'anchor' institution then can be useful politically as the locus for certain manoeuvres within capitalism. This indeed is the lens through which to view the convergence of strategies in Ireland described above: the national spatial strategy (literally) 'grounds' other strategies, such as the strategy for higher education, clearly 'anchoring' it in place and space and time. We might best understand the political economy of spatial strategy (especially as it applies to smart cities), therefore, via a closer investigation of the kinds of entities the strategy wishes to 'place'.

Such metaphorical formulations as the university as 'anchor' of course are not arbitrary nor historically – nor ideologically – accidental, as Steven Shapin (2012) shows in his compelling examination of the use of another metaphor for the university, that of the 'ivory tower'. The notion of the university as an 'ivory tower' emerged in the 1930s and was part of a wider discourse around political commitment – the question was whether professors and students should act 'responsibly' and join the fight against the Fascists or whether, morally, they could retreat and disregard contemporary political and social reality. The term increasingly was pejorative in its usage; in an address in the University of Pennsylvania in 1940, Roosevelt proclaimed: 'This is no time for any man to withdraw into some ivory tower and proclaim the right to hold himself aloof from the problems, yes, and the agonies of his society' (cited in Shapin 2012: 14). Correction and reform of the university proceeded through the war years, leading, to a point, in the resolution of the 'disengagement-commitment' problem after the Second World War by which time universities had been brought into greater alignment with the state. After the Second World War, there came the construction of what Shapin refers to as the 'military–industrial–academic complex', and such is the power of that complex that 'the ivory tower of old has become an arm of the state and an arm of industry, and the students inside reach out toward the labour market and toward political influence' (Kerr cited in Shapin 2012: 16).

The notion of the 'anchor' has emerged at an important time in thinking about the role of universities and, interestingly, at a time when the very discourses that preoccupied many in the 1930s, particularly around ideas of engagement and responsibility, have been – to an extent – revived. The 'anchor' is a more flattering formulation to many academics, certainly, than 'ivory tower'; where the 'ivory tower' – with its roots in religion and mythology[2] – suggests separation, fantastic abstraction and isolation, the 'anchor' can be seen to represent attachment, solidity and relevance. But where the 'ivory tower' constructs the university as a place – in the form of a building, however fantastical – the 'anchor' is a metaphor of instrumentality, pitching the debate about universities not so much towards the kinds of places they *are* but rather to the kinds of *uses* they have, an important shift in thinking (Goatly 2007: 103).

The use of universities

Invariably, the focus in much of the literature has been on the *economic* usages of universities as city anchors and on their economic contribution to cities and regions. It is possible to list these contributions by way of summary of recent 'anchor' literature (see, e.g., Adams 2003; Ehlenz 2018; Goddard et al. 2014; Harris and Holley 2016; Penn Institute for Urban Research 2010). Universities, we can note first of all, are major employers by virtue of their scale and complexity, often among the largest employers in particular locations. Second, as institutions of scale, they are major purchasers of local goods and services and thus have considerable effect on the local market and local service provision. Third, universities attract students, including students from outside the city and often from abroad, all of whom contribute to the local economy through their own expenditure – on accommodation, food and various services. According to Ehlenz (2018: 88), urban physical revitalization efforts by universities can be viewed as part of the recruitment effort, as universities 'seek to sell students not only on their campuses, but also their neighbourhoods', within which context 'physical revitalization becomes a strategic investment'. Fourth, these students, in turn, provide a cadre of flexible, low-cost, often casual workers to local enterprise. These impacts by virtue of the scale and breadth of the operation of the organization, are an expression of 'mechanical "demand" effects' (Valero and van Reenen 2019).

Also of course the core activities of teaching and research have an economic impact on the university's city and further afield – the economic impact of 'supply', as it were, to add to the demand effects listed above. Through the education of students, universities contribute to what is now termed 'human capital'. 'Skilled workers are more productive than unskilled workers', Valero and Van Reenan (2019: 53) indicate, and universities increase the pool of skilled workers and increase the level of skills of the workers already in place. Felsenstein (1996: 1568) contends that, 'by raising the average level of human capital locally, the university increases productivity of all labour in the metropolitan area,' adding that

> the human capital effect can also have an effect on business location decisions. The existence of a university-generated, skilled-labour pool can attract existing firms from other places and can also lead to an increase in local new firm formation rate.

Finally,

> in a knowledge-based society, the university moves from a secondary status to become an equal player with government and industry as the source of growth poles for economic development based on new knowledge that it generates or existing knowledge whose transfer it facilitates.
>
> (Etzkowitz 2018: 296)

Research activity within the university generates this new knowledge; this is then made available for utilization by others (as Felsenstein [1996: 1570] notes, 'the university presence in this area is felt in the production of knowledge that is sold to export markets or that will help local firms and services become more competitive'), or, in some cases, is used by the university itself to create intellectual property that is directly commercialized. The value of universities here is typically measured in the patents they produce as well as in the translation of knowledge into economic activity by associated firms and entrepreneurs through various collaborative agreements of one kind of another (which may involve, for instance, co-sponsorship of a particular research programme, the sharing of physical laboratories or the on-campus hosting of companies and the provision of business support to them within 'incubators') (see, e.g., Holley and Harris 2018).

It is immediately evident that the utilitarian, instrumental nature of the anchor metaphor carries over into thinking about the university as an anchor institution, with the focus in the description above less on the *nature* of the organization and more on its *use*. In itself this gives expression to a shift in thinking about universities in the twentieth century from a traditional vision of the university as involving 'the production of high culture, critical thinking, and exemplary scientific and humanistic knowledge, necessary for the training of elites', to a vision that involves the university in 'the production of average cultural standards and *instrumental knowledge* [...] useful for training the qualified labour force demanded by capitalist developments' (de Sousa Santos 2010: 60, emphasis added).It is interesting in this regard that the usefulness of the university is considered in terms of 'impact', understood and measured in various ways. Drawing on such a metaphorical field associated with power and force encourages a goal-directedness in our thinking about the organization that is so described. (We read, in the same vein, of universities as 'drivers' of economic development, where forceful metaphorical fields are also deployed.) Worth noting also in passing is of the entity 'having a stake', which seems to combine both territorial usages (as in, 'to stake a claim') and usages linked to participation via the word 'stakeholder'. While the origins of 'stakeholder' are uncertain, it does seem to have appeared in management literature in the 1970s and to have been a deliberate play on words like 'shareholder' or 'stockholder'. The notion of 'having a stake' confers legitimacy, according to Freeman (2010: 45, 46), who goes on to say that a stakeholder in an organization (or, for our purposes, in a city) is 'any group or individual who can affect or is affected by the achievement of the organization's objectives'. The 'stake' in this sense is future-directed and teleological in that it is linked to the (future) 'achievement of objectives' – the association of the image of the 'stake' with gambling (as in, 'to stake a bet on') underlines this goal-directed notion attaching to it, as does the rootedness of the word in 'shareholder' where the future goal is profit. The metaphor also, if we press hard enough, here admits the notions of winning and losing into our understanding of the organization, eschewing figuratively any attempt to position such an organization as advancing equality.

The anchor metaphor as deployed above points towards a broad, neo-liberal marketization of higher education; that is, both on calibrating the use of the organization against the wider market and in positioning the institution in a higher-education 'marketplace' within which students are conceived as consumers for whom colleges compete (see, e.g., Levidow 2004). The neo-liberal university – and to be sure the 'anchor' set out above describes such an organization – therefore is market-led in two related ways. First of all, in 'bringing economic rationality, consumer choice and the disciplining of the market and its accompanying new managerialist forms of administration to bear on knowledge production and dissemination', neo-liberalism has shifted how knowledge is produced and disseminated, how universities are organized and run and how universities are thought of and represented (Ward 2012: 5). Ward (2012: 6) writes that 'market efficiencies and economic fundamentals' determine the courses developed and taught (based on the types of skills determined to be needed by the market), 'while simultaneously creating the competitive pressures necessary to force educational institutions and teachers and professors to become more flexible and to produce the best product possible for the lowest possible cost'. Second, increasingly universities are directed towards 'employability' and labour force development, seeking what one writer calls a 'grim alignment' between higher-education institutions (and other institutions of the state) and corporate capital and transnational corporations (Giroux 2004). In these circumstances, institutions such as universities are 'guided and governed by the logic and imperatives of transnational corporations and the broader economic goals', rather than by ends that are self-defined (Germic 2009: 127).

One may certainly position the 'anchor' university within the smart city as an extension of the 'military–industrial–academic complex' above. Extrapolating from the two understandings of the smart city proposed by Kitchin (2014), we can determine two distinct, if related, ways in which the university plays a role in smart city development in this context. As Kitchin (2014: 2) suggests, on the one hand, the smart city proposition is linked closely to an economic growth proposition built on the so-called knowledge economy, with the smart city 'one whose economy and governance is being driven by innovation, creativity and entrepreneurship, enacted by smart people'. The university, in this case, can be seen to provide many of these important component parts: strong research and development expertise, equipment and effort, including in specific 'high-value' domains; the 'smart people', that is, educated workers; creativity that arises naturally within the experimental domains that are universities, not to mention the cultural activity that is attracted by the scale and nature of the university as an entity; business schools, in many cases, out of which arises support and education for entrepreneurs. Universities, moreover, as 'anchor' institutions possess the kind of stability and immunity from institutional failure – the 'institutional stamina' (Bunnell and Lawson 2006: 41) – that permits these experiments to fail without serious (commercial) penalty. On the other hand, according to Kitchin (2014: 2), a smart city 'focuses on ICT and its use in managing and regulating the city from a largely technocratic and technological perspective', embedding technology into the fabric of the city, 'everyware', which 'works to make a city knowable and controllable in new, more fine-grained, dynamic and interconnected ways'. Universities, similarly, have in themselves become proving grounds for the deployment of smart technologies; 'smart universities' and 'smart campuses', terms now more frequently in use, see universities use integrated information systems to enrol and monitor students, as well as carry out core administrative tasks, and the use of so-called virtual learning environments (VLEs) as teaching platforms is now ubiquitous. The European Commission, notably, has declared the need for an educational 'reset' to take account of the rapid digitalization of society that includes more extensive use of digital tools in teaching coupled with a plan for 'improving digital literacy, skills and capacity at all levels of education and training and for all levels of digital skills', with significant consequences for universities (European Commission 2020: 4). Some universities have adopted smart technology to monitor energy usage, among other things, and make that data available to the public (Vasileva et al. 2018). In these and other ways, the university can function as a 'growth pole' for smart technologies and a laboratory for smart developments, can 'anchor' smart cities in these respects very effectively.

Strategic priorities in Ireland

The vision of higher education set out in Ireland's *National Strategy for Higher Education* is largely neo-liberal in the terms sketched out above. 'Our economy depends on – and will continue to depend on – knowledge and its application in products, processes and services that are exported', the strategy tells us early on, going on to set out the demands that are placed on higher-education institutions in the service of that economy: 'the educational level of the Irish population has to be raised', not as an end in itself but in order to create 'a workforce capable of dealing with the increasingly complex demands of the global economy'. For the same reason, 'people who are already employed need to raise their level of qualification and broaden their educational base' and 'unemployed people need new educational opportunities that are attuned to the demands of the new economy'. Finally, 'a significant research effort has to be expended on priority areas where we, as a country, have the talent, experience and resources that will enable us to succeed on a global scale' because 'research has strong potential to create the new knowledge that can be used to create new enterprise opportunities, and to improve quality of life throughout society', with the prescription that 'higher education institutions must become more active agents in knowledge transfer than before and gain greater value from inherent intellectual property by engaging more effectively with enterprise' (Department of Education and Skills 2011: 29, 33, 38; for more detailed analysis of the Irish context, see, e.g., Holborow 2012a, 2012b; Holborow and O'Sullivan 2017; Holland et al. 2016; Mercille and Murphy 2015).

The elaboration of a particular notion of equality in the *National Strategy for Higher Education* is revealing. Equality in the strategy is linked to participation and participation is required in order to fuel 'the further expansion of higher education' that is 'inevitable and essential if we are to fulfil our aspirations as an innovative and knowledge-based economy' (Department of Education and Skills 2011: 33). Equality, in other words, is not pursued as an end it itself but as a means to increase the volume of graduates. How those graduates are to be formed is also set out: they must have an 'entrepreneurial imagination'; they should be equipped with certain core, not specialist, skills that will enable them to bring greater flexibility to the workplace; they should also display strong skills in maths and science because of the 'technological orientation of our leading companies'; they should take programmes of study that are the result of institutions taking a more 'responsive' approach to programme development (referencing those programmes against 'wider social, economic, environmental and civic challenges' as set by the 'external' environment; and, finally, those programmes should be delivered 'flexibly' to allow for people who 'want to – and need to – move between employment and education', the workplace and the classroom (Department of Education and Skills 2011: 35–37). Equality, in other words, is framed within the broad neo-liberal approach and is linked to the fulfilment of, especially, workforce and 'human capital' development strategy.

The new universities envisaged for Ireland and described in the *National Strategy* are a particularly important instrument for the implementation of this neo-liberal agenda and, indeed, as new organizations represent an institutional *tabula rasa* on which that neo-liberal agenda can find, to date, largely uncontested expression. Among the functions of the technological university, under the Techno-logical Universities Act 2018, are included the requirement that the university acts to 'support entrepreneurship, enterprise development and innovation in business, enterprise and the professions through teaching and the conduct of research and through effective transfer to those and other sectors of knowledge arising from that research', to 'collaborate with business, enterprise, the professions, the commu-nity, local interests and related stakeholders', 'to promote the involvement of those stakeholders in the design and delivery of programmes of education and training', to 'ensure that, in so far as possible, innovation activity and research undertaken by the technological university reflects the needs of those stakeholders', to 'support the development of a skilled labour force' and the 'mobility of staff and students of the technological university into and out of the labour force through collabor-ation with business, enterprise, the professions and related stakeholders' and, 'in so far as possible in the performance of its functions', to promote 'an entrepre-neurial ethos' (Technological Universities Act 2018: n.pag.).

Importantly, these new universities also have a critical role to play in the real-ization of Ireland's spatial strategy. *Project Ireland 2040* suggests that, 'by creating institutions of scale and strength, multi-campus technological universities will bring greater social and economic benefits to their regions through a strengthened role in research and innovation and the delivery of a broad range of high-quality education' (Government of Ireland 2018: 90). The centre points of Ireland's spa-tial strategy are Ireland's cities; *Project Ireland 2040* strongly favours 'more con-centrated growth' in Ireland's five cities (Dublin, Cork, Limerick, Galway and Waterford) and indicates that 'in our plan we are targeting these five cities for 50% of overall national growth between them'. Partly the strategy is designed to correct a 'regional imbalance' that has seen a considerable growth in population in Dublin at the expense of other locations:

> At the moment Dublin, and to a lesser extent the wider Eastern and Midland area, has witnessed an overconcentration of population, homes and jobs. We cannot let this continue unchecked and so our aim is to see [...] 75% of the [future] growth to be outside of Dublin and its suburbs.
>
> (Government of Ireland 2018: 11)

'As the largest centres of population, employment and services outside the Capital, the four cities other than Dublin, provide a focus for their regions,' the strategy says, with the regional cities therefore bearing the load of rebalancing against the capital (Government of Ireland 2018: 20). In other words, Irish regional cities are conceived in the strategy as the country's 'growth machines' (see Molotch 1976). Technological universities are imagined as an important vehicle of regional rebalancing and will be located in all of the regional cities.[3] The regional dimension is embedded into the very fabric of these organizations; the functions of the technological universities are framed – indeed contained – by an overarching requirement that these universities have 'particular regard to the needs of the region in which the campuses of the technological university are located' (Technological Universities Act 2018).

While these universities are required to respond to the 'needs of the region' (however defined), there is surprisingly little in the national strategy on the physical footprints of these entities. Indeed, the national strategy sidesteps spatial considerations by proclaiming that 'developments in information and communications technologies enable higher education to be delivered in ways never before possible, and allow students to access a wide range of resources, *free from limitations of space and time*' (Department of Education and Skills 2011: 48, emphasis added). A section on 'physical resources' in the *National Strategy for Higher Education* is notable for its brevity but also for the implied understanding of space it sets out. The framework within which institutional spaces are considered is that of efficiency in space utilization, with the strategy encouraging 'increasing the efficiency of space usage in the [higher-education] sector' through, for instance, lengthening the academic year and facilitating the kinds of flexible provision (e.g. night-time delivery of programmes) emphasized earlier (Department of Education and Skills 2011: 120). Here, consistent with the overall ideological project, space also is commodified and the goal is to manipulate and exploit it as efficiently as possible. Thomas Docherty (2011: 73) makes the point very well:

> Space, as a commodity, is itself to be exploited; and its exploitation will lead to further manipulations of space that will encourage further exploitation of the resources of the planet we call home. Behind this is an ideological drive in which citizens will start to 'know their proper place', as it were; and, in this, I mean to hint that there is a tacit political and ideological drive here, and one that is meant to 'contain' (if I can pursue the spatial metaphor) the potential or latent demands of the human subject and spirit for edification and expansion of consciousness into unforeseen modes of thought.

The underlying assumption, highlighted by Docherty here, is that higher-education institutions, anchored in physical places, can be the vehicle by which that space is utilized 'efficiently'. The underlying approach to space in the neo-liberal university, then, involves the *disciplining* and *containment* of space that it might yield greater return (in the shape of efficiency). It is interesting to note in this context that the European Commission's approach to smart cities places emphasis on the smart city as 'a way to do urban politics for less money', as Smigiel (2018: 340) puts it, 'a narrative of cost-efficiency that makes them adaptable to other multiscalar political strategies, for example, austerity politics'.

I suggest a similar project is at work in the larger strategy as it relates to the creation of new city-based, regional universities. David Harvey (2000: 31) contends that 'the accumulation of capital has always been a profoundly geographical affair', in that 'geographical re-orderings and restructurings, spatial strategic and geopolitical elements, uneven geographical developments, and the like, are vital aspects to the accumulation of capital and the dynamics of class struggle'. Capital strives, in periods of turbulence, to create 'fixes' by which, as suggested above, contradictions and tensions within capitalism are resolved by certain spatial reorderings and restructurings. These restructurings 'serve to facilitate regime legitimation, the reproduction of labour and, above all, the production and circulation of capital' (Breathnach 2010: 1181). I propose that the anchor university, described in the ways set out above, does not so much anchor the city in which it is based but rather serves to anchor *capital* in the city that will be disciplined to capital's end. The city is not anchored by the university, in other words; the university, as the vehicle for the neo-liberal state, is anchored by the city. As Peck et al. (2009: 49, 58) have suggested, 'cities have become strategically central sites in the uneven, crisis-laden advance of neoliberal restructuring projects' with many cities 'geographical targets and institutional laboratories for a variety of neoliberal policy experiments'. The creation of the technological university in Ireland, with its strong region-centred profile and its alignment with the national spatial strategy that emphasizes 'compact growth' in Ireland's cities, is, I suggest, a neo-liberal policy experiment such as is described above – one means for the 'urbanization of neoliberalism' (Peck et al. 2009: 65).

Neo-liberal urbanization

Peck et al. (2009) describe, in a useful schema, a number of what they call 'destructive and creative moments of neoliberal urbanization' to which the technological university 'anchors' can usefully be linked. We may point to three in particular. These involve, first of all, 'reconfiguring the institutional infrastructure of the local state'. This requires 'dismantling [...] bureaucratized, hierarchical forms of local public administration' and assaulting 'traditional relays of local democratic accountability' in favour of 'new networked forms of local governance' and the 'incorporation of elite business interests in local policy and development' (Peck et al. 2009: 59–62). Irish higher-education policy has been strong on the greater inclusion of business interests in decision-making, including at the level of the curriculum and the strengthening of association between the new universities and business, and enterprise is an important feature of the technological university. The anchor university is a means by which these interests can find greater representation.

Second, the neo-liberal urbanization experiment involves 'reworking labour market regulation'. The university described above has a particular focus on labour-market activation through the creation of work-linked programmes of study, the integration of work-based elements into the curriculum and the widening of participation with the purpose of increasing the number of 'work-ready' graduates. Peck et al. (2009: 59–62) suggest that neo-liberal urbanization has involved the 'dismantling of traditional, publicly funded programmes' and the 'implementation of work-readiness programs aimed at the conscription of workers into low-wage jobs'. While these are not obviously the case in Ireland, the strong policy imperative around the involvement of universities explicitly in creating labour market supply is consistent with this move. What one can suggest is that the consistent emphasis in higher-education policy on the *volume* of graduates, particularly in domains linked to technology, is designed to undermine the possibility that workers within these domains will generate monopoly power by ensuring an abundance of avenues for training workers in these areas (Harvey 2015: 120). The so-called skills agenda in this analysis is driven not by an abundance of vacancies but by a need to create a surplus of skilled workers, therefore ensuring that the cost (to capital) of trained workers is reduced. We might also suggest that the emphasis in regional universities on regional rebalancing, as the national spatial strategy has it, involves the production of a labour force (with its ecological-political consequences) outside the centre of power (the capital city in this case). This is a familiar strategy within capitalism: the geography of social reproduction is rejigged 'so that the costs of social reproduction [...] are borne away from where most [of] the benefits accrue' (Katz 2001: 715).

Finally, neo-liberal urbanization involves 're-representing the city'. Peck et al. (2009: 59–62) point to the prevalence of ' "entrepreneurial" discourses and representations focused on urban revitalization, reinvestment and rejuvenation' displacing 'performative discourses of urban disorder, "dangerous classes" and economic decline'. The strong focus in the new universities on entrepreneurism and the 'entrepreneurial mindset', as we have seen, is consistent with this shift in urbanization under neo-liberalism. It is in the context of 're-presenting the city' that we may also best understand the 'smart city imaginary' and the role of universities in smart city discourse (Cugurullo 2018: 113). Gonella (2019: 9) writes of the 'mainstream S[mart] C[ity] narrative as presented by most of the current outlines' as often talking 'of an urban reality that does not exist'. 'Real problems that are at the root of "un-smartness" of a city,' Gonella declares, 'like poverty, inequality, unemployment, illiteracy, corruption, lack of sanitary and educational structures, are just not addressed whatsoever' in the typical and dominant smart city narrative; that narrative is, in this sense, a distorted re-presentation of urban reality (Gonella 2019: 9). The 'smart university', the 'anchor', may be seen to form part of that same strategy, involving a rhetorical reframing of urban experience in terms of, for instance, 'innovation' and the 'landmark' role of a university being displaced into its use function in supporting certain business interests, rather than as a physical location in which certain dimensions of urban experience are manifested, described and analysed or, as I examine later, wherein certain forms of citizenship may be explored.

These various interventions associated with 'neo-liberal urbanization' are of course the outcomes of state-written strategies and come thus with the imprimatur of the state. While neo-liberalism has involved the purposeful 'withdrawal of the state from many areas of social provision' (Harvey 2005: 3), with the state moving 'from being a purveyor of collective well-being, equality and general social welfare' to 'an information conduit' for entrepreneurs and consumers, ensuring they continue to be 'informed of their options in the marketplace' (students of course in this scenario are primarily consumers), 'a manager or auditor' who verifies if economic goals are being achieved and 'accountability mandates' being followed and 'an agent who would establish a market where none existed before' (Ward 2012: 6), that withdrawal has not been entirely complete. Some have suggested that the state has been transformed into a different *kind* of state, with the nation state replaced by the market state:

> The nation state is responsible for groups; the market state enhances the opportunities of individuals [...]. In the nation state, the economic arena is the workplace and factory: men and women are workers and producers. In the market state, the economic arena is the market place: men and women are consumers.
>
> (Rutherford 2005: 299)

Historically (as Oleson [2014] has shown), however, neo-liberalism has not always involved the state 'getting out of the way' of capital. In the 1990s, during the so-called roll-out phase of neo-liberalism, more prevalent was an aides-faire as much as a laissez-faire approach by the state, with the state often playing 'a more active role in facilitating the accumulation of capital by intervening in the market, for example, through among other things, generating public investments in infrastructure and urban development projects in order to support market logics and competition' (Oleson 2014: 292). I contend that the creation of new universities in Ireland coupled with the national spatial strategy represents such an intervention. State sponsorship of smart city initiatives, arguably, fall into the same category.

Alternatives and responses

As Brenner (2004: 76) is keen to point out, however, 'state spatiality' is 'not a thing, container, or platform, but a socially produced conflictual, and dynamically changing matrix of sociospatial interaction', 'a presupposition, an arena, and an outcome of continually evolving political strategies'. Pinson and Journel (2016: 139, emphasis added) argue, in fact, that 'neoliberalism does not only land in cities or impact urban governance; cities are basically crucial cradles of neoliberalization, provide fundamental material bases for this process, but also for its *contestation*'. While the kinds of organizations conceived in the Irish national strategy as described above seek to 'anchor' cities in particular ways determined by a neo-liberal state, this strategy – these spaces – may yet be tested.

MacGregor (2004: 144) remarks on the 'cultural shift' that has occurred in the wake of neo-liberal state policies, whereby 'those included in the economy and society have to exercise responsibility to provide for themselves and their families'; neo-liberalism has involved the elevation of what one may term the 'entrepreneurial self', where there is an increased emphasis on personal responsibility for one's (particularly) economic fate. Rose describes in more detail the construction of a life made up of a series of different enterprises and quotes Gordon who speaks of how

> the whole ensemble of individual life [...] structured as the pursuit of a range of different enterprises, a person's relation to all his or her activities, and indeed to his or her self, [has] 'the ethos and structure of the enterprise form'.
>
> (Gordon cited in Rose 1999: 138)

This 'cultural shift' involves a reconfiguration of the relationship between the public and the private spheres, and indeed Rose (1999: 166) suggests that the neo-liberal rationale has involved reaching a position where 'individuals can best fulfil their political obligations in relation to the wealth, health and happiness of the nation not when they are bound into relations of dependency and obligation, but when they seek to fulfil themselves as free individuals'. For Rose (1999: 166), we find in neo-liberal states that 'citizenship is no longer primarily realized in a relation with the state, or in a single 'public sphere', but in a variety of private, corporate and quasi-public practices from working to shopping' with the citizen compelled to 'enact his or her democratic obligations as a form of consumption'. In the university, similarly, the pursuit of learning for the purposes of individual self-actualization (usually understood in terms of employability) now eclipses any notion of learning for its own sake; 'university students are increasingly approaching knowledge not as a journey of discovery or a process of transformation but as a purely instrumental endeavour, which may bring a better social status and salary in the future' (Mavelli 2018: 485), and the public institution of the university has been transformed into an organization ideologically and practically built in order to guarantee that individual self-actualization – this much is evident from the Irish national strategy.[4] The public role of the university as 'anchor' is to offer a venue for consumption wherein (neo-liberal) citizenship may be realized. The spatial construction of universities arguably mirrors this move towards greater individuation and privatization of learning. While a detailed examination of the footprints of Irish universities is beyond the scope of this chapter, we may point towards some common features of university campuses that are immediately recognizable in the Irish context, features that militate against a sense of the university as a 'public' institution and promote a culture of 'separateness and containment' (Stanton 2005: 38). So, as Dever et al. (2014: 12) suggest, 'to provide ease of access for faculty, staff and students, the university builds parking lots around the school, often at the edges of campus, abutting the larger community' and providing a barrier between the university and the community. Further, 'amenities, such as open space, recreational facilities, etc., are located on campus in a controlled environment allowing for limited interaction with community members', something subject to surveillance and security, often not accessible at all (Dever et al. 2014: 12). To this we might add, in the Irish context, the construction of many universities away from city centres on out-of-town suburban sites.

A countermove would be to liberate universities as public spaces and support an equality agenda based less around access to future economic opportunity and employment and the enhancement of 'human capital' and a more active appreciation of interdependence and community. This liberation might begin to be achieved, first of all, by reforming educational discourse and the curriculum to shift emphasis from learning as a private endeavour, an 'investment' in self-actualization, to recognize, with John Dewey, that school is 'a form of community life' (Dewey 1929: 293). This shift in educational discourse might then be mirrored in a shift in the discourses surrounding citizen participation in smart city life, typically a paradigm wherein citizen participation is 'often synonymous with "choice" and the market, with the predominant citizen roles being: "consumer" or "user" [...], "resident" [...], or "data product"' (Cardullo and Kitchin 2019: 813). The opportunity exists to model new modes of participation in civic life through new modes of talking about and participating in university life and to force into being a new set of discursive practices around smart cities.

From a practical point of view, the recovery of the university campus as a public space involves recognizing and exploiting space for its representational potential – again as a model for how such space can be recovered elsewhere in the (smart) city. Mitchell (1995), drawing heavily on Lefevbre, points towards two visions of 'public space'. The first vision is where such space is conceived as 'open space for recreation and entertainment, subject to usage by an appropriate public that is allowed in', space that is thus 'a controlled and orderly retreat where a properly behaved public might experience the spectacle of the city'. Public space, in this formulation, is conceived of as a representation of space by Lefevbre (see Lefevbre 1991), to be contrasted with 'representational space', where 'public space is taken and remade by political actors; it is politicized at its very core; and it tolerates the risks of disorder (including recidivist political movements) as central to its functioning'. The former vision 'is planned, orderly, and safe' and 'users of this space must be made to feel comfortable, and they should not be driven away by unsightly homeless people or unsolicited political activity'; in the latter, the public space 'is a place within which a political movement can stake out the space that allows it to be seen', a space where 'social groups themselves become public' (Mitchell 1995: 115). The anchor university as conceived in the remarks above proposes itself very much as a 'representation of space' – safe, controlled, an orderly retreat; a more radical vision would be of a university more obviously 'representational'. Multiple strategies might here be involved, above and beyond making institutional space available for political gatherings and action (Ong [2006: 503] speaks of the opening up of 'venues of political performance and claims' enabled by technology). Notions of the university as a kind of *heterotopia* and a place apart might be critiqued; universities should encourage exercises that dismantle the power relations at work within the university itself, allowing for a process of 'unlearning the internalization of institutional learning, from clock-watching to hierarchies of expertise' (Jeppesen and Adamik 2017: 240). In particular, there might be an erosion of the power relations associated with the notion of 'expertise' and the creation of a different form of public life in the shape of the collegiate community (see Noveck [2015] for some reflections on expertise and urban governance). This might involve more sustained and systematic investigations of the relationships between formality and informality in the learning environment (see Devlin and Porter 2011). It might also involve greater scrutiny and interrogation of the value systems embedded in the data gathering and analysis that takes place within and between universities and across the wider educational system, from examination results and student records to institutional rankings. In the end, a 'representational' campus, in practical terms, would seem to involve a campus without physical barriers (including means of surveillance) to public access to classrooms, laboratories and other spaces within university campuses. This would be a radical challenge to educational commodification. Conceptualizing and modelling such a campus would raise interesting structural questions about the funding of universities, among other things, and in turn raise useful questions for public access across all urban environments.

Harvey (2013: 23) has pointed out that part of the neo-liberal assault on cities has been

> to create new systems of governance that integrate state and corporate interests and, through the application of money power, assure that control over the disbursement of the surplus through the state apparatus favours corporate capital and the upper classes in the shaping of the urban process.

In this way, he says, 'we see the right to the city falling into the hands of private or quasi-private interests' (Harvey 2013: 23). The liberation of the university as a public space has to do with the relationship between the institution and community, that is, with constructing (or renewing) particular models of collaborative governance and spatial stewardship. Nye and Schramm (1999: 11) usefully rehearse a number of potential models of community–university partnership, starting with the 'paternalistic/theory testing relationship' in which 'the university poses both the questions and the tentative answers, and then uses the community as a laboratory to test its theories' to the 'university as your resource' model in which the university 'sees itself as subservient to the community's needs, available to help as needed but not to set the agenda'. In the end they advocate for 'the empowerment or capacity-building model', which 'emphasizes the building of the power and capacity of local community organizations and residents to formulate and carry out their own planning, research, and implementation', working alongside university staff (Nye and Schramm 1999: 11). In terms of architecture and spatial planning, one would expect such a university to address questions such as those put by Lyndon (2005: 3):

> Do the patterns of open space and building that are conventionally associated with 'campus' have a place within neighbourhoods that the institutions infiltrate? Conversely, should the apparatus of the city have something to say about how campus spaces are formed? [...] Should not places of learning be designed so that they lead their inhabitants to encounter a larger community, new perceptions of capability, and expanded understanding of their position in the natural and built places they inhabit?

Answering these questions would necessarily involve meaningful and formal collaboration with neighbours, which would in turn mean the meaningful involvement of locals in university governance and decision-making. Universities are particularly well-equipped to pursue a community 'anchor' role understood in this way because, as Bunnell and Lawson (2006: 41) put it, they have the 'ability to command attention', the ability 'to bring powerful and influential public agencies together', more than local communities they have the ability to 'organise and orchestrate a complex planning process involving multiple parties' and 'to sustain the planning process' because they can deploy the 'institutional stamina' identified earlier to 'pursue the time-consuming steps needed to take a community vision from the concept stage to a refined form where it could gain official public acceptance'. We may need to go further. According to de Lange and de Waal (2013), notions of 'togetherness' – 'a fittingly nauseating name for an old ideal in planning theory', says Jacobs (1992: 62) – should be rejected in favour of more radical reinventions of our approach to collective issues and, ultimately, to equality and citizenship. De Lange and de Waal (2013: n.pag.) advocate for the governance of citizen engagement to be based on peer-to-peer networking rather than 'the parochialism inherent in bottom-up community models and the paternalism of top-down institutional participation policies'. 'Networked peer-to-peer tools', they write, 'instead of seeking consensus', are 'tools that allow room for managing differences'.

Conclusion

The creation of collaborative and cooperative, 'public' universities utilizing smart and readily available technology and constructed in peer-to-peer rather than hierarchical modes of organization might begin to counteract existing systems of governance within the urban process, serving indeed as a means to 'anchor' in a different way the interests of the community and act as an agency that allows citizens' rights to public space be exercised and equality to begin to be properly examined. In a sense what is proposed here is that the 'right to the city' could be at least partially facilitated through the 'right to the university' conceived as a form of urban commons and decoupled from the neo-liberal paradigm – including from existing smart city paradigms – sketched out above. Describing universities as such venues is a challenge and suggests the need for a different metaphorical field than that provided by 'anchor' or indeed by the wider vocabulary of the smart city.

NOTES

1. The phrase is F. Scott Fitzgerald's. Considering Hollywood, the narrator of *The Last Tycoon*, says, 'It can be understood too, but only dimly and in flashes. Not half a dozen men have ever been able to keep the whole equation of pictures in their heads' (Fitzgerald 1960: 5–6).

2. 'In the twelfth century [the ivory tower] stood for the casing in which the salvation of the world was segregated for a while in order to grow for its role in the world. The Virgin Mary was compared to an ivory tower because she had carried the Saviour in her pure womb until He entered the world.' (Rüegg 2011: 16)
3. There are, it must be noted, nuances here that are beyond the scope of this chapter. Each technological university will be created from the amalgamation and re-designation of a number of existing institutions, some of which are currently located in the regional cities, some in towns elsewhere in the various regions. The primacy of one site over another has not been established within these various consortia; I follow here the logic of the national spatial strategy, which clearly indicates the priority of the city in regional development terms.
4. Carol Christ's comments on the marketing literature of certain American colleges and their use of metaphors of family and community to encourage a sense of belonging offers an interesting topic of further study (see Christ 2005).

REFERENCES

Adams, C. (2003), 'The meds and eds in urban economic development', *Journal of Urban Affairs*, 25:5, pp. 571–88.

Berman, M. (1982), *All That Is Solid Melts into Air: The Experience of Modernity*, Harmondsworth: Penguin.

Breathnach, P. (2010), 'From spatial Keynesianism to post-Fordist neoliberalism: Emerging contradictions in the spatiality of the Irish state', *Antipode*, 42:5, pp. 1180–99.

Brenner, N. (2004), *New State Spaces: Urban Governance and the Rescaling of Statehood*, Oxford: Oxford University Press.

Bunnell, G. and Lawson, C. (2006), 'A public university as city planner and developer: Experience in the "capital of good planning"', *Planning, Practice & Research*, 21:1, pp. 25–43.

Cardullo, P. and Kitchin, R. (2019), 'Smart urbanism and smart citizenship: The neoliberal logic of "citizen-focused" smart cities in Europe', *Environment and Planning C: Politics and Space*, 37:5, pp. 813–30.

Christ, C. T. (2005), 'Living in public', *Places*, 17:1, pp. 22–25.

Cugurullo, F. (2018), 'The origin of the smart city imaginary: From the dawn of modernity to the eclipse of reason', in C. Lindner and M. Meissner (eds), *The Routledge Companion to Urban Imaginaries*, London: Routledge, pp. 113–24.

de Lange, M. and de Waal, M. (2013), 'Owning the city: New media and citizen engagement in urban design', *First Monday*, November, 18:11, n.pag. https://doi.org/10.5210/fm.v18i11.4954. Accessed 30 May 2020.

Department of Education and Skills (2011), *National Strategy for Higher Education to 2030*, Dublin: Department of Education and Skills.

Department of Education and Skills (2020), *Connectedness and Collaboration through Connectivity: Report of the Technological Universities Research Network to the Department of Education and Skills*, Dublin: Department of Education and Skills.

de Sousa Santos, B. (2010), 'The university in the twenty-first century: Toward a democratic and emancipatory university reform', in M. Apple, S. Ball and L. A. Gandin (eds), *The Routledge International Handbook of the Sociology of Education*, Abingdon: Routledge, pp. 274–82.

Dever, B., Blaik, O., Smith, G. and McCarthy, G. (2014), *Defining a Successful Anchor Strategy: Understanding and Engaging Anchor Institutions*, Cambridge, MA: Lincoln Institute of Land Policy.

Devlin, R. and Porter, L. (2011), 'Informal urbanism in the USA: New challenges for theory and practice', *Planning Theory & Practice*, 12:1, pp. 144–50.

Dewey, J. (1929), 'My pedagogic creed', *Journal of the National Education Association*, 18:9, pp. 291–95.

Docherty, T. (2011), *For the University: Democracy and the Future of the Institution*, London: Bloomsbury.

Ehlenz, M. M. (2018), 'Defining university anchor institution strategies: Comparing theory and practice', *Planning Theory & Practice*, 19:1, pp. 74–92.

Etzkowitz, H. (2018), 'Innovation governance: From the "endless frontier" to the triple helix', in P. E. A. Meusburger (ed.), *Geographies of the University*, Knowledge and Space, vol. 12. New York: Springer Open, pp. 291–312.

European Commission (2020), *Digital Action Plan 2021–27: Resetting Education and Training for the Digital Age*, Brussels: European Commission.

Felsenstein, D. (1996), 'The university in the metropolitan arena: Impacts and public policy implications', *Urban Studies*, 33:9, pp. 1565–80.

Fitzgerald, F. S. (1960), *The Last Tycoon*, Harmondsworth: Penguin.

Freeman, R. E. (2010), *Strategic Management: A Stakeholder Approach*, Cambridge, UK: Cambridge University Press.

Germic, S. (2009), 'The neoliberal university: Theory and practice', *Alif: Journal of Comparative Poetics*, 29, pp. 127–48.

Giroux, H. (2004), 'Neoliberalism and the demise of democracy: Resurrecting hope in dark times', *Dissident Voice*, 7 August, http://dissidentvoice.org/Aug04/Giroux0807.htm. Accessed 14 September 2018.

Goatly, A. (2007), *Washing the Brain: Metaphor and Hidden Ideology*, Amsterdam: John Benjamins.

Goddard, J., Coombes, M., Kempton, L. and Vallance, P. (2014), 'Universities as anchor institutions in cities in a turbulent funding environment: Vulnerable institutions and vulnerable places in England', *Cambridge Journal of Regions, Economy and Society*, 7:2, pp. 307–25.

Gonella, F. (2019), 'The smart narrative of a smart city', *Frontiers in Sustainable Cities*, 1, p. 9.

Government of Ireland (2018), *Project Ireland 2040: National Planning Framework*, https://npf.ie/wp-content/uploads/Project-Ireland-2040-NPF.pdf. Accessed 24 March 2021.

Harris, M. and Holley, K. (2016), 'Universities as anchor institutions: Economic and social potential for urban development', in M. Paulson (ed.), *Higher Education: Handbook of Theory and Research*, New York: Springer, pp. 393–439.

Hart, P. and Tindall, K. (2009), 'Understanding crisis exploitation: Leadership, rhetoric and framing contests in response to the economic meltdown', in P. Hart and K. Tindall (eds), *Framing the Global Economic Downturn*, Canberra: ANU Press, pp. 21–40.

Harvey, D. (2013), *Rebel Cities: From the Right to the City to the Urban Revolution*, New York: Verso.

Harvey, D. (2015), *Seventeen Contradictions and the End of Capitalism*, London: Profile Books.

Harvey, D. (2017), *The Ways of the World* (2nd ed.), London: Profile.

Harvey, D. (2000), *Spaces of Hope*, Edinburgh: Edinburgh University Press.

Harvey, D. (2005), *A Brief History of Neoliberalism*, Oxford: Oxford University Press.

Hay, C. (1999), 'Crisis and the structural transformation of the state: Interrogating the process of change', *British Journal of Politics and International Relations*, 1:3, pp. 317–44.

Holborow, M. (2012a), 'Austerity, capitalism and the restructuring of Irish higher education', *Irish Marxist Review*, 1:2, pp. 24–36.

Holborow, M. (2012b), 'Neoliberalism, human capital and the skills agenda in higher education: The Irish case', *Journal for Critical Education Policy Studies*, 10:1, pp. 93–111.

Holborow, M. and O'Sullivan, J. (2017), 'Austerity Ireland and the neo-liberal university: Hollow enterprise', in J. Nixon (ed.), *Higher Education in Austerity Europe*, London: Bloomsbury, pp. 107–26.

Holland, C., Lorenzi, F. and Hall, T. (2016), 'Performance anxiety in academia: Tensions within research assessment exercises in an age of austerity', *Policy Futures in Education*, 14:8, pp. 1101–16.

Holley, K. and Harris, M. (2018), ' "The 400-pound gorilla": The role of the research university in city development', *Innovation Higher Education*, 43, pp. 77–90.

Jacobs, J. (1992), *The Death and Life of Great American Cities*, New York: Vintage.

Jeppesen, S. and Adamik, J. (2017), 'Street theory: Grassroots activist interventions in regimes of knowledge', in R. H. Haworth and J. M. Elmore (eds), *Out of the Ruins: The Emergence of Radical Informal Learning Spaces*, Oakland, CA: PM Press, pp. 223–44.

Katz, C. (2001), 'Vagabond capitalism and the necessity of social reproduction', *Antipode*, 33:4, pp. 709–28.

Kitchin, R. (2014), 'The real-time city? Big data and smart urbanism', *GeoJournal*, 79, pp. 1–14.

Kuipers, S. (2006), *The Crisis Imperative: Crisis Rhetoric and Welfare State Reform in Belgium and the Netherlands in the early 1990s*, Amsterdam: Amsterdam University Press.

Lefevbre, H. (1991), *The Production of Space*, Oxford: Blackwell.

Lefevbre, H. (2003), *The Urban Revolution*, Minneapolis: University of Minnesota Press.

Levidow, L. (2004), 'Neoliberal agendas for higher education', in A. Saad-Filho and D. Johnston (eds), *Neoliberalism: A Critical Reader*, London: Pluto Press, pp. 152–62.

Lyndon, D. (2005), 'Caring for places: Caring for thought', *Places*, 17:1, p. 3.

MacGregor, S. (2004), 'The welfare state and neoliberalism', in A. Saad-Filho and D. Johnston (eds), *Neoliberalism: A Critical Reader*, London: Pluto Press, pp. 142–48.

Marx, K. (1977), *Selected Writings*, Oxford: Oxford University Press.

Mavelli, L. (2018), 'Citizenship for sale and the neoliberal political economy of belonging', *International Studies Quarterly*, 62, pp. 482–93.

Mercille, J. and Murphy, E. (2015), 'The neoliberalization of Irish higher education under austerity', *Critical Sociology*, 43:3, pp. 371–87.

Mitchell, D. (1995), 'The end of public space? People's park, definitions of the public, and democracy', *Annals of the Association of American Geographers*, 85:1, pp. 108–33.

Molotch, H. (1976), 'The city as a growth machine: Towards a political economy of place', *American Journal of Sociology*, 82:2, pp. 309–32.

Noveck, B. S. (2015), *Smart Citizens, Smarter State: The Technologies of Expertise and the Future of Governing*, Cambridge, MA: Harvard University Press.

Nye, N. and Schramm, R. (1999), *Building Higher Education–Community Development Corporation Partnerships*, Washington, DC: Department of Housing and Urban Development, Office of University Partnerships.

Oleson, K. (2014), 'The neoliberalisation of strategic spatial planning', *Planning Theory*, 13:3, pp. 288–303.

Ong, A. (2006), 'Mutations in citizenship', *Theory, Culture and Society*, 23:2–3, pp. 499–531.

Peck, J., Brenner, N. and Theodore, N. (2009), 'Neoliberal urbanism: Models, moments, mutations', *SAIS Review*, XXIX:1, pp. 49–66.

Penn Institute for Urban Research (2010), *Anchor Institutions and Their Role in Metropolitan Change White Paper on Penn IUR Initiatives on Anchor Institutions*, Philadelphia, PA: Penn Institute for Urban Research.

Pinson, G. and Journel, C. M. (2016), 'The neoliberal city: Theory, evidence, debates', *Territory, Politics, Governance*, 4:2, pp. 137–53.

Rose, N. (1999), *Powers of Freedom: Reframing Political Thought*, Cambridge, UK: Cambridge University Press.

Rüegg, W. (2011), 'Themes', in H. de Ridder-Symoens (ed.), *A History of the University in Europe: Volume 4, Universities Since 1945*. Cambridge, UK: Cambridge University Press, pp. 3–30.

Rutherford, J. (2005), 'Cultural studies in the corporate university', *Cultural Studies*, 19:3, pp. 297–317.

Shapin, S. (2012), 'The ivory tower: The history of a figure of speech and its cultural uses', *British Journal of the History of Science*, 45:1, pp. 1–27.

Smigiel, C. (2018), 'Urban political strategies in times of crisis: A multiscalar perspective on smart cities in Italy', *European Urban and Regional Studies*, 26: 4, pp. 336–48.

Stanton, B. H. (2005), 'Cognitive standards and the sense of campus', *Places*, 17:1, pp. 38–41.

Taylor, H. L. and Luter, G. (2013), *Anchor Institutions: An Interpretive Review Essay*, New York: Anchor Institutions Task Force.

Technological Universities Act (2018), http://www.irishstatutebook.ie/eli/2018/act/3/enacted/en/html. Accessed 21 March 2021.

Valero, A. and van Reenen, J. (2019), 'The economic impact of universities: Evidence from across the globe', *Economics of Education Review*, 68, pp. 53–67.

Vasileva, R., Rodrigues, L., Hughes, N., Greenhalgh, C., Goulden, M. and Tennison, J. (2018), 'What smart campuses can teach us about smart cities: User Experiences and open data', *Information*, 9:10, p. 251.

Ward, S. (2012), *Neoliberalism and the Global Restructuring of Knowledge and Education*, New York: Routledge.

SECTION 2

CITY DESIGN

5

Universal Smart City Design

*Eoghan Conor O' Shea, Institute of Technology,
Carlow, Ireland*

Introduction

> If we draw an analogy between the computer matrix of data management and the city, then it is precisely the spaces of disjunction between the rows and columns of the data entries that represent the forgotten spaces, the disavowed places, and the bits eradicated because of the noise and redundancy they generate.
>
> (Boyer 1996: 9)

What occurs in the interstices of that matrix of data, in the awkward and unruly physical spaces of the city? The design of cities, and the buildings and spaces that fill them, has always been a matter of negotiation between the current and future needs of citizens and visitors, and the wants of its administrators or rulers, while incorporating technologies in conjunction with the capabilities and practices of fabricators and builders. And there have always been disavowed spaces and marginalized people. The smart city, being the latest aspect of this complex palimpsest of urbanity, is likely no exception. This is a new cityscape that offers boundless opportunities to citizens and governors alike – harvesting this data-rich environment has the feeling of trawling an ocean teeming with fish. But – to quickly mix metaphors – the smart city has to be mindful of the fox in the henhouse, who gets caught in a frenzy and harvests far more than could ever be eaten, leaving waste and desolation behind.

That is not to underplay the potential beneficial experiences for citizens and decision-makers alike, and these will be explored later in the chapter. The physical manifestation driven by the smart city concept include what is implied in the 'problematic urban visions' highlighted by Ayona Datta (2018: 410) where information and communications technology (ICT) will drive economic growth and prosperity. Yet this is familiar territory, driven not just by 'smart' growth but growth due to any assets or specific opportunities – and that Datta notes in an Indian context the smart city meant to 'set for itself parameters of western modernity and urbanism'.

What, however, of the experience for someone as an inhabitant, as commuter, as consumer, as meanderer, as someone who felt disavowed by the unsmart city who now is hungry for new possibilities? It is unclear how different the city will feel in the flesh, apart from better access to Wi-Fi, access to digital information and services and perhaps a better coordinated transport infrastructure. What is not clear is any possible effect on the fabric and the physical experience of the city, especially for those feeling isolated in the unsmart city. In their introduction to *Creating Smart Cities*, leading smart cities researcher Rob Kitchin and his colleagues note that 'issues of citizenship and ethics are a significant blind spot in much smart city rhetoric, and [...] creating inclusive and principled cities means a radical rethink in how smart cities are framed and implemented' (Kitchin et al. 2019: 11). This chapter seeks to posit one framework that might be deployed in order to analyse the inclusive element of the ethical problem raised by Kitchin et al. (2019): the tangible, physical experience of the smart city for the many groups of people who use it, which to date has been the subject of little academic scrutiny. A democratic city, as is currently evident in American politics, can serve 51 per cent of the population while ignoring 49 per cent. While citizen experience has been the subject of analysis, the tangible experience of the city, particularly for those in the margins of debate and decision-making, can often be ignored.

This chapter provides a review of inclusivity as it appears in discussions of the smart city, before moving on to the citizen herself. This chapter also provides various perspectives of the smart citizen as subject or participant. This concept of citizen is sketched through her appearance in the history of urban design, the smart city and inclusive/universal design. At its core the chapter will examine how universal design (UD) can offer a critical tool for reviewing how the affordances offered by a smart city impacts or enables people across all spectra of ages, abilities, genders and cultural backgrounds. UD principles (CUD 1997), and subsequent theoretical development, are utilized as a framework for interrogating different affordances of the smart city and a limited number of perspectives of the smart citizen.

At the time of writing this chapter, the experience of urban life has been severely affected by the COVID-19 pandemic. This has upended both planners' and citizens' perspective of the affordances cities should offer in terms of the role of technology in everyday life and the spatial organization of public, semi-public and private realms. In seeking to address some of the tensions and new difficulties posed on individuals and employers, government has embraced the techniques of activists to respond, in some instances with something akin to state-sponsored guerrilla urbanism. This sudden ability to listen and act may also have revealed fleeting glimpses of what universal smart city design might look like.

Inclusive smart cities

In geospatial terms the city is a slippery concept. It is in flux, in a continuous cycle of dematerialization. Arata Isozaki (1967: 403) viewed the city as being 'in a liquid state of constant organic reproduction and division'. Like the human body where individual cells die and are replaced – and no matter the physical age no part of the body is more than 10 years old – the city can be both ancient and young simultaneously. And like the human body, cities never *are*, they are in a process of becoming something else. The concepts of the smart city and UD are also both simultaneously old and new. Their names and updated meanings date from the late twentieth century – although both have an ancestry that stretches far back in history in parallel with concepts of evolution through technological progress, and evolving social attitudes concerning human difference. And as concepts they continuously evolve. The smart city as an idea feels simple, yet, as the *Boston Smart City Playbook* (MONUM 2016) puts it, 'We don't really know what that means. Or at least, not yet'. UD principles too have become more broad ranging, with initial principles grounded in anthropometric concerns evolving toward embracing cultural and gendered differences (Hamraie 2013; Tauke et al. 2015), and amplifying the focus on the empowering and social integrative potential of incorporating UD (Steinfeld and Maisel 2012).

Technotopia

The role of technology in cities is as old as the processing of the first materials that conjoined to define communal spaces. Accessibility and usability evolved with cities, with steps used in place of steep ramps, lamps to light streets for ease of use and security, paving to make footing more secure and reliable in all weather conditions, escalators and elevators to move people from floor to floor easily and efficiently. The symbiotic relationship between technology and accessibility is self-evident (Pullin 2009; Tobias 2003), albeit that the conception of who access is granted to has historically been relatively narrow where, as Hahn (1986: 273) noted before a general progression in regulations and standards, 'in terms of ease or comfort, most cities have been designed not merely for the disabled but for a physical ideal that few human beings can ever hope to approximate'. Progress has been made since Hahn's observation although, as will be noted later in the chapter, not sufficiently. There are, in affluent settlements, a greater presence of kerb cuts in pavements, automatic opening doors, automatic closers, elevators, escalators, travellators and induction loops for augmenting hearing. And yet the role of technology is problematic, as it can create new ways of doing things with more chance of failure and no backup. It can also, in the case of smart cities, do 'mental harm' in 'dumbing down its citizens' (Sennett 2010: 144). Jascha Franklin-Hodge (2019: x), a technology company founder turned public official, noted that a 'tendency to overlook deeper questions of values and trade-offs [...] is one of the blind spots of many technologists'. Bruno Latour (2008) describes the reliance on 'life supports' as a vital concept in considering the role of technology; the more a technology moves us from the familiar toward a new, strange paradigm (like a rocket ship to the moon, for instance) the more trouble we are in if the technology fails. If the life supports are insufficiently robust, then the passengers will have little hope. If a lift doesn't work and if it were the only means of navigating between floors then it creates a physical displacement of those passengers that is hard to resolve. To use a smart city example, if internet access is unavailable when workers are operating from their homes during a pandemic on cloud-based platforms, then the illusion of the remote office quickly fades back to the cluttered domestic situation it briefly displaced.

Beyond solving small issues, city planners have toyed with technology as a panacea and cities have suffered as a result, due to the 'wicked' nature of city design problems. The city wall, once a technological innovation and set to preserve cities and towns in times of warfare, also served as a clear device for creating or reinforcing a sense of 'other' for those outside the walls, behind which 'the sheltered being gives perceptible limits to his shelter' (Bachelard 1997: 83). In his book *The Smart Enough City*, Ben Green (2019) points to role of the car seen as the pumping bloody supply in the architect/planner Le Corbusier's visions of vertical cities fed horizontally by motorcar-laden arteries – which unfortunately inspired unsustainable urban sprawl leading to empty city centres across the world, including cities such as New York and Detroit. This reliance upon the technology of the motorcar as the cure for all transportation ills led to ever increasing numbers of cars and exponential increases in traffic congestion. Autonomous vehicles, a modern panacea, have demonstrated similar blind spots when tested in the complexity of real-world situations: one virtual demonstration of the efficiencies of systems fully populated with autonomous vehicles failed to consider the need for pedestrians to cross the street at a busy junction (Green 2019).

Cardulla et al. (2019) show that this tendency for smart cities to follow a 'technological solutionist approach' by allowing private corporations to take the lead toward a techno-utopian governance model. Smart technologists are promoted and harnessed for their promise of efficiency, and not their efficacy at making a more inclusive and equal society.

In built spaces, this includes data harvested from a passive citizenry. Shannon Mattern (2019), who regularly describes the interface between smart city and physical experience, describes a matrix of web-active kiosks in New York by Google's parent company Alphabet Inc. to replace redundant phone kiosks, but also to harvest data from service users to an unclearly defined end in a service provided by a private organization.

UD is not immune to this type of criticism. Tobias (2003: n.pag.) points to an 'uncritical belief in the benefits of technology' as 'automatically superior'. The geographer Rob Imrie (2012), a long-time observer of UD concepts and implementation, agrees that UD has a tendency to promote technical solutions to complex multidimensional problems in buildings. Both concepts are in danger of promoting solutions 'fuelled by user-friendly technology which stupefies its citizens', as Richard Sennett (2010: 158) accused the prescriptive smart city of doing. Sennett (2010) points to examples of smart cities such as Songdo in Korea and Masdar on the outskirts of Abu Dhabi, both built from the ground up explicitly to be smart cities of the future. Yet, for Sennett (2010: 158–67), both disappointed, failing not only economically but also containing only faint echoes of a messy, busy, negotiated city space. Both have also suffered from being labelled as gated cities for the wealthy (Ouroussoff 2010). As Gordon and Walter (2019: 329) point out, it is vital to ask not, 'How can we make civil life more efficient with technology?' but rather, 'How can we use technology to make civic life more meaningful?'

Inclusion of smart citizens

Richard Sennett characterized the radical planners of the 1960s, including Jane Jacobs, as having the 'sociologically naïve' notion that '[b]uilding should follow dwelling' (Sendra and Sennett 2020: 115). He lamented, however, that as people in developing countries grew wealthier, their instinctive response was to ask, 'Who can we keep out?'

The history of cities is littered with examples of people left as marginalia, sketched in roughly, acted upon and limited to passive roles. The philosopher Giorgio Agamben differentiates between the citizens of Greek cities, active participants (*bios*, life in the political state) and the people who have no citizenship or who are stripped of it (*zoē*, or bare life) (Davis 2013: 14) and liable to be acted upon with no direct agency. Lennart Davis develops the parallels between the position of *zoē* and *bios* and the views of the impaired body in society: cast as the 'ethnic other, the abject, the disabled', which is an excluded subject in a 'neoliberal [...] postmodernity' (Davis 2013: 14). This would similarly exclude the *zoē* subject from consideration in the neo-liberal casting of the smart city project, warned against by Kitchin, Cardullo and Green (Cardullo et al. 2019; Green 2019; Kitchin 2015).

111

To guard against inequality, Amartya Sen (1992) highlighted that additional affordances are needed to make all people capable of basic functionings, and providing these affordances would give people similar access to well-being, comfort to assess their social condition and access to the tools to bring about social change where it is needed. The physical design of the environment has a significant role here, which is confirmed in the United Nations Convention on the Rights of Persons with Disabilities (CRPD), which highlights the physical design of built spaces as affecting people's ability to socialize, to visit public services, to be educated and – perhaps of most importance to the neo-liberal project of the smart city – to play an active role in the workforce. The framework it references is UD, defined in the CRPD as the 'design of products, environment, programmes and services to be usable by all people to the greatest extent possible, without the need for adaption or specialized design' (United Nations 2007).

Capabilities of smart citizens

The capabilities of Sen, later codified to a degree by philosopher Martha Nussbaum (2008), are linked by Inger Marie Lid (2010) to look at how both physical and inclusive design strategies seek to create affordances in built environments, in products and in service provision that enable and support use by the greatest extent of people – a universal population, hence UD. UD goes beyond accessible design, which amounted to insertions that render built spaces more usable and easier to navigate, but make people who rely on these insertions – often people with disabilities – more visible. This was at odds with a social model of disability that emphasized a criticism of disabling environments, which Selwyn Goldsmith (2001) characterized as architectural disability. The social model as a critical approach pinpointed the blame for disability in environments that failed to provide affordances to allow everyone to achieve basic levels of capability. UD as a means to achieve these basic levels of capability for citizens is omnipresent throughout the CRPD. The CRPD deploys UD as an approach for assessing environmental factors (United Nations 2007).

The promises of the smart city are inclusive in that everyone is capable of participating equally on the free space of a digital platform in order to carry out necessary services and payments, to critique governance and to vote. Participatory workshops have become de rigueur during the incubation period of all smart city projects (Mattern 2020). Yet these promises are immaterial to someone who cannot fulfil their part of a social contract based on rationality, on autonomy. Nussbaum (2006: 159–60) warns of the necessity to connect human dignity to vulnerability and to 'bodily need, including the need for care', and to see the social contract as one of recognizing basic capabilities of citizens and that must respond to human need and dependency.

Ayona Datta (2019) has probed into the concept of the smart citizen and points to a smart city initiative where the Indian Ministry of Urban Design has prepared plans based on extensive participation with what amounted to 12 per cent of the population of participating cities. Elsewhere, Datta (2016) alludes to an assumption of smart citizens as active digital citizens. What of those who are less, or inactive? These are people in danger of being classified as part of Agamben's *zoē*.

Universal smart city design

There are numerous frameworks with which to examine the affordances offered to users by inclusive built environments (Imrie and Luck 2014; O Shea et al. 2014). UD has gained the most traction internationally and is in effect a critical theory and a design theory, aimed at two levels of explanatory discourse (D'Souza 2004). The affordances of built spaces and services can be highlighted through the UD filter to reveal their effectiveness at enabling or empowering people with diverse abilities and backgrounds (Froyen 2012). UD literature also looks at solutions, guidelines on how to create or refurbish built space, ICT services and educational approaches to become more usable and accessible to a wider public (Story et al. 1998).

This section will concentrate upon the interactions between physical and virtual settings and the UD approach and principles will be utilized to as a frame to discuss how citizen-centric a smart city is and can be. Smart cities have and will pose unforeseen demands on both, as crisis or evolution in cultural or social practice alter how the person engages with the city and how it is navigated and utilized. It makes use of the seven principles of UD (CUD 1997), which are still the most common way of categorizing the various elements to be considered in how *universally designed* an environment or interface is. Evolutions of these principles will be referred to where appropriate.

Principle 1: Equitable use

This is the principle that most explicitly addresses values, and in further development has been broken down into smaller categories. It speaks to an equivalence of experience in any activity for all citizens, regardless of how circumstances of embodiment affect performance. At a small scale the front door of a building should allow everyone to gain access to it – if there are steps then other means to arrive there, such as a ramp, should create an equivalent arrival sequence and no separate entrance should be required for some arrivals.

This idea of creating an equally satisfying experience requires an understanding of the emotions and frustrations that built spaces and cities can generate. At an urban level, Green (2019) describes a community in Ohio, where the instinctive approach to solve the problem of unequal access to a prenatal class was a one-off technological smart fix such as the provision of autonomous vehicles. However, to create an equitable solution required a multimodal approach: apps that unified transportation information across a number of services and providers; free and reliable access to Wi-Fi in the area, so all service users could easily access this information; and a unified payment card and app for all transport services that was easy to top up, either online or with cash through physical kiosks at key locations. The final relatively 'unsmart' cash-based machines were critical for those with limited access to cashless infrastructure, and provided a failsafe for others. This was selective physical infrastructure working in tandem with the use of smart technologies and required pulling the problem apart and engaging directly and meaningfully with the service users.

The following are three UD goals, a selection from the eight described by Steinfeld and Maisel (2012), which further unpack the concept of equitable use.

Social integration

Social integration refers to the treatment of all groups with dignity and respect. The design of built spaces integrates the social importance of environments, products and services that promote and enable social interaction and participation in all matters. This include matters of civic import such as casting a vote, procuring services from a municipal authority or a private shop or business; socializing in a casual setting; or visiting an amenity or a place of scenic or historical significance.

The limiting of movement to within 2 km of where people lived in Ireland between March and June of 2020, still meant many (but not all) could work from home due to smart infrastructures. This brought attention to the consequences of the disruptive nature of this innovation. While much work could continue, it began to highlight a type of spatial poverty where people sought psychological fulfilment in being out and out about in their own areas, and the reassurance of seeing and integrating with others in the public realm. Not all areas allowed for this: car parks near beauty spots in many parts of the country were forced to close to stop people seeking places to walk and see others outside of their areas.

Personalization

Personalization addresses the need for people to have the right to expression through design, to have choice in how that expression is manifested. It can mean providing

114

choice in public buildings for how to design interactions by providing different types of setting, and to choose the level of privacy they desire (Steinfeld and Maisel 2012: 163). A desire for privacy can mean a reluctance to exposing details in an online environment and having the choice to carry out transactions and activities in person – ideally in universally designed service engagement environments. In the COVID-19-related scenario, personalization would have been addressed by providing sufficient private or semi-private opportunities to interact, as an alternative to providing public spaces to accommodate this.

Cultural appropriateness

Cultural appropriateness addresses the need 'for respecting and reinforcing' local customs and existing social and cultural practice, and the context within which interpersonal relations between citizens and those providing services or in positions of power take place (Steinfeld and Maisel 2012: 90). This is granular detail that can really only be accessed by close collaboration and by continuous interaction between cultural groups. Observation is needed of attitudes to social interaction, of the language information is relayed in, the composition of homes and the streetscape and the reinforcement of prevailing cultural practices that should be maintained and supported (Kaliski 1999). There is a suspicion that many participative processes related to smart city initiatives, particularly where run by private organizations, may amount to merely a box-ticking exercise to some degree (Mattern 2020).

Principle 2: Flexibility in use

Flexibility means choice: a designed element or artefact has to work for people of all strengths and abilities and offer various means of engagement. The placement height of a handrail affects how many people can use it comfortably – two handrails might be placed on a stairway to make sure smaller people and young children who may be unsteady on their feet can equally find support from it, even if that rail is redundant for many people. Cities too have redundancy: buildings will be temporarily vacant, streets will occasionally be empty, cars will sit unused for up to 22 hours a day. Smart cities have to manage flexible access to services and conveniences through different avenues of access: by foot, car, public transport, through multiple online means. Similarly, consideration needs to be given to voting and other avenues for engaging with participative democracy. In over 250 Brazilian cities community voting for local service provision has had a relatively seamless transition from physical voting to online voting (Baiocchi and Ganuza 2014).

Flexibility is tested in times of stress – can the smart city respond to the advice to avoid public transport where possible during the COVID-19 pandemic? If so, can it allow remote working and provide the necessary infrastructural and traditional amenity supports to go with? We have already seen that cities that offered flexibility in working methods, allowing a switch between physical and virtual connections to the workplace, placed a sudden demand for a flexible urban landscape within which the home was embedded. This is a flexibility that many people with disabilities fought hard for with much resistance, only to find with some frustration that it became suddenly an acceptable solution when this aligned with corporate interests (Malowney 2020). Inflexible attitudes that had previously shut people out of workplaces despite a desire to work in a way that relaxed dramatically in 2020 with the COVID-19 pandemic and suddenly became mainstream.

Principle 3: Simple and intuitive use

When an affordance is provided it should be easy to understand how it works in relation to an activity that is to be completed. Any form of threshold condition – such as moving past a door into a room, or between rooms, where we will encounter a door handle, for example – relies on us understanding quickly how it works. The lever handle on a door is intuitive, it relates to our body, slips into our hand and we are effectively led into making it function for us. Equally, we could operate the handle with a closed fist, or an elbow if we had functional problems with our hands or did not want to risk contamination during a pandemic. The same is required of ICT services under this principle – it should feel simple and easy to navigate the system toward essential services.

Smart cities need similarly intuitive consideration of threshold conditions, particularly when navigating between physical and virtual spaces. Where vulnerable populations cannot be expected to intuit how access to services is managed, a reciprocal system is needed to reach out to these populations. In Helsinki, the smart city infrastructure ensured that during the COVID-19 pandemic they could reach out in conjunction with non-governmental organizations (NGOs) and church organizations to every resident over 70 years of age to provide personalized services for food and pharmacy needs (Wahba and Vapaavuori 2020).

Principle 4: Perceptible information

We should be able to pick out important information in different modalities – visually, aurally, through touch. This could be through olfactory means potentially – a bakery section of a supermarket will often announce itself through smell far more strikingly than through any other sense. Similarly, but for less salubrious reasons, a toilet may be easy to discern for a blind person. Important information should be legible in multiple modes – a reception desk placed in front of a bright window would make lip-reading difficult for someone with hearing difficulty. This principle advocates a multi-sensorial experience for important information, so that it is available to all citizens regardless of the sensory systems available to them. In the smart city it is principally the screen embedded in buildings, kiosks, furnishings 'and behind these screens [are] floods of data' (Mattern 2014). There are other smart infrastructures – Melbourne's Southern Cross railway station terminal uses a smartphone app that combines Global Positioning System (GPS) and Bluetooth alerts, provided by twenty wireless beacons around the station. Audio alerts provide real-time information on escalator or lift malfunctions, as well as descriptive advice on the immediate directional choices that need to be made (Salman 2018)

Yet it is not just screens that present information. During the COVID-19 pandemic we have had to deal with streets whose layout suddenly altered to respond to citizens suddenly hungry to explore streets again, while maintaining social distance. New information and rapid (smart?) responses to changing need was manifest in hand-drawn white lines (see Figure 5.3) that appeared on the Dublin quays to designate hastily required cycle lanes (Sticky Bottle 2020); in Dingle, County Kerry hastily erected bollards quickly created wider pedestrian paths and impromptu pedestrian streets (see Figure 5.1 and 5.2). Guerrilla urbanists have become expert in this type of expression of desire (Pask 2010) – a skill set that could potentially make them planners of expediency in the smart city

Principle 5: Tolerance for error

Tolerance for error means choice, the ability to go backward as well as forward, allowing people to carry out delicate transactions in a comfortable environment, be they physical or virtual. In ICT it means a failsafe to make sure you don't make irreversible decisions that affect your interactions. In building and cities it can mean avoiding situations where 'wrong' decisions don't result in injury or psychologically damaging situations. These are communications and supports built into environments, many indeed mandated by regulation, which allow us to make mistakes without great risk of injury. We can go close to the edge of a drop or steps without falling due to guarding or tactile warnings. In the case of stairs, a shallow pitch and frequent landings would offer some measure of safety in the case of a fall. Tolerance for error can also be related to robustness, that a visually impaired person could bang into a piece of furniture and not have to dread the sound of something falling from the surface and smashing, drawing unwanted attention.

The digital environment can be designed to be similarly robust and allow citizens to move some face-to-face transactions to a virtual setting, and in doing so to support navigation without fear of giving up access to sensitive personal information (Kitchin 2020). There is comfort for some in this information being

FIGURE 5.1: Expanding footpaths in Dingle, Kerry. Photo by author.

volunteered to a person, in a place where cold feet and a cancelled transaction can be understood by a real person – there needs to be faith that such consents are capable of being reversed (Kitchin 2020).

Principle 6: Low physical effort

For buildings and products, this principle points to a consideration not to make undue demands of bodies – allowing them to maintain a neutral position during any action, not demand too much energy for a task or require sustained effort

FIGURE 5.2: New pedestrian street in Dingle, county Kerry. Photo by author.

or repetitive actions (Story et al. 1998: 35). A door may be heavy and difficult to open or stairs might be steep and demanding to climb with no handrail to allow support on either side.

The demands of a traditional city can be physical – conveniently placed benches can offer walkers a place to take a break if a journey proves too much or they could be Wi-Fi hotspots. The smart city can offer alternative means to accessing services and provisions and make journeys more a choice than a chore or a requirement. And yet, the possibilities of surveillance has excited private companies, where monitoring of client activities through fitness trackers now can affect health insurance premiums, with a possibilities of reward for more active clients (Carver 2018).

Principle 7: Size and space for approach and use

This is the most explicitly architectural principle. In buildings this can mean enough space to approach and open a door, to approach and use a convenience such as a computer terminal, a reception desk, a toilet or sink, or to navigate across

FIGURE 5.3: Hacked cycle lanes on Dublin city quays. Photo by Ray McAdam.

a room or along a pavement. In the dystopian vision of the smart city shown in the movie *The Matrix* (Wachowski and Wachowski 1999), the space required by individuals shrank to a point barely larger than the body, which was plugged in and drained of excess energy – a perverse concept of egalitarianism. Yet in the current dystopian times at the time of writing, the call is for more space, for better space such as the intrusions into Dublin and Dingle previously referred to. Space where people can breathe and relax and escape the confines of tightly layered home/work/school/play/sleep space. While many jobs have disappeared for some during the

COVID-19 pandemic, for others work, education and socializing moved into virtual spaces, separation distances become necessities rather than preferences: they become universal rather than marginal. The disabling effect of health concerns is universally felt in space, although it does not affect everyone equally (Booth 2020). The impact of this is apparent in shops that force all but one patron out on to the street to queue, or footpaths that have invaded the streets and deprived the cars of precious driving lanes and parking spaces.

Discussion: Wellness in the coordinated smart city

Sennett (2010: 144) prefers a smart city that 'coordinates but does not erase messier activities' of the life of the city. While Songdo and Masdar are unappetizing as a model to follow, they are, as Sennett (2010) notes, very easy to live in – and herein lies the danger of a stupefying effect filled with passive citizens. Gerontologists (Nahemow and Lawton 1973) and occupational therapists (Iwarsson 2003) have warned against environments that fail to pose physical challenges and describe the need for a good fit, balancing the physical and psychological challenges and affordances on offer. The bespoke smart cities of Songdo and Masdar disappointed because experience of place was diminished. Contrast this with the spilling of citizens on to the streets in Ireland, when suddenly everyone was requested not to venture more than 2 km from their home. While there was confusion and anxiety about many aspects of experience, the experience of place was amplified and intensified: my local city of Kilkenny became a landscape suddenly dense with walkers and wheelers.

The wellness goal of UD, identified by Steinfeld and Maisel (2012), balances the focus of ergonomic affordances that mitigate against undue demands on the body, with social and psychological affordances that satisfy deeper and more personal needs. Wellness indicates the level of satisfaction attained, and yet our sense of what signifies a sense of wellness can be subject to rapid and radical change. The smart city concept, at its most optimistic, points to the value of technology in enriching our overall experience of place, layering additional information to alleviate disorientation and to drive curiosity about where we are and the things we have the potential to do there. The promise is that technology can fill gaps that the traditional (unsmart) city can never do.

Roboticist Hans Moravec (Moravec 1988: 15) points to a useful paradox: machines tend to be good where humans are weak, and vice versa. The key is to understand where the boundaries lie, and to intermingle processes where human minds and computer artificial intelligence (AI) blend rather than work in silos. Although chess machines have been largely dominant in the human versus machine battle since Gary Kasparov was defeated by Deep Blue in 1997, the most successful chess-playing entity is a reasonable club player in partnership with a computer (Litt 2020). This is a partnership of mutual respect, where human lets computer do what it is good at, making modest adjustments as necessary. This partnership will defeat grandmaster/computer pairings, where human and computer get in each other's way. Each smart citizen should be allowed to play this role, to attune themselves to the possibilities of partnership with the virtual presence of the city, rather than feel controlled by or a need to control this presence.

In this way the smart citizen is a person of almost infinite possibilities, and as a collective can achieve these possibilities: their attributes range across a broad spectrum of body types, ages and abilities. The smart citizen needs a medium to express her voice in order to describe what is needed for her to perform in a smart city, to be able to point out any barriers to social interaction, be they physical, social or cultural. Where her voice is silent it needs to be sought out.

The ground-up 'clever city' approach of Ross Atkin (2015) addresses much of this. It presents a bottom-up version of the smart city where problems highlighted by citizens are the basis for developing digital technologies, designed with citizens who hold on to existing social and cultural practices that increasingly have been utilized to reach consensus. Similarly Ben Green's 'smart-enough city' looks at successions of smart insertions co-created with empowered citizenry. Combining the approaches of Green or Atkin with an acknowledgement of Martha Nussbaum's advocacy of the dignity of dependency to seek out the voices of the disenfranchised, and layering in the analytical lens from the principles discussed in the previous sections, would move in the direction of a universal smart city design.

Conclusion

While the smart city is a growing topic for analysis and discussion, the inclusive smart city has seen less attention, particularly with a focus on the capabilities of its citizens and affordances that will need to be provided. Neither has there been significant scholarship in the spatial impacts of the smart city, the types of demands it will place with resultant manifestation in the physical shape and form of future cities. This chapter contains a flawed and far from complete analysis, motivated to pull together some strands for the benefit of more focused future research.

The smart city concept rests heavily on technological solutions applied without deep consideration for the potential contingent consequences. Impositions of experimental technological or utopian solution have had disastrous consequences, and misplaced confidence in the unfailing ability of greenfield smart cities to soar, such as Songdo and Masdar, have led to underwhelming results. The same is true of all experiments: in speaking of the novel, the author Brian Moore said that, 'To my mind, one cannot write truly experimental books unless they are masterpieces' (Kilgallin and Moore 2019: 112). It is easy to fail with experiments, especially with a god-like author as opposed to organic organizations.

To get the best out of the smart city concept, technology should be allowed to do what it is best at doing, and not be allowed to take responsibility for value judgements. Better partnerships, fed by community-generated information, in conjunction with people who can direct smart technology toward coordinating what is best for citizens. The technology of the smart city is not value-free – it affects how we use the spaces of the city, and changes our perceptions of the affordances needed within the physical spaces around us. This was revealed during the COVID-19 pandemic, in periods where citizens were forced to make use of the affordances of smart technology while working from home, and then seek previously unsolicited affordances from the spaces around their homes that might support sufficient diversions and interactions to maintain their well-being. The consequences of accepting the possibilities of smart technologies are unpredictable, and not all welcome. The universal smart city design is one lens through which to examine these affordances, and decide whether the locales we live in are to be constructed to make the flexible living promised by smart city technology into something that enhances our quality of life.

REFERENCES

Atkin, R. (2015), *Manifesto for the Clever City*, http://theclevercity.net/. Accessed 13 July 2020.

Bachelard, G. (1997), 'The poetics of space', in N. Leach (ed.), *Rethinking Architecture: A Reader in Cultural Theory*, London: Routledge.

Baiocchi, G. and Ganuza, E. (2014), 'Participatory budgeting as if emancipation mattered', *Politics & Society*, 42:1, pp. 29–50. https://doi.org/10.1177%2F0032329213512978. Accessed 30 May 2020.

Booth, R. (2020), 'Coronavirus inquiry "could transform racial inequality in UK"', *The Guardian*, 1 July, http://www.theguardian.com/world/2020/jul/01/coronavirus-inquiry-could-transform-racial-inequality-in-uk. Accessed 15 July 2020.

Boyer, C. M. (1996), *Cyber Cities: Visual Perception in the Age of Electronic Communication*, New York: Princeton Architectural Press, http://choicereviews.org/review/10.5860/CHOICE.34-2792. Accessed 12 August 2020.

Cardullo, P., Di Feliciantonio, C. and Kitchin, R. (2019), *The Right to the Smart City*, Bingley: Emerald Publishing.

Carver, L. F. (2018), 'Why life insurance companies want your fitbit data', The Conversation, http://theconversation.com/why-life-insurance-companies-want-your-fitbit-data-103732. Accessed 7 December 2020.

Center for Universal Design (CUD) (1997), *The Principles of Universal Design, Version 2.0*, Raleigh: Center for Universal Design/North Carolina State University.

Datta, A. (2016), *Smart Cities and Citizenships: Critical Challenges and Action Points*, Geneva: United Nations Conference on Trade and Development, https://unctad.org/system/files/non-official-document/ecn162016p12_Datta_en.pdf. Accessed 5 December 2020.

Datta, A. (2018), 'The digital turn in postcolonial urbanism: Smart citizenship in the making of India's 100 smart cities', *Transactions of the Institute of British Geographers*, 43:3, pp. 405–19.

Datta, A. (2019), ' "Citizens become netizens": Hashtag citizenships in the making of India's 100 smart cities', in C. Coletta, E. Evans, L. Heaphy and R. Kitchen (eds), *Creating Smart Cities*, Abingdon: Routledge, pp. 131–43.

Davis, L. J. (2013), *The End of Normal: Identity in a Biocultural Era*, Ann Arbor: University of Michigan Press.

D'Souza, N. (2004), 'Is universal design a critical theory?' in S. Keates, J. Clarkson, P. Langdon and P. Robinson (eds), *Designing a More Inclusive World*, London: Springer-Verlag, pp. 3–9.

Franklin-Hodge, J. (2019), 'Foreword', in B. Green, *The Smart Enough City: Putting Technology in Its Place to Reclaim Our Urban Future*, Strong Ideas, Cambridge, MA: MIT Press, pp. ix–xii.

Froyen, H. (2012), *Universal Design, a Methodological Approach*, Limburg: Institute for Human-Centered Design.

Goldsmith, S. (2001), Universal Design, Oxford: Architectural Press.

Gordon, E. and Walter, S. (2019), 'Meaningful inefficiencies: Resisting the logic of technological efficiency in the design of civic systems', in R. Glas, S. Lammes, M. de Lange, J. Raessens and I. de Vries (eds), *The Playful Citizen*, Amsterdam: Amsterdam University Press, pp. 310–34.

Green, B. (2019), *The Smart Enough City: Putting Technology in Its Place to Reclaim Our Urban Future*, Strong Ideas, Cambridge, MA: MIT Press.

Hahn, H. (1986), 'Disability and the urban environment: A perspective on Los Angeles', *Environment and Planning D: Society and Space*, 4:3, pp. 273–88.

Hamraie, A. (2013), 'Designing collective access: A feminist disability theory of universal design', *Disability Studies Quarterly*, 33:4, n.pag., http://dsq-sds.org/article/view/3871/3411. Accessed 11 September 2015.

Imrie, R. (2012), 'Universalism, universal design and equitable access to the built environment', *Disability and Rehabilitation*, 34:10, pp. 873–82.

Imrie, R. and Luck, R. (2014), 'Designing inclusive environments: Rehabilitating the body and the relevance of universal design', *Disability and Rehabilitation*, 36:16, pp. 1315–19.

Isozaki, A. (1967), 'Invisible city', in J. Ockman (ed.), *Architecture Culture 1943–1968: A Documentary Anthology*, Milan: Rizzoli, pp. 402–07.

Iwarsson, S. (2003), 'Accessibility, usability and universal design: Positioning and definition of concepts describing person-environment relationships', *Disability and Rehabilitation*, 25:2, pp. 57–66.

Kaliski, J. (1999), 'The present city and the practice of city design', in J. Chase, M. Crawford and J. Kaliski (eds), *Everyday Urbanism*, New York: Monacelli Press, pp. 89–109.

Kilgallin, T. and Moore, B. (2019), 'Interview: Tony Kilgallin in conversation with the late Brian Moore', *Reading Ireland: The Little Magazine*, p. 112.

Kitchin, R. (2015), 'Making sense of smart cities: Addressing present shortcomings', *Cambridge Journal of Regions, Economy and Society*, 8:1, pp. 131–36.

Kitchin, R. (2020), 'Civil liberties or public health, or civil liberties and public health? Using surveillance technologies to tackle the spread of COVID-19', *Space and Polity*, 24:3, pp. 362–81. https://doi.org/10.1080/13562576.2020.1770587. Accessed 30 May 2020.

Kitchin, R., Coletta, C., Evans, L. and Heaphy, L. (2019), 'Creating smart cities', in C. Coletta, E. Evans, L. Heaphy and R. Kitchen (eds), *Creating Smart Cities*, Abingdon: Routledge, pp. 1–18.

Latour, B. (2008), 'A cautious Prometheus? A few steps toward a philosophy of design', in *Proceedings of the 2008 Annual International Conference of the Design History Society, Falmouth, Cornwall, 3–6 September*, Irvine, CA: Universal Publishers, pp. 2–10, http://www.bruno-latour.fr/node/69. Accessed 30 May 2020.

Lid, I. M. (2010), 'Accessibility as a statutory right', *Nordic Journal of Human Rights*, 28:1, pp. 20–38.

Litt, X. (2020), 'Chess shows that humans and AI work better together', *Irish Examiner*, 17 January, https://www.irishexaminer.com/opinion/commentanalysis/arid-30975938.html. Accessed 6 December 2020.

Malowney, T. (2020), 'This pandemic is an opportunity to learn from the disability community: We are experts in resilience', *The Guardian*, 29 July, http://www.theguardian.com/commentisfree/2020/jul/29/this-pandemic-is-an-opportunity-to-learn-from-the-disability-community-we-are-experts-in-resilience. Accessed 5 December 2020.

Mattern, S. (2014), 'Interfacing urban intelligence', *Places Journal*, April, n.pag., https://placesjournal.org/article/interfacing-urban-intelligence/.

Mattern, S. (2019), 'Where code meets concrete', *Urban Omnibus*, https://urbanomnibus.net/2019/09/where-code-meets-concrete/. Accessed 30 December 2019).

Mattern, S. (2020), 'Post-it note city', *Places Journal*, February, n.pag., https://placesjournal.org/article/post-it-note-city/. Accessed 30 May 2020.

Mayor's Office of New Urban Mechanics (MONUM) (2016), *Boston Smart City Playbook*, https://monum.github.io/playbook/. Accessed 13 July 2020.

Moravec, H. P. (1988), *Mind Children: The Future of Robot and Human Intelligence*, Cambridge, MA: Harvard University Press.

Nahemow, L. and Lawton, M. P. (1973), 'Toward an ecological theory of adaption and aging', *Environmental Design Research: Selected Papers*, 1, pp. 24–32.

Nussbaum, M. C. (2006), *Frontiers of Justice: Disability, Nationality, Species Membership*, Cambridge MA: Harvard University Press

Nussbaum, M. C. (2008), 'Who is the happy warrior? Philosophy poses questions to psychology', *Journal of Legal Studies*, 37:S2, pp. S81–113.

O Shea, E. C., Pavia, S., Dyer, M., Craddock, G. and Murphy, N. (2014), 'Measuring the design of empathetic buildings: A review of universal design evaluation methods', *Disability and Rehabilitation: Assistive Technology*, 11:1, pp. 13–21.

Ouroussoff, N. (2010), 'In Arabian Desert, a sustainable city rises', *New York Times*, 25 September, https://www.nytimes.com/2010/09/26/arts/design/26masdar.html. Accessed 7 December 2020.

Pask, A. (2010), 'Public space activism: Toronto and Vancouver', in J. Hou (ed.), *Insurgent Public Space: Guerrilla Urbanism and the Remaking of Contemporary Cities*, New York: Routledge, pp. 221–40.

Pullin, G. (2009), *Design Meets Disability*, Cambridge MA: MIT Press.

Salman, S. (2018), 'What would a truly disabled-accessible city look like? ', *The Guardian*, 14 February, https://www.theguardian.com/cities/2018/feb/14/what-disability-accessible-city-look-like. Accessed 7 December 2020.

Sen, A. (1992), *Inequality Reexamined*, Cambridge MA: Harvard University Press.

Sendra, P. and Sennett, R. (2020), *Designing Disorder: Experiments and Disruptions in the City*, London: Verso.

Sennett, R. (2010), *Building and Dwelling: Ethics for the City*, London: Penguin Books.

Steinfeld, E. and Maisel, J. (2012), *Universal Design: Creating Inclusive Environments*, Hoboken, NJ: John Wiley & Sons.

Sticky Bottle (2020), 'Liffey cycle route on Dublin's quays – video first look', http://www.stickybottle.com/latest-news/video-first-look-at-new-liffey-cycle-route-on-dublins-quays/. Accessed 23 June 2020.

Story, M. F., Mueller, J. L. and Mace, R. L. (1998), *The Universal Design File: Designing for People of All Ages and Abilities*, Raleigh: Center for Universal Design/North Carolina State University.

Tauke, B., Smith, K. and Davis, C. (eds) (2015), *Diversity and Design: Understanding Hidden Consequences*, New York: Routledge.

Tobias, J. (2003), 'Universal design: Is it really about design?' *Information Technology and Disabilities Journal*, 9:2, n.pag., http://people.rit.edu/easi/itd/volume9/number2/tobias.html. Accessed 19 January 2012.

United Nations (2007), *Convention on the Rights of Persons with Disabilities*, http://heinonline.org/hol-cgi-bin/get_pdf.cgi?handle=hein.journals/eurjhlb14&section=31. Accessed 6 July 2016.

Wachowski, L. and Wachowski, L. (1999), *The Matrix*, Los Angeles, CA: Warner Brothers.

Wahba, S. and Vapaavuori, J. (2020), 'A functional city's response to the COVID-19 pandemic', World Bank: Sustainable Cities, https://blogs.worldbank.org/sustainablecities/functional-citys-response-covid-19-pandemic. Accessed 6 December 2020.

6

The Design and Public Imaginaries of Smart Street Furniture

Justine Humphry, University of Sydney
Sophia Maalsen, University of Sydney
Justine Gangneux, University of Glasgow
Chris Chesher, University of Sydney
Matt Hanchard, University of Glasgow
Simon Joss, University of Glasgow
Peter Merrington, University of Glasgow
Bridgette Wessels, University of Glasgow[1]

Introduction

Design is dependent on an imaginary future object or outcome. In smart cities, this imaginary is frequently framed as an efficient and connected city for smart citizens. This city is underpinned by smart and connected infrastructure – city services, transport and street furniture – are connected, Wi-Fi enabled and embedded with sensors (Kitchin and Dodge 2011). The smart citizen is enabled by this connectivity. As critics note, however, the imagined smart public lacks inclusivity and the emergence and operation of the smart city is rarely seamless. There is a discrepancy between design imaginaries and lived reality.

In this chapter we engage with this disconnect through a focus on the design and public imaginaries of smart street furniture with respect to smart kiosk and smart bench projects. We look at the kinds of publics and audiences imagined in the marketing and design of smart street furniture, exploring the tensions and alignments between these imaginaries alongside the actual groups who most use these devices. In doing so we ask whether and how any social justice goals can be met when these imaginations are disconnected from the realities of street life and the communication needs of citizens (and non-citizens) with unequal levels of access to resources and capital.

We do this by using textual and framing analysis of the representations of street furniture on websites, signage, promotional material and technical documentation and combine this with interviews and observations of the design and use of the objects *in situ*, drawing upon fieldwork conducted in Glasgow on InLink kiosks and in London on Strawberry Energy benches. Combining these allows us to identify the similarities and differences between the imaginaries and realities of smart street furniture. In revealing these tensions, we identify a middle-ground imaginary, a compromise, which can help us better understand the intersection between smart imaginaries and lived realities, and that in turn can help us to design inclusive smart infrastructure.

This chapter proceeds as follows. First, we explain the research conducted and methods used as well as the analytical framework adopted for this chapter. We discuss how the public has been framed in the smart city through the different types of smart citizen imaginaries as variously absent, active or passive. Next we describe smart street furniture with particular reference to the smart kiosks and benches that form the basis of this study, before providing an overview of methods and our analysis. We show that there is a discrepancy between the corporate-led public imaginaries and the actual users of the street furniture – as well as more gradations within the actual active and passive users. The absence of marginalized users in representing these devices suggests they will be taken up among more well-connected, mobile, urban citizens. However, we found these not to be the main users of these kiosks and benches, and instead these played an important role for people who were precariously connected – the homeless and gig workers. While the findings can help to develop more inclusive furniture that addresses actually existing publics, there is also an opportunity to question the model or understandings of the public and connect these with more expansive imaginations and goals that go beyond the instrumental uses of the public for the purposes of their data value.

Smart citizens: Imaginaries of the smart citizen

Smart cities, it is generally envisioned, are inhabited by smart citizens. Debate about where and how the public is incorporated into the smart city has been persistent since the early smart cities emerged, and has continued through new iterations of smart cities. Early critiques of the smart city pointed out the absence of people in the city at all. Smart cities it seemed, were for technology, and citizens were an afterthought (Greenfield 2013). Responding to this critique, cities adopting smart city policy and practices made efforts to highlight the role of citizens, with technology reframed not as the priority but as an enabler (Barns et al.

2017). In this reframing, citizens were envisioned either as active or passive in relation to the technology, but critically data – its generation and analysis – underpins both.

Gabrys (2014) has written on the citizen as sensor as she discusses how the intersection of the city and computational technologies have produced a new modality of citizenship. In the smart city, citizenship becomes operationalized through generating, analysing and managing data, rather than existing as a fixed subject (Gabrys 2014: 34). But the extent to which people purposely engage or are even able to engage in these practices varies.

Framings of active citizenship reference users who purposely generate their own data or make use of city data to shape and manage urban life. Since 2000, open data initiatives, crowdsourcing and events such as hackathons have become central tools of citizen engagement, with smart citizens frequently portrayed as actively participating in urban problem solving and entrepreneurial activities, through local government and industry events (Hollands 2008). The extent to which these events reflect citizen agency is open to critique (Cardullo and Kitchin 2019a, 2019b; Joss et al. 2017). As Perng (2019: 420–21) notes, such events encourage 'entrepreneurial citizenship and civic paternalism […] what is engineered tends to be neoliberal citizenship'. However, such events have the potential for citizens to engage with shaping urban futures and, as Perng (2019: 432) goes on to explain, they can disrupt neoliberal co-optation, by repurposing state and privatized resources, and build civic infrastructure.

Although this reframing placed people back into the smart city, it was not a vision inclusive of a diverse citizenship. Those who were not technologically savvy, or who were unable to comfortably access events were unaccounted for. Hackathons, for example, have been critiqued for their predominance of White, middle-class, non-disabled, male participants, excluding others along the lines of gender, socio-economic class, disability and race. This resulted in bias in selecting which problems were addressed through such events, as they reflected the problems experienced by this narrow group of participants and were therefore not broadly inclusive (Gabrys 2014; Maalsen and Perng 2016, 2017; Mattern 2014).

The framing of passive smart citizenship also relies on data. Unlike the user-generated data of active participation, this data is often unconsciously generated by an individual's everyday digital footprint as they interact and move through urban spaces. Citizen profiles begin to build through, for example, use of a smart transport card, free Wi-Fi connections, electronic purchases and geolocation services. Data traces create data bodies – a fragmentation of the individual into discrete data units characteristic of systems of modulatory control. However, as Iveson and Maalsen (2019) argue, in networked cities, citizenship exists on a spectrum between modulatory and disciplinary control, and individuals can be reassembled from their 'dividual' data bodies (Deleuze 1992: 5). Willingly or not, citizens of the smart city generate data that can then be used by public and private interests to manage, shape and control the city.

A smart citizen therefore is variously portrayed as actively engaged or passive (Cardullo and Kitchin 2019a; Shelton and Lodato 2019). The smart citizen either intentionally uses smart city apps and infrastructure producing and interacting with data; or at other times the citizen is a passive user, a citizen sensor unknowingly generating data as they go about their daily lives. Regardless of whether active or passive, moves to make smart cities 'citizen-centric' remain grounded in 'pragmatic, instrumental and paternalistic discourses and practices rather than those of social rights, political citizenship, and the common good' (Cardullo and Kitchin 2019b: 813).

Notably, despite a shift to the 'citizen-centric' smart city (Cowley et al. 2018), this discourse is largely divorced from the long history of literature and debates about the public, public space and the public sphere. McGuire (2008) notes that intellectual scholarship on the value of the public emerged in part as a result of the massive transformations wrought by media and urban change in the twentieth century, corresponding with a withdrawal from public life into the privatized space of the suburban home. Modern urban life was a focus of narratives of loss as well as renewal, with the street a site and motif for the political potential of the public (Habermas 1993; Jacobs 1961; Lefebvre [1967] 1996; Sennett 1977). Central to these accounts was a shared optimism in the idea that bringing together strangers in common space would bring about healthier, more vibrant, inclusive places, as well as a radicalized social consciousness. As many have pointed out, however, there is an inherent contradiction in the structuring of the public that has historically excluded groups on the basis of gender, class and race. This has led to struggles for the widening of representation (Mitchell 1995) and underscored the important relation between the political agency of citizens and the design of urban spaces.

How does this 'citizen-centric' vision translate to the infrastructure of the actually existing smart city? Smart street furniture offers a valuable opportunity to look further into interpretations and imaginaries of who is a citizen of the smart city. This is because street furniture is always imagined with civics in mind. It is necessarily public and provides a public service, whether that is a place to sit or a place to communicate, or in the provision of public connectivity or information. Critically analysing the design, policies and use of smart street furniture provides insights into the types of smart city public imaginaries embedded in the furniture. It also reveals the disconnects, tensions and materialization of this public in its actual use. In this chapter we look at how smart citizens are envisioned in smart street furniture through the lens of their design and marketing. We analyse these imaginaries alongside observations and vox pops with members of the public carried out on Strawberry Energy benches in London and InLink kiosks in Glasgow.

Seeing public imaginaries through smart street furniture

Street furniture is designed with certain publics in mind and is an often contested public resource. The use and users of public benches, for example, are subject to informal reprobation or formal strategies of discouragement or prohibition. Some cities are notorious for installing 'bumproof benches' (Davis 2006: 233) that intervene in the benches' affordances by making them too short, curved, diagonally angled or obstructed by handrails and are therefore unsuitable to lie down upon (Bergamaschi et al. 2014). Another population that is subject to regulation is teenagers, who also like to 'sit up high with their feet propped, they lean and they huddle' (Owens 2007: 161). In many American cities, planners deliberately space out benches along a walkway to discourage groups of teens assembling. Teens have responded by gathering at night on play equipment that is used by younger people. In many places, loitering, curfews and vagrancy laws have been applied specifically to target these public bench users.

The distinctive attribute of the smart bench, as opposed to other smart infrastructures, is that it displaces only another bench. It does not necessarily make a new claim on public space that kiosks, wayfinders and new advertising hoardings might. Unlike smart city command and control systems such as artificially intelligent public surveillance systems, or digital advertising space, the smart bench offers a public amenity that provides charging and connectivity for mobile communication devices, which itself displaced the public phone. It can serve particularly those who lack access to these resources and are not necessarily rate payers, such as people experiencing homelessness and budget travellers. It continues to offer that basic affordance of sitting, and fosters the etiquette of sharing a public resource.

Kiosks, on the other hand, are diverse in their appearance and application, with more recent iterations providing an informational role within a self-service paradigm. The term 'kiosk', with its roots in the Persion word *kūshk*, refers to a pavilion with a roof or roof struts and open walls. These flexible structures were adapted in many different cultural contexts, as a way to reach out to and interact with people in the immediate vicinity in a variety of ways. Used by the upper classes in the Ottoman Empire in their summer gardens as a servery for refreshments, and by the European monarchy to host musicians, the kiosk found a more common use in the twentieth century in a westernized context as a booth in which a vendor sells newspapers, magazines, fruit and other consumables to the public on the street. The self-service interactive kiosk is a further adaptation that accompanies the development of computers. It is a structure that houses the equipment required to deliver an automated service with a monitor and terminal providing an interface to end users.

Methods and analysis

For the research carried out on smart street furniture, we focused on two types of furniture: InLink kiosks in Glasgow and Strawberry Energy smart benches in London. At the time of the research, InLink kiosks were being rolled out in several cities in the United Kingdom by a joint venture formed in 2017 between Intersection, a US company, and Primesight (now Global), a UK advertising agency, in partnership with British Telecom (BT).[2] Strawberry Energy is a Serbian crowd-funded start-up company created in 2011 and launched its first UK smart bench in 2015. It has now rolled out smart benches in 30 cities across 17 countries.

The selection of smart street furniture was made to explore the new types and combinations of technologies and services, and to compare the ways in which people encountered, perceived and interacted with these. A comprehensive discussion of the project methodology can be found in (Wessels et al. forthcoming) but we briefly detail them here.

In this chapter we draw upon data from InLinkUK and Strawberry Energy websites and publicly available corporate documents to identify and compare the imagined users with the users that emerge in practice. We analyse the content available with particular reference to the type of users they imagine.

We also draw upon field observations, vox pops and stakeholder interviews undertaken by the project team in Glasgow and London from July to November in 2019. A total of three InLink kiosks in Glasgow (Sauchiehall St, Buchanan St and Hope St) and three Strawberry Energy benches in Southwark borough in London (Southwark Bridge Rd, Borough Rd and Elephant Rd) were observed for our research. The observed sites were selected for the diversity of location and potential different users. Observations and vox pops were conducted at selected times to reflect a range of uses and interactions: two weekdays and one weekend day for three set periods of time – morning, lunchtime and early evening.

Researchers took field observations and conducted a series of vox pops, totalling 30 for the InLinks and 45 for the benches, to observe how people interacted with these devices, and to ascertain the public's opinions of the street furniture. Vox pop participants were recruited by engaging passers-by who were asked a series of questions to gauge their awareness of smart street furniture and its functions, their perceptions as well as their actual uses (or non-uses) of this new type of furniture.

Interview and observation data was analysed thematically in NVivo in a collaborative process involving all members of the project team with regular meetings to ensure consistency, iteratively reflect and discuss emerging themes. For this chapter we also draw on textual analysis and framing approaches to analyse the imaginaries of the smart citizen as this manifests in smart street furniture. Media frames, a development of Goffman's (1974) 'social frameworks' theory, are the means by which readers and audiences are guided towards certain ideas, values and meanings in their consumption of texts (Entman 1993). Media frames have been the subject of extensive research to ascertain how news media coverage shapes mass opinion – also known as 'agenda setting'. Extending this approach, Woolgar (1990) argued that technologies can similarly be read as texts and that designers, like authors, 'configure the user' in the way that ideas about the user's capacity and future actions are programmed into their design. Frames thus work textually, in representations and other semiotic practices, and materially, in the features and affordances of a technological artifact.

InLinkUK and Strawberry Energy's imaginaries of the end users of smart kiosks/benches

The ways in which end users are envisioned by the corporations behind smart street furniture play a crucial role in how their products are developed and designed. Indeed, corporations' imaginaries of the potential end users of their urban infrastructures are inscribed in the representations of users as well as in the functionalities and affordances these infrastructures offer. Drawing on analysis of corporate documents made publicly available by InLinkUK and Strawberry Energy (e.g. terms of use, devices specifications, press kits and blog posts as well as audiovisual and written material amassed on their websites), this section examines how the two corporations imagined the end users of their products, paying attention to the frames employed. This in turn sheds light on how their imaginaries informed the particular design and provision catered by smart kiosks and smart benches.

Young, mobile and connected

Both InLinkUK and Strawberry Energy prioritize improving the connectivity of cities (and citizens) in the design and promotional material for their smart street furniture. Potential end users of their products are represented as young, mobile and connected. End users are pictured engaging with the kiosks and benches remotely using their smartphones (connecting to Wi-Fi) and directly by making use of inbuilt facilities to sustain their existing connectivity (charging phone

133

facilities). On its former website, InLinkUK stated that one of the key features of the kiosks was to 'connect to ultrafast Wi-Fi using your own device' (InLinkUK 2019a: n.pag.). In its press kit, the company further explains that links connect 'the fastest available internet service to the fastest commercially available Wi-Fi equipment and opens all that bandwidth for people to use – no data caps or time-outs' (InLinkUK 2019a: n.pag.). Similarly, on the company's website, Strawberry Energy portrays a pictorial series of young professionals sitting on the benches in groups or individually to rest while using or charging their phones. Benches are presented as places of informal socialization that are enhanced by access to Wi-Fi and charging facilities. Fitting within this imaginary, benches are described as 'providing energy, connectivity and relevant local information on the go' (Strawberry Energy 2020: n.pag.).

Smart and sustainable

The ideal of environmental sustainability also finds a place in the marketing of these smart street furniture products. Strawberry Energy describes its mission as developing 'solar powered smart urban furniture for smart and sustainable cities' (Strawberry Energy 2020: n.pag.), locating both its infrastructures and potential end users within 'people-centric' smart city discourses and emerging ideas of smart citizenship (Cardullo and Kitchin 2019a, 2019b; Joss et al. 2019). Users of Strawberry Energy benches are portrayed as participating in and engaging with their local environment. Strawberry Energy's mission relies on the active participation of citizens who can utilize smart furniture with access to Wi-Fi and charging facilities while taking part in the collection of real-time information about their local environment (via a mobile app). The Strawberry Energy app enables 'smarter navigation through the city' (Strawberry Energy 2020: n.pag.), allowing its users to connect to the Strawberry Energy bench network while encouraging them to share local information collected from the benches' sensors on social media platforms and websites. Users here are envisioned within the framework of smart citizens who are actively engaging with smart technologies in urban environments, generating (purposely or inadvertently) data in real time, which is allegedly used to improve public spaces (and the company's services).

As shown above, both InLinkUK and Strawberry Energy's strategies and visions draw on an imaginary of young urban, mobile and already connected users. Connectivity needs are assumed to be temporary gaps in access that can be 'enhanced' to achieve the seamless ideal. In addition to the numerous limitations of this type of participation (see Cardullo and Kitchin 2019a), representations of end users exclude vulnerable populations such as low-income and poorly connected communities who rely heavily on freely accessible Wi-Fi systems. Indeed, while end users of the kiosks and benches are understood by corporations as mobile and connected, this does not reflect the actual uses of these infrastructures and the ways in which these are adopted and reappropriated by different groups of users, such as, for example, the use of the kiosks' free call facility by the homeless population (see Halegoua and Lingel [2018] for failure to include marginalized groups in the vision of the LinkNYC). As pointed out by Halegoua and Lingel (2018: 4647), one of the issues behind this type of smart street furniture is that they 'need to adopt more inclusive imaginations of the public and imagine more varied uses of public connection'.

Essential, but for whom?

A complicating feature of these imaginaries is that, despite the absence of marginalized users represented in promotional material, the design of the InLink kiosks and Strawberry Energy benches includes features and services that are suggestive of a less connected 'public user'. This idea was also echoed in the interviews with commercial providers and local council officers. The CEO of Strawberry Energy, interviewed in September 2019, described his benches as follows: 'For the people it's just a bunch of useful services, completely free of charge, designed around their needs.' Similarly, InLinkUK identifies one of the key contributions of its InLink kiosks as providing 'essential free services to enhance the public realm' (InLinkUK 2019b). In addition to free Wi-Fi and charging facilities like the benches, these have the added features of an emergency call button, free telephone service and a social services directory accessible through the inbuilt touchscreen tablet.

Commercial providers recognize the ongoing value and business case for extending connectivity in the context of an 'infrastructural gap' (Dalakoglou 2016) and evidence of the persistence of access issues and disparities among citizens. In this sense, the offer of public connectivity is important for building support and justification for new smart urban initiatives. At the same time, this 'public user' imaginary is under-articulated, without a clear sense of for whom these services are vital or why. The framing of these connectivity services as 'essential' has performative value and is strategically deployed, reinforcing the need for such services to bolster and boost the model of connected citizenship so central to smart cities. Frames are not only rhetorical devices that guide audiences to read meanings in a particular way, they also perform a range of ideological and mediating functions, helping to bring about a certain reality (Butler 1999; Hall 2001). These tensions between the imaginaries, design and uses of smart street furniture point to a more complex process at work in the emergence of smart cities and the citizens they are designed for.

Imagined publics versus actual publics

Does the imagined public as described above translate to the actually existing city? In this section we draw upon our observations of the smart benches and kiosks to analyse the relationship between the designers' and technology providers' imaginations as represented in public documents and the behaviours of actual users. Our observations and analysis revealed multiple and sometimes contradictory public imaginaries envisioned by city planners and technology designers. These imaginaries emphasize active smart citizens as the main users characterized by the dominant frame of the young, urban, mobile and connected user. However, we found a more diverse range of user types and practices and have detailed these in relation to the imaginaries of active users and passive users. Most notably we found a disconnect between the images of young, urban, mobile and highly connected users who are prominent on the vendor websites and materials, and the observed users that predominantly included vulnerable groups such as the homeless. An additional imagined user – the public imagined by the user (or non-user) – emerged when people we interviewed reflected on who they thought would be the primary users of the smart street furniture.

The passive user

A large number of the people we spoke to and observed around the InLink kiosks in Glasgow and Strawberry Energy smart benches in London had not registered the kiosks and benches. Neither were they aware of the new kinds of functionalities these new types of furniture offered. This was illustrated in replies like this one from a person in Glasgow when asked if they had noticed the InLinks in the city before:

> Er no, I haven't [...] what's it for? Is it to make free calls [laughs] to anywhere in the UK? [...] I just thought it was like an advertising board, I guess! [laughs] Um what is it for? Just that I guess? [...] I would think bus times, it kind of looks like a bus timetable but I don't know! [laughs]
>
> (Vox pop, Glasgow, Sauchiehall St, 4 July 2019)

A similar sense of puzzlement was observed in London when passers-by were asked the same question about the smart benches, though in their case, the prior affordance of these as a place to sit was more readily recognized. This group conformed to aspects of the passive user of smart street furniture, in that they were characterized by a lack of use of these objects and a certain indifference to their existence, while at the same time, may also be unaware that they are using features of the street furniture:

I haven't used them but I've seen 'em around, especially on this side of the river. I haven't seen 'em up on the north side yet. But that doesn't mean, I mean, I've not been looking for it to be honest.

(Vox pop, London, Southwark Bridge Rd, 4 July 2019)

We found a number of people were unsure if they had used the Wi-Fi service of the kiosk or bench, as reflected in this participant's comment:

I might be or I might be on data, it depends because sometimes if I'm passing by and it's a Wi-Fi thing that I don't know and hasn't logged me in, I'll just have the data instead so that I can get any messages or whatever.

(Vox pop, Glasgow, Sauchiehall St, 4 July 2019)

This kind of passive use is likely to occur as a result of the automatic connectivity built-in to the Wi-Fi network. Records of users who have previously connected are created in their smartphone's automatic connection to Wi-Fi as they move through the city and pass either the InLinks or smart benches. The automatic yet passive connectivity is enabled by the user's previous actions. If they signed up to the telecommunication provider's Wi-Fi at some time in the past, their devices will continue to connect without them deliberately connecting each time. This automation also means that the user is passively generating data about their presence in the place. As we discussed above, passive smart citizenship emerges from the digital footprint that an individual produces as they move through urban spaces and this data can be used to manage and shape the city.

The InLinks have another kind of user who has varying levels of awareness of their interaction with street furniture: the consumer of advertising. It is their attention to the advertisements on the digital screens that justifies the money that advertisers spend to have their content displayed, even if most people may seem to ignore it. The InLinkUK network is funded through advertising on the devices' two 135.7 cm high-definition (HD) digital screens, which stand on either side of these free-standing structures (InLink 2019b). As highlighted in the opening quote to this section, many interviewees thought that advertising was the only purpose of these kiosks, and had not noticed the interactive service available. For example, one passer-by who took part in a vox pop in Glasgow only noticed the kiosk when it was pointed out to them and guessed one of its functionalities by reading the inscription on the screen: 'Make free calls to anywhere in the UK here'. Prior to this moment of discovery, this person thought that the kiosk was 'an advertising board'. Meanwhile, others did not notice the InLinks or advertisements until they had their attention drawn to it as shown in the following excerpt:

Interviewer: Have you noticed these around?
Respondent: Not till this very moment, yes.

(Vox pop, Glasgow, Buchanan St, 27 June 2019)

We found that the researchers played an important role as intermediaries, drawing attention to these objects and providing an opportunity to reflect on and discover them *in situ*. In this process, many of these up-until-now passive users expressed an interest in these objects and the services they offered. They also revealed some of the reasons behind their non-use, which was related to multiple factors including sufficient data plans and internet connectivity through their smartphones, a lack of clear signage and an already existing familiarity with the city.

These passive users did not discover the kiosks and benches through need but had the potential to become more intentional active users (indeed, some of the active users described later in the chapter started using the kiosks and benches after seeing other people using them). Similarly, when given an opportunity to reflect on the possible use of their data when connected to such services, we found that individuals took a more active stance, engaging in questions and giving opinions. There is a long history of critiquing the existence of the passive mass media consumer (see, e.g., de Certeau 1984; Krajina 2014), and as such, being 'unaware' or 'indifferent' does not necessarily translate into a lack of activity or agency. These findings suggest a more complex relation than that captured in the imagined figure of the passive user.

Nevertheless, seemingly passive users still generate data and are an important audience for the city, markets and third parties who have an investment in their data trails. These are variously generated through access to data granted at the point of agreement to signing up to free Wi-Fi. Moreover, for advertisers, passive consumption of advertisements represents a potential market return. Indeed, despite the shift from traditional media to online advertising, outdoor advertising is a growing industry and in a process of global consolidation (Iveson 2012). Iveson (2012) suggests that exclusive advertising deals in city centres and new ways to monetize digital screens are the main drivers behind this growth and the emergence of new kinds of private–public street furniture partnerships. Passive users are an important factor in the success of such projects.

The active user

The active user intentionally interacts with the kiosk or bench. The active user is not continuously mobile but may be stationary for periods of time as they use the services provided by the street furniture, such as charging a phone or using a free call facility. In other cases, they may remain mobile but their movement is determined by access to free Wi-Fi. However, unlike the young urban professionals envisioned by the vendors, our observations show that these users, particularly for the kiosks, are predominantly those with insecure access to internet and telecommunications. The two main groups of active users were the homeless and gig economy workers.

We frequently observed people who seemed homeless using the free call function of the InLinks. The inclusion of a free phone service in the kiosk design is a distinctive aspect of the InLinks and an important part of its business case to local councils. This function allows callers to connect to any number within the United Kingdom and can help those without other forms of communication to maintain contact with family members and connect to services. One middle-aged homeless man we spoke to explained the benefit of these over the old pay phones, since they did not cost money and did not require an unwieldy amount of change. Another elderly rough sleeper explained how he used the free phone facility to stay in touch with his brother.

The following excerpt from our field observations of the InLinks in Glasgow is illustrative of the kinds of encounters we observed:

> Three homeless people used the kiosk in the morning, two together (they had a piece of paper with a number, type it on the screen, it failed to go through and they left immediately). Half an hour later another man (who was chatting with the two previous ones earlier) also tried to make a phone call. Got really frustrated as it did not work and cursed the kiosk and left.
>
> (Fieldwork notes, Sauchiehall Street, Glasgow, 4 July 2019)

Our observations and vox pops indicated the phone facility was vital for those members of the public who were without a working mobile phone to contact family and make appointments with services such as the local job centre, but there were drawbacks. Our observations showed that the kiosks also weren't always reliable infrastructures of connectivity, with calls sometimes failing to connect. Callbacks could not be received, which limited the utility of the phone service and the open design of the kiosk (unlike the traditional phone 'booth') meant that callers had to speak loudly to be heard and lean into the kiosk to hear the phone conversation. Importantly, the kiosks provide connectivity to those who can't afford mobile phones and data. These users are rarely depicted in the designer and technology providers' visions of the smart city, but in our observations show that smart street furniture has significant benefits for them.

Platform economy workers were also regularly observed using the kiosks to charge their phones and connect to the Wi-Fi. The services offered by the InLinks

139

were valuable for them to do their work by being able to charge their handsets and connect when waiting for jobs:

> Respondent: Just now I was charging my phone because most of the time I go around with a power point with me, but today I forgot my power point so this was the emergency thing, to back up here! [laughs] It's very good, it's very helpful, yeah [...] Er I use them when my phone is dying because I work with my phone some-times, a lot of times it happens to me my phone dies and I forgot my power point at home, so I can use them to back up my charge, yeah.
>
> (Vox pop, Glasgow, Sauchiehall St, 4 July 2019)

Smart cities are interconnected with the gig economy. Both are mediated by digital platforms and the entrepreneurial aspects of platform capitalism and labour are valued by smart cities. Gig workers are, however, largely absent from the imaginaries of the product material analysed above.

While not purposely contributing data in the same way as participants in citizen science initiatives or urban data hackathons discussed earlier, these users are still actively generating data. By making use of the services, they generate a footprint similar to that of the passive user, except that in active and purposeful use, more data will be generated – for example, through records of phone and data use.

Unlike the kiosks, the smart benches were predominantly engaged with for their original and 'non-smart' function – that of providing a place to sit. These attracted a wider range of users in our observations: workers on their lunch break, daytime shoppers, tourists, students; parents with children, elderly men and women. Several people were seen using their mobile phone while seated. There were also signs that the benches had been used by people to rest for longer periods including overnight (e.g. fresh cigarette butts and bottles were seen deposited next to the bench early in the morning). This was despite the built-in bar that divided this model of bench into two smaller sections, preventing it being used to fully recline. Several people also noted the use of the benches by people who appeared to be sleeping rough, a point of contention for wider take up by some groups who saw this as problematic.

> They look very modern. Yeah, I mean they're good for, I've seen a lot of er, I don't know whether it's the right crowd, but homeless using them to charge their speakers, their phones, stuff like that because they don't really have access to charging amenities.
>
> (Vox pop, London, Borough Rd., 3 July 2019)

It was often difficult to determine if bench users and passers-by were using the free Wi-Fi service available through a third-party internet provider in partnership with Strawberry Energy. However, in our attempts at the three different sites, we were only able to connect to this service at one bench. We were able to access the environmental data from the Strawberry Energy app but noted that this was only accessible from a smartphone and that the accuracy of the readings appeared to be incorrect (with types of available data also differing across the two bench models). We did observe the charging facility being used but the charging cables were observed to be often broken. Various other issues prevented us from using the environmental data via the downloadable app – slow downloads from the bench Wi-Fi, the app wouldn't open on the mobile phone and the app was only partially functional (the bench location was not visible on Google Maps at one site).

Active users of the benches are not exclusively the urban young professionals envisioned by the vendors, though these were among the user groups observed. However, while active users are imagined as those who interact with data services, the benches were by and large used as traditional benches rather than for their smart functions. Furthermore, even if users might try to engage in these, there were a number of barriers to use. The active user imaginary is dependent not only on alignment with the actual user but also usability of the devices and their data-generating features.

The imagined other user

The third type of user that emerged was the 'other user' imagined by the public. This user was frequently referred to in relation to an individual's use or non-use of the furniture. For example, while someone might say they have no need to use the features of the kiosk or bench, they envision it being useful for others. These 'others' are predominantly those who need the connectivity affordances of the infrastructure, for example those that don't have data on their mobile plan or who can't afford to call from their own mobile, and those that are visiting or unfamiliar with the city. The homeless, tourists and students featured in these imaginaries – groups of people who either don't have the resources to be consistently digitally connected and therefore use the benches and kiosks for their connectivity affordances, or who are unfamiliar with the area and use the wayfinding and information services provided by the furniture. For example, these two participants reflect on the benefits of the kiosks for the homeless, in particular, the ability to keep them connected whether by charging their phones or using the free call function:

> My first thought was um the individuals who are homeless need to have access to being able to call resources. It's great, I mean it will charge their phones, they don't always have access to power. So just that alone is a huge help.
>
> (Vox pop, Glasgow, Buchanan St, 27 June 2019)

> I have seen more people using the free phone calls. I mean mostly homeless people, I must admit, um but it's good for them, so at least they have access to contacting people that they need to, social security and stuff like that, whoever.
>
> (Vox pop, Glasgow, Sauchiehall St, 4 July 2019)

Similarly, a council officer in Southwark borough reflects on the positive attributes of the smart benches, in particular the benches' ability to serve a range of people from tourists to the homeless:

> I mean, the people who use them are quite varied. I've noticed a lot of tourists use them, because they're in the north of the borough, which is used as a tourist area anyway, but we get lots of tourists using them. Homeless people use them quite a lot I've noticed, and people have opinions about that, whether it's positive or negative. I think it's positive that somebody can go and charge their phone up somewhere, they're just as entitled as anybody else to use them. And you do see people kneeling, charging their phone up, and maybe they've run out of battery. I think it's all very positive.
>
> (London stakeholders interview, 11 October 2019)

Use is not always without contention, however, with some participants negatively responding to the use of the benches by the homeless, throwing into question who they think the furniture is for:

> It's a good idea, if for example I was working and I want a break, to sit on, but you can't sit on them because the homeless people are using it most of the time, so you won't be able to make use of the chair, that they lie on it or they don't want anybody to sit, they occupy the whole space.
>
> (Vox pop, London, Southwark Bridge Rd, 3 July 2019)

These respondents were reflecting on observations they had made of the benches and kiosks – the observed uses and the observed users. Drawing upon this they highlighted the benefits of the infrastructure but also positioned it as something that other people with less resources than themselves use. The provision of connectivity, information, data and free calls was seen as positive. This was predominantly seen as beneficial for the homeless, students and tourists, who they had seen make use of the furniture, groups of users that are not reflected in the technology providers and designers material. This points to the existence of a larger 'public' that is 'smart' than that envisioned by smart furniture vendors and cities, one that is more inclusive in the way the smart citizen inhabits public space and the public sphere.

These three types of user show the disconnect and fragmentation about what policy-makers and designers imagine as a smart public. There is a disconnect between active and passive use, and frequently, the main users are likely not the ones primarily imagined in the design phase or policy. Imaginaries of a smart citizen frequently conjure images of a digitally connected and mobile citizen, and rarely do we see homeless groups or precarious gig economy workers factored in this.

Discussion and conclusion

Smart cities are built on the promise that they will make cities more efficient and improved. Smart street furniture plays a role in providing these improvements, promising citizens of the smart city information and communication services in exchange for data or advertising space. While there has been debate over the smart city's vision of the smart citizen, the designs and implementation of smart street infrastructure give us some insight into the design and technology providers' imaginaries of citizens. By comparing these visions with the public use and perceptions of smart street furniture, we can see how these imaginaries translate to the reality of the city, and potentially use these insights to create a more inclusive smart city that goes beyond rhetoric and performance.

While the citizen imaginaries represented in the design and technology provider material painted a picture of young urban, mobile and connected users, our analysis revealed a more diverse group of users. We categorized these as active and passive users dependent on the intention with which they interacted with the street furniture at the time of observation; and the 'imagined other user', a user constructed by a member of the public when thinking about who the kiosk or bench would serve.

Active users intentionally engage with the street furniture, either using its physical capabilities – charging points, free call services, places to sit or lean – or its digital services – using free Wi-Fi. While there are similarities between some of these characteristics and those of the design imaginaries – namely mobility, urban based and connectivity – there are also disconnects. Rather than young urban professionals, these active smart citizens are those who inhabit more precarious positions within the urban. They are the gig workers and the homeless, citizens who are predominantly absent from the design and technology provider material, and who are rarely discussed as citizens in the smart city literature more broadly.

Passive users are more likely to be the urban, young, connected and mobile professional envisioned by the designers and technology providers. However, because of their mobility and connectivity they do not use the kiosks or benches in the way that is envisioned. Passive users predominantly have the privilege of their own phones and data, meaning they have less need to rely on the free services offered by the furniture. Passive users may automatically connect to Wi-Fi as they move through the city, having previously signed up to the service provider, but they don't actively use or seek out that connectivity. At the same time, passive users have the potential to become active users and have a more complex relation to advertising and data consumption than suggested in corporate-held public imaginaries.

The 'imagined other user' is interesting in that it provides insights into the smart citizen from the perspective of the existing publics. The majority of the literature on the citizen in the smart city addresses the citizen as envisioned by local government, policy-makers, designers and technology service providers. The 'imagined other user' is, however, a user that emerges from both active and passive users' reflections and imaginations of who smart street furniture is for. The publics' 'imagined other user' offers an interesting critique of the users imagined by the design and technology providers, as well as local government. As noted earlier, public space has always excluded along lines of gender, class and race, and the absence of homeless and less affluent users from the discourses and designs surrounding the smart furniture described here, highlights that exclusion exists in the imagined smart citizen. But the publics' vision of the 'imagined other user' based on their observations and reflections of the use of the kiosks and benches shows that a more inclusive vision of the smart citizen can emerge.

Charles Taylor's (2002) 'social imaginary' is suggestive of the kind of broader public imaginary captured in this third imagined user group. According to Taylor (2002: 106), these imaginaries are not the 'possession of a small minority' but 'shared by large groups of people, if not the whole society', in turn rendering possible a 'shared sense of legitimacy'. This highlights a number of contradictions with regards to the smart kiosks' and benches' imaginaries. The citizens' imaginaries upon which private corporations developed the kiosks and benches were noticeably divergent from the imaginaries portrayed by the public. Furthermore, Taylor (2002: 106) points out that the social imaginaries are deeper and broader than 'the intellectual schemes people may entertain when they think about social reality in a disengaged mode'.

We might conclude that this disengaged mode is precisely what comes about as a result of the off-the-shelf designs that prioritize the passive data user in current implementations of smart street furniture. This demonstrates some of the normative and global visions of 'smart citizens' of key providers in the private sector as well as their lack of inclusivity and imagination of different end users and contexts. This in turn feeds into a perceived lack of legitimacy (that is, it is only

144

for advertising) as well as controversies at the street level as seen in New York (Halegoua and Linge 2018). On the other hand, the imagined other users points to a broader and more inclusive (that is, widening access to digital facilities) social imaginary. However, it also points to some tensions between those in need of the provision and those who do not need it or only in rare cases.

These three user types – active, passive and 'imagined other' – illustrate that the affordances of smart infrastructure can serve diverse publics dependent on their needs and a refashioning of the public and public space. Reliance on the connectivity afforded by the furniture varies dependent on a users' own access to mobile technology, data and mobility. Those who have their own phones and data plans, predominantly the young, urban professionals envisioned by the providers and designers, need and use the furniture less than those who are not as materially resourced and mobile. Instead, the primary users were those who are predominantly absent in the imaginaries of the designers, providers and governments when discussing the smart city. These are the homeless and precarious gig workers who rely on the types of street furniture described here to connect to services, family and friends, to charge phones and to access data – all of which are activities that require them to stay put while they use the kiosk or bench. This is not the mobile urban professional.

The discrepancies between the imagined users and the actual users, however, are useful for informing the design of smart street furniture that can be more inclusive. Both design and policy visions of the smart citizen rarely reflect on the disadvantaged, instead framing the smart citizen as actively involved in the smart city through citizen science, participating in hackathons and generating and using data in a purposeful way. Here we have shown that the smart citizen also includes the homeless and the precarious. These observations can be used to inform a more inclusive smart city and vision of the smart citizen. Doing so can potentially help to better design smart cities to provide for diverse publics – from the most disadvantaged to the more privileged. It can also help reveal what is behind investments in public connectivity through smart street furniture. Connecting and opening up and aligning public–private partnerships with the broader, deeper, more representative existing public sphere can lead to more inclusive cities but also in a way that does not produce people as merely data citizens or individuals.

NOTES

1. Author order notes: the first four authors are the core authors and listed by contribution. The remaining authors have been listed alphabetically.
2. The InLinkUK joint venture has dissolved and the InLinks are now fully owned by BT, an arrangement that was announced in late December 2019.

ACKNOWLEDGEMENTS

This research was made possible through a grant from the University of Sydney and the University of Glasgow Partnership Collaboration Awards (PCA) 2019 round.

REFERENCES

Barns, S., Cosgrave, E., Acuto, M. and Mcneill, D. (2017), 'Digital infrastructures and urban governance', *Urban Policy and Research*, 35:1, pp. 20–31.

Bergamaschi, M., Castrignanò, M. and De Rubertis, P. (2014), 'The homeless and public space: Urban policy and exclusion in Bologna', Revue Interventions économiques, 51. https://doi.org/10.4000/interventionseconomiques.2441. Accessed 14 June 2021.

Butler, J. (1999), *Gender Trouble: Feminism and the Subversion of Identity*, London: Routledge.

Cardullo, P. and Kitchin, R. (2019a), 'Being a "citizen" in the smart city: Up and down the scaffold of smart citizen participation in Dublin, Ireland', *Geo Journal*, 84, pp. 1–13.

Cardullo, C. and Kitchin, R. (2019b), 'Smart urbanism and smart citizenship: The neoliberal logic of "citizen-focused" smart cities in Europe', *EPC: Politics and Space*, 37:5, pp. 813–30.

Certeau, M. de (1984), *The Practice of Everyday Life*, Berkeley, University of California Press.

Cowley, R., Joss, S. and Dayot, Y. (2018), 'The smart city and its publics: Insights from across six UK cities', *Urban Research & Practice*, 11(1), pp. 53–77.

Dalakoglu, D. (2016), 'Infrastructural gap: Commons, state and anthropology', *City*, 20:6, pp. 822–31.

Davis, M. (2006), *City of Quartz: Excavating the Future in Los Angeles*, London: Verso.

Deleuze, G. (1992), 'Postscript on the societies of control', *October*, 59, pp. 3–7.

Entman, R. M. (1993), 'Framing: Toward clarification of a fractured paradigm', *Journal of Communication*, 43:4, pp. 51–58.

Gabrys, J. (2014), 'Programming environments: Environmentality and citizen sensing in the smart city', *Environment and Planning D: Society and Space*, 32, pp. 30–48.

Greenfield, A. (2013), *Against the Smart City: A Pamphlet*, New York: Do Projects.

Goffman, E. (1974), *Frame Analysis: An Essay on the Organization of Experience*, Cambridge, MA: Harvard University Press.

Habermas, J. (1993), *The Structural Transformation of the Public Sphere: An Inquiry into a Category of Bourgeois Society*, Cambridge, UK: Polity Press.

Halegoua, G. and Lingel. J. (2018), 'Lit up and left dark: Failures of imagination in urban broadband networks', *New Media & Society*, 20:12, pp. 4634–52.

Hall, K. (2001), 'Performativity', in A. Duranti (ed.), *Key Terms in Language and Culture*, Oxford: Blackwell, pp. 180–83.

Hollands, R. G. (2008), 'Will the real smart city please stand up?' *City*, 12:3, pp. 303–20.

InLinkUK (2019a), 'Home page', https://www.inlinkuk.com/. Accessed 1 December 2019.

InLinkUK (2019b), 'InLink Product Statement V3.0', May, https://planning.islington.gov.uk/NorthgatePublicDocs/00510721.pdf. Accessed 1 December 2019.

Iveson, K. (2012), 'Branded cities: Outdoor advertising, urban governance, and the outdoor media landscape', *Antipode*, 44:1, pp. 151–74.

Iveson, K. and Maalsen, S. (2019), 'Social control in the networked city: Datafied dividuals, disciplined individuals and powers of assembly', *Environment and Planning D: Society and Space*, 37:2, pp. 331–49. https://doi.org/10.1177/0263775818812084. Accessed 14 June 2021.

Jacobs, J. (1961), *The Death and Life of Great American Cities*, New York: Random House.

Joss, S., Cook, M. and Dayot, Y. (2017), 'Smart cities: Towards a new citizenship regime? A discourse analysis of the British smart city standard', *Journal of Urban Technology*, 24:4, pp. 29–49.

Joss, S., Sengers, F., Schraven, D., Caprotti, F. and Dayot, Y. (2019), 'The smart city as global discourse: Storylines and critical junctures across 27 cities', *Journal of Urban Technology*, 26:1, pp. 3–34.

Kitchin, R. and Dodge, M. (2011), *Code/space: Software and Everyday Life*, Cambridge, MA: MIT Press.

Krajina, Z. (2014), *Negotiating the Mediated City: Everyday Encounters with Public Screens*, London: Routledge.

Lefebvre, H. ([1967] 1996), *Writings on Cities* (trans. E. Kofman and E. Lebas), Oxford: Wiley-Blackwell.

Maalsen, S. and Perng, S.-Y. (2016), 'Encountering the city at hacking events', in R. Kitchin and S.-Y. Perng (eds), *Code and the City*, London: Routledge, pp. 190–99.

Maalsen, S. and Perng, S.-Y. (2017), 'Crafting code: Gender, coding and spatial hybridity in the events of PyLadies Dublin', in S. Luckman and N. Thomas (eds), *Craft Economies*, London: Bloomsbury, pp. 223–32.

McGuire, S. (2008), *The Media City: Media, Architecture and Urban Space*, London: Sage.

Mattern, S. (2014), 'Interfacing urban intelligence', *Places Journal*, April, n.pag., https://placesjournal.org/article/interfacing-urban-intelligence/. Accessed 4 February 2020.

Mitchell, D. (1995), 'The end of public space? People's park, definitions of the public, and democracy', *Annals of the Association of American Geographers*, 85:1, pp. 108–33.

Owens, P. E. (2007), 'No teens allowed: The exclusion of adolescents from public spaces', *Landscape Journal*, 21:1, pp. 156–63.

Perng, S.-Y. (2019), 'Anticipating digital futures: Ruins, entanglements and the possibilities of shared technology making', *Mobilities*, 14:4, pp. 418–34.

Sennett, R. (1977), *The Fall of Public Man*, New York: Alfred A. Knopf.

Shelton, T. and Lodato, T. (2019), 'Actually existing smart citizens', *City*, 23:1, pp. 35–52.

Strawberry Energy (2020), 'Home page', https://strawberrye.com/. Accessed 4 February 2020.

Taylor, C. (2002), 'Modern social imaginaries', *Public Culture*, 14:1, pp. 91–124.

Wessels, B., Humphry, J., Gangneux, J., Hanchard, M., Chesher, C., Joss, S., Maalsen, S. and Merrington, P. (forthcoming), *The Design, Use and Governance of Smart Kiosks and Benches: Insights for Policy and Practice*, Glasgow and Sydney: University of Sydney, University of Glasgow.

Woolgar, S. (1990), 'Configuring the user: The case of usability trials', *Sociological Review*, 38:1_suppl, pp. 58–99.

7

Co-creating Place and Creativity Through Media Architecture The InstaBooth

Glenda Caldwell, Queensland University of Technology

Introduction

Easy access to information through ubiquitous computing, mobile devices and Web 2.0 has increasingly become part of our daily lives and deeply affects how we experience urban environments and interact with local communities. For example, Figure 7.1 shows people walking along a footpath in Chongqing, China. This image exemplifies how a city has adapted its physical infrastructure and urban design to accommodate pedestrians' use of technology in daily life.

However, the question arises: how does the use of technology impact on the creation of place? What does it mean to the communities who live, work and play in these cities? Media architecture is defined as 'an overarching concept that covers the design of physical spaces at architectural scale incorporating materials with dynamic properties that allow for dynamic, reactive or interactive behavior' (Brynskov et al. 2013: 1–2). The research in this chapter explores how a design intervention in a public space, which combines media and architecture, can enable active and creative citizenship in relation to place. Acknowledging that it is the memories and meanings that we attach to public spaces that create place (Arefi 2004; Carmona et al. 2010; Jackson 1994; Trancik 1986), this chapter examines a particular facet of media architecture – 'do-it-yourself' (DIY)/'do-it-with-others' (DIWO) media architecture (Caldwell and Foth 2014, 2017) – to uncover how these combinations within citizen-focused design can assist in developing and understanding community. DIY has given people the skills to create what they like without being an expert (Francisco 2007; Gauntlett 2007). The shift away from top-down approaches to one focused on co-production was first referred to by the

ChinaAfricaBlog @ChinaAfricaBlog · 15 Sep 2014
#Chongqing City has set up "exclusive sidewalk for mobile phone users " to
avoid possible crashes via @PDChina #china

↰   ⇄ 3   ♥ 2   •••

FIGURE 7.1: ChinaAfricaBlog, sidewalks for mobile phone usage in Chongqing, China. Twitter,
15 September 2014.

arts collective Furtherfield in 2006 as 'do-it-with-others' (DIWO) (Garrett 2012).
Applying a DIY or DIWO approach to the design process of media architecture
not only provides a bottom-up outcome but also a means of communication and
expression for local communities (Caldwell et al. 2016; Fredericks et al. 2016).

Using technology and varied media, the InstaBooth, a prototype of DIY/DIWO
media architecture, was developed as a tool for situated community engagement. In
2014–15 the InstaBooth was designed, fabricated and deployed by academics from
the QUT Design Lab, School of Design, Queensland University of Technology.
The design process of the InstaBooth was based on participatory principles and
involved end users in a series of co-design workshops discussed in more detail in
other publications (Caldwell et al. 2016; Johnstone et al. 2015). The InstaBooth
has been introduced to different communities around Brisbane and south-east
Queensland in a range of contexts; based on qualitative interviews with InstaBooth
participants, this chapter uncovers the participants' experience with the design
intervention to question the meaning that such media architecture can provide to a
community. The findings indicate that combining digital and tangible media with
architecture can provide greater opportunities for the co-creation of place and creativity within urban environments by enabling a novel discussion platform. The

150

research presented in this chapter informs architectural studies or urban design and planning as well as illuminates how some communities feel about current communication opportunities within south-east Queensland.

This research emerges from urban informatics, which is the 'study, design, and practice of urban experiences across different urban contexts that are created by new opportunities of real-time, ubiquitous technology and the augmentation that mediates the physical and digital layers of people networks and urban infra-structures' (Foth et al. 2011). In the following section, background information on place, people and media architecture contextualize our research project and the theories that have guided its implementation.

Background and research design: Place, community and media architecture

While the concept of 'place' has been interrogated from many perspectives, the work of Yi-Fu Tuan (1974, 1977) focuses on examining how people attach meaning to place. Tuan (1977) argues that spaces gain value and develop into places by increasing personal use and knowledge about the location. From an urban-planning and architectural perspective, the value of place is a desirable outcome when designing urban environments (Arefi 2004; Carmona et al. 2010; Jackson 1994; Trancik 1986). As the connection of people to digital spaces (such as Web 2.0) continues to increase through the use of mobile technologies we must acknowledge that digital spaces can also become places. Harrison and Dourish (1996) identify that meaningful places can be established within digital space by users participating, adapting and appropriating the space.

As defined by Altman and Low (1992), place attachment is an emotional bond between people and places that includes social relationships. This definition is supported by Massey (1994: 121), who claims that places are 'porous networks of social relations', and Manzo and Perkins (2006), who argue that place attachments affect both individuals and neighbourhoods. It is place attachment that drives people to care for their street, look after their neighbour and participate in community activities (Manzo and Perkins 2006). Therefore, when we consider how to make better places it is important to consider what places mean to both individuals and communities. This understanding is relative to many factors, such as the questions being asked and the purpose of the investigation or creation (Geertz 1992). The findings presented in this chapter are not intended to be universal or generalizations; rather, they explore the different dimensions of meaning creation and connection to place that certain people have experienced when engaging with the InstaBooth. Their position is not of nowhere but of situated users (Geertz 1992).

Current literature indicates place attachment and a sense of community are often closely related when considering particular geographic locations (Manzo and Perkins 2006; Pretty et al. 2003). A sense of community pertains to the social and emotional relationships that people have with others and involve feelings of inclusion and belonging, shared interests or personal histories (Perkins and Long 2002). Along with place attachment, Manzo and Perkins (2006) argue that a sense of community through social inclusion, connection and trust contribute to the level of participation of individuals in community activities. This link to participation is a valuable concept that assists in urban-planning initiatives and interaction design (Harrison and Dourish 1996). In understanding a sense of community and place attachment it is critical to highlight that these are concepts that mean different things to each individual or community; therefore, it is valuable to acknowledge difference as much as similarity.

Manzo and Perkins (2006) propose a framework where the ideal conditions leading to positive community engagement rely on an individual's experience of their community and place through three different levels of interaction and interpretation: *cognitive* (place identity and community identity), *affective* (place attachments and sense of community) and *behavioural* (participation and action within the community). Participation can create empowerment, which in turn allows people to feel a sense of control over their surroundings. While not everyone feels place attachment or finds a sense of community, by understanding the benefits of these the concepts can be used to increase participation in the community from more people.

The InstaBooth – as a tool for situated community engagement – is a project in media architecture. Media architecture focuses on the architectural design of spaces that incorporate digital media (Brynskov et al. 2013) and Haeusler (2017) claims that increased use of technology drives this emerging discipline. Technology in media architecture such as digital facades, LED lighting, projection mapping and large urban screens have typically been used to support entertainment or advertising in public spaces. However, alongside Haeusler (2017), there are a growing number of artists, architects, academics and designers who are questioning the purpose of technology use and how to make media architecture that is more meaningful or useful to the surrounding community.

In line with this shift and building on the notions of DIY urban design (Douglas 2014), DIY citizenship (Ratto and Boler 2014) and DIY urbanism (Iveson 2013), DIY/DIWO media architecture (Caldwell and Foth 2014, 2017) has been proposed as a concept to encourage a more open and participatory type of media architecture and this deeply informed the creation of the InstaBooth. Our initial intention behind the InstaBooth was to promote engagement and interactivity to enable citizen control (Caldwell and Foth 2014). However, during the deployment process, it became evident that the media content creation within the InstaBooth has a much broader significance that goes beyond the technology used in media architecture. Focusing our attention on understanding media as a term – which encompasses the different means, tools, formats and materials through which people communicate – allows us to create architectural spaces that can be appropriated or adapted by local communities.

Media architecture and urban informatics are transdisciplinary areas of design and research that attempt to understand 'the city as an ecology that consists of technological, social and architectural layers' (Foth et al. 2011). Theories from urban informatics, human computer interaction (HCI) and architecture were brought together in this research by employing a research through design (RtD) approach (Dow et al. 2013). The purpose of RtD is to develop and implement designed artefacts with the intention to learn about particular facets of human experience (Dow et al. 2013; Frayling 1993).

RtD is a holistic approach that incorporates the design process, the object and its impact on end users. This research contributes to promoting the value and impact that RtD offers by empowering people to reflect on the meaning of place through creative practices. These approaches are not novel but assist to inspire participants to view the world around them differently and to reflect and potentially create change within their local communities.

The InstaBooth

In an attempt to combine the above perspectives of place, community and media architecture, and our underpinning approach of RtD, the InstaBooth (Figure 7.2) was developed as a community engagement tool combining different media within an architectural structure and space. The InstaBooth was designed, fabricated and deployed to align with the DIY/DIWO media architecture concept outlined above (Caldwell and Foth 2014, 2017). The InstaBooth purposefully stimulates creativity and meaningful experiences through the sharing of ideas and concerns via digital and physical media.

Fundamental to the InstaBooth is participation, as its design process relied on participatory design and co-design principles (Bodker and Pekkola 2010; Muller 2003; Muller and Kuhn 1993; Sanders and Stappers 2008), and it was intended to generate situated community engagement. Its aim was to create a platform for communities to express their voices by asking them questions and asking them to share their thoughts in an unstructured and playful way. Its modular design accommodated a range of bespoke interactive technologies, both analogue and digital, designed to facilitate the engagement process by offering different materials and

FIGURE 7.2: The InstaBooth at the ABC studios, Brisbane, Queensland.

ways to collect feedback (Johnstone et al. 2015). The appearance and interactions of the InstaBooth were designed to appeal to different demographics and foster discussion about a range of topics such as change management, policy development and urban planning (Guaralda et al. 2019).

Once the InstaBooth was deployed in public spaces, the responses of the public, either through digital or tangible media, became the content within the InstaBooth. Sanders and Stappers (2008: 6) refer to co-creation as 'any act of collective creativity'. Within the InstaBooth users interacted with content created by others, adapted and appropriated the interactions and content and also reflected on the creative process of doing so. Therefore, aligning with Sanders and Stappers (2008), we argue that the InstaBooth content was co-created by its users.

The InstaBooth was deployed in seven locations across south-east Queensland between April and November 2015. In this chapter, we discuss two of the InstaBooth deployments to examine the research question: how does the InstaBooth, a DIY/DIWO media architecture design intervention, impact on place?

Deployment 1: Brisbane Writers Festival

From 17 August to 6 September 2015 the InstaBooth was invited to participate in the Brisbane Writers Festival (BWF). The annual festival takes place at the State Library of Queensland and the theme of the 2015 festival was 'minds wide open'. One of the key events was 'Brisbane 2050: Imagining Our Future City', which presented a panel of experts including Bernard Salt, Elizabeth Farrelly, Goeff Woolcock, Andrew Gutteridge and Marcus Foth. The audience participants were urban planners, artists, economists and community leaders who discussed the future of Brisbane for 2050 with the panellists. The InstaBooth project and team were invited to support this event by assisting the BWF organizers to conduct community engagement. The purpose was to gather data from the local community before the Brisbane 2050 event to inform the discussion around Brisbane's future. Prior to the festival's commencement, the InstaBooth was situated in the foyer of the Australian Broadcast Corporation's (ABC) studios in South Bank, Brisbane and was promoted for two weeks through ABC media channels, including radio and online publications.

For BWF, the InstaBooth was relocated to the festival location of the State Library of Queensland (Figure 7.3). The BWF volunteers assisted in attending the InstaBooth. The InstaBooth was set up asking a range of questions to stimulate

FIGURE 7.3: The InstaBooth at the 2015 Brisbane Writers Festival.

(a)　　　　　　　　　　　(b)

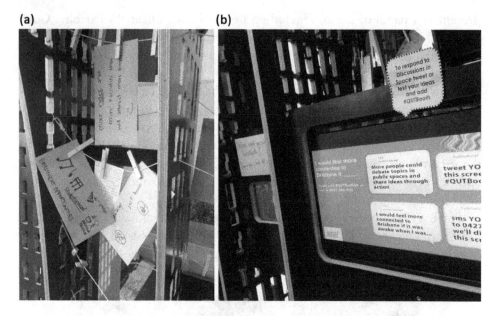

FIGURES 7.4a and 7.4b: Responses on display within the InstaBooth at the 2015 Brisbane Writers Festival.

discussion and responses around what people wanted to see for Brisbane in 2050. Six different interactions were set up within the InstaBooth and each one employed digital or physical media to present a different question around the topic and provided different mechanisms and media through which users could respond. These included writing a note, drawing a picture, tweeting or texting a response, dropping a physical pin on a corkboard, dropping a virtual pin on a Google map or voting for pictures via an Instagram feed. All of the responses were collected anonymously, most of which were visible to other users by pinning responses to a cork board, pegging drawings to a clothes line or displayed on a digital screen as seen in Figures 7.4a and 7.4b.

Deployment 2: Pomona

From 17–21 October 2015, the InstaBooth was placed on the main street in the regional Queensland town of Pomona (Figure 7.5). Similarly to the BWF deployment, the local community group, Heart of Pomona, invited the InstaBooth team to assist in conducting community engagement around the future vision of Pomona. The results of the engagement process were to be presented to the local council to inform the development of the upcoming Pomona master plan. The configuration of the InstaBooth echoed the BWF deployment where the questions and

FIGURE 7.5: InstaBooth in Pomona, Queensland.

interactions promoted discussion for the future vision of Pomona. In both deployments, the InstaBooth team worked closely with community stakeholders to create the questions that were asked through the interactive components and to decide on the best way to present them within the InstaBooth – such as through the graphic design of papers, materials and digital interactions.

Methods

Galletta (2013: 45) claims that '[s]emi-structured interviews incorporate both open-ended and more theoretically driven questions, eliciting data grounded in the

157

experience of the participant as well as data guided by existing constructs in the particular discipline within which one is conducting research'. With the InstaBooth project, the best way to engage with users was one-to-one directly after participants interacted with the InstaBooth. Using semi-structured interviews allowed for open-ended responses and the ability to inquire further on certain topics that arose. Different to the questions asked to the public through the interactive components of the InstaBooth (which were developed with community stakeholders), the questions asked during the semi-structured interviews were developed by the research team. In these cases, the stakeholders (BWF and the Heart of Pomona) were more interested in capturing the ideas and feelings of the local community in regards to the future of Brisbane or Pomona. The semi-structured interview questions were developed by the research team to address research aims such as understanding the quality of the experience people had within the InstaBooth. Therefore, the stakeholders were not involved in the development of the interview questions.

After capturing basic demographic information such as age, gender, occupation and postcode, the semi-structured interview questions for both the BWF and Pomona deployments were:

- What did you do in the InstaBooth?
- Did you do any of the drawings or write any of the notes?
- What were you thinking when you made your drawing or left a note?
- What aspects of the InstaBooth did you enjoy the most?
- Did other people's responses influence how you interacted with the InstaBooth?
- What did interacting with the InstaBooth mean to you?
- Do you feel connected to other people in any way from interacting with the InstaBooth?
- Do you think something like the InstaBooth can make a change?
- Has this experience changed you or influenced your thoughts on (Brisbane or Pomona) in any way?
- Why did you come to the InstaBooth? Did you know about it beforehand?
- Have you learned anything about (Brisbane or Pomona) through the InstaBooth?
- If you could put the InstaBooth anywhere you wanted, what would you do with it or how would you like people to use it?
- What kind of questions would you like to ask through the InstaBooth?

During both BWF and Pomona fourteen interviews were conducted and analysed at each deployment by the research team. Collectively, interview participants included eight males and twenty females ranging from the ages of 18 to 75. The number of interview participants does not reflect the number of InstaBooth users during each deployment. Due to the complexity of the InstaBooth and limitations of research personnel, the exact number of InstaBooth users was not recorded. However, based on the number of papers with comments and drawings within the InstaBooth, we can estimate that during BWF there were approximately 22 contributing users per day over seven days, and in Pomona there were approximately 26 contributing users per day over the five-day deployment. These numbers are similar to participant numbers from other deployments of the InstaBooth in different contexts, regardless of population size, associated event or deployment location. These numbers exclude InstaBooth visitors who did not contribute to the paper questions or who may have only looked at the comments left by others.

The names used in this chapter are fictitious to ensure anonymity of participants. The interviews varied in length from approximately 5 minutes to 25 minutes. This chapter focuses on the analysis of the responses from participants to the question: *What did interacting with the InstaBooth mean to you?* Thematic analysis was the qualitative method used by the research team to analyse the interviews, which illuminated an emerging pattern of reoccurring themes within the data (Braun and Clarke 2006; Vaismoradi et al. 2013). As a result, when examining the responses to the question, the team identified four categories of meaning, which are discussed in the following section.

Findings

The structure of this section is based on the community experience framework developed by Manzo and Perkins (2006), which uses cognitive, affective and behavioural dimensions to indicate three levels of interaction leading toward positive community engagement. This framework reveals two layers of the data: perspectives from the individual and views on the community. When participants were asked what interacting with the InstaBooth meant to them, through thematic analysis the following themes emerged: providing a platform, place of learning, feelings on community and hope for the future. Table 7.1 summarizes the themes, the number of instances that associated words were found in the transcripts and how they relate to the dimensional framework developed by Manzo and Perkins (2006).

The following sections discuss each of the categories in more depth.

Cognitive dimensions

As described by Manzo and Perkins (2006: 344), the cognitive dimension refers to 'one's sense of self as informed by neighborhood places and by social interactions/neighboring respectively', including place identity and community identity.

159

Code	# of references, out of 28 interviews	Theme	Community experience dimension
Voice	36	Providing a platform	Cognitive
Places	63	Place of learning	Cognitive
Learning	11		
Feelings	42	Feelings in community	Affective
Community	75		
Hope	17	Hope for the future	Behavioural
Future	19		

TABLE 7.1: Key themes

Providing a platform

Participants perceived the InstaBooth as providing a platform to voice their ideas. It became a place in the public space that allowed them to find a sense of expression and a vocalized sense of themselves. This became evident as participants frequently referred to the InstaBooth using terms such as: listening post, forum, platform, soapbox, physical petition, venue for discussion and arena. Each of these terms refer to some aspect of vocalizing and sharing ideas with others.

The following participant referred to the InstaBooth as somewhere to have a say:

Yes, it [the InstaBooth] was somewhere like when you're seeing things happening within your own suburb, that you don't think anybody else is looking at it the same way or there's nowhere to address it to. This was somewhere where you could have a say and it's accessible.

(Lucy, BWF)

Lucy heard about the InstaBooth through the ABC radio station and purposefully went to BWF to find it. She wanted to have a say because she felt there was nowhere to address her feelings about what was happening around her neighbourhood.

In the following excerpt George talked about the InstaBooth as a platform and a petition. He summarized how many other people saw the InstaBooth and how it could be used by society:

160

People always need a platform to air their wants and needs and their voice. If you can get enough voices, I mean look at the power of petitions on the internet, I mean if enough people say the same thing, enough people agree on the same thing, then as far as I'm concerned this is a petition in real life in the box.

(George, BWF)

The InstaBooth being 'a petition in real life in the box' is a powerful statement and signifies that George saw the InstaBooth as something much more than just a box with media in it. George could see the potential of allowing people to share their ideas through the InstaBooth and that change could occur as a result.

The benefit of the InstaBooth is that it is a structure designed to display and share ideas with others. The InstaBooth does not pertain to a city council or a political party, and has a neutral agenda, as it was placed in public spaces. The interviews made it clear that people appreciated that it is open and visible yet anonymous. They tended to feel comfortable with the InstaBooth and felt that they could be honest about sharing their thoughts, even acknowledging that they had the ability to disagree with others.

Place of learning

Many of the participants revealed that the InstaBooth allowed them to see things from the perspectives of others, which prompted new ways of thinking about certain issues or ideas. Through viewing other people's comments, users learned new things about other members of their community while also learning about themselves. Some users said that the InstaBooth caused them to 'think outside the box'.

The following quote from George expresses the inspiration he received from another user's comment: 'There was another sort of a multicultural comment on there, which kind of stoked my thinking as well. I had to agree that it's something I'd really like to see' (George, BWF).

The word 'stoked' refers to something that fuelled George's ability to think differently. This indicates that George was learning from the comments of others. The way questions were asked and how media for users to interact with appeared in the InstaBooth also inspired thoughtful feedback: 'I think having that availability of pick and choose which ways [...] which methods you want to choose would really kind of stoke people's thinking and sort of get them thinking a bit more outside the box' (George, BWF). George refers to the different methods of communication within the InstaBooth that helped people to think 'outside the box' about the responses they were leaving. Another participant reinforces this statement by discussing the creative elements of the interactions that caused her to think about the questions being asked in a novel way: 'I guess it made me feel like

I was heard. Also, it's a creative process too so it made me think outside the box' (Kylie, BWF). The participants acknowledged the creative process of interacting and providing responses to the questions as a means through which they could find different perspectives towards the issues discussed within the InstaBooth. The inspiration participants found from the responses of others enriched their experience and many indicated that they learned about the desires of other people in their community. Freely sharing ideas through the InstaBooth created a place of learning about how individuals see the world and about the community as a whole. The comments contributed to the InstaBooth by its users does not reflect whether the opinion is from an expert, a novice, a local or a visitor. The knowledge that is created through experiencing the InstaBooth is primarily based on the individual and the meaning they create from it.

Affective dimensions

The affective dimensions refer to the emotional connections to a neighbourhood or neighbours. It also includes the emotional relationships to people created within particular places, also known as place attachments (Manzo and Perkins 2006).

Feelings on community

During both deployments of the InstaBooth the questions asked focused on creating a discussion on the future of the city or town. This line of questioning inherently caused people to reflect on their existing relationships with their community and what the place where they live means to them. In her interview, this participant revealed her thoughts about the importance of a sense of community:

> [It] just [made me] really stop and think about what I did like about the town. I guess when you live in there, you can just get caught up in your day-to-day activity, so it was good to reflect and really analyse what is important to me in a sense of community and what maybe can be done better, especially having young children, thinking about their needs being in a small town as well.
>
> (Kylie, Pomona)

In Kylie's interview, she expressed her thoughts about how the sense of community could be better for young children in Pomona. She was also worried about their needs, which indicates that she felt that children are often overlooked in the planning process. For Kylie, the InstaBooth was an opportunity to think about Pomona in a different and focused way.

Many participants saw the InstaBooth as reflecting the feelings or sense of community in their location. For some it reinforced their thoughts and others found a greater appreciation of their community. By collecting the voices of InstaBooth users, whether it be through their written notes, drawings or tweets, the InstaBooth acts like a mirror for the community to view itself.

Behavioural dimensions

The behavioural dimension refers to 'socially oriented behaviour', such as participation in neighbourhood activities (Manzo and Perkins 2006). The InstaBooth users in both deployments demonstrated socially oriented behaviour by leaving their comments and expressing their ideas.

Hope for the future

While many of the responses at both deployments dealt with notions of time, it was through the interviews that participants expressed that the InstaBooth symbolized hope for the futures of Brisbane and Pomona.

> What did it mean to me? It meant hope. It actually was a hopeful experience because it was a vision I think of the future. It employed all different varieties of mediums to engage with that [...] I had to let go of my preconceived idea about having to do things a certain way to conform to whatever category I was working with. At the end of the day, all I really needed to do was leave a comment in whichever medium I felt comfortable, so that was great [...] I felt this was hopeful because it gives everybody [...] it gives a broad range of options to people to engage with the InstaBooth to be able to leave a comment.
>
> (Amanda, BWF)

The link between the vision of the future and asking people their thoughts about the future filled Amanda with hope. It was not only the questions that were asked but the different media through which they were asked and collected that instilled this optimistic view. Amanda had preconceived ideas about how to interact with the InstaBooth, but when she discovered that she did not have to conform to any prescribed way of responding she engaged with the InstaBooth in a more meaningful way. The feeling of hope also stemmed from the fact that she could see how the InstaBooth engaged with a variety of people: there are options for everybody and anyone can leave a comment.

Amanda's experience is similar to others who find the InstaBooth a space for thinking about (in this instance) how they would like to see the future of their town or city. For most of these people the future of Brisbane or Pomona is intertwined with their own futures and positions within society. Even though through the InstaBooth many people commented on what they were unhappy with, Amanda saw the InstaBooth as a symbol of positivity. To her, a shared conversation about the future is hopeful because it means that there are people who are concerned with improving the place, which could lead towards a brighter future for everyone. Even though there are no immediate effects or solutions that were occurring as a result of people's contributions to the InstaBooth, that did not seem to matter to most people: users were happy to have an opportunity to learn from others.

Discussion

The recent research of York et al. (2015: 329) proposes 'that neighborhood context structures an individual's personal social network'. The size and strength of social networks created within a neighbourhood is based on several factors, including socio-economic status, gender, age and proximity to community-based institutions (York et al. 2015). Therefore, an individual's experience of a community differs from one person to the next as their personal networks vary. The findings in this chapter make evident that in Brisbane many people feel disconnected from a sense of community and that they are not part of the larger conversation of what the future of Brisbane will be like. In an interview with Martin, one of the participants from BWF, he talks about the lack of a sense of community that he feels:

> Well I think the key thing is how can we be a better community? […] I think a lot of things that break down in community […] there's increasingly things like refugees, people getting poorer, people getting wealthier, middle-class people, people who don't know each other. Brisbane used to be a smaller city, that there's no longer that communal thing as much […] I mean they're in groups, like clumps and things like that, but I just don't see that community that you might have in a small community […] you lose that in the big city but can they bring that back somehow? […] genuine community engagement with other people and learning more.
>
> (Martin, BWF)

Martin feels that communities in big cities are breaking apart due to the great range of needs that people have in contemporary society. He remembers Brisbane feeling more communal but now that it is a big city a community core has been lost, which aligns with classic urban theory (York et al. 2015). For Martin, meaningful experiences such as learning are a part of community engagement.

The deployment of the InstaBooth in Pomona helped us to compare our results between that of a city such as Brisbane to that of a small regional town. The majority of users in Pomona had a positive consensus toward the town and a strong sense of community; they loved how it was and did not desire change. However, while people tended to agree that Pomona was great how it was, users were still able to learn through the InstaBooth about themselves and the community.

The InstaBooth participants who were interviewed both in Brisbane and Pomona predominantly felt as though there are few opportunities to share their thoughts or voice their concerns in a public way. The citizens appeared to feel that whatever options do exist, those in authority are not actually listening to what people have to say. Users were largely supportive, interested and even excited about the InstaBooth as they saw it as their opportunity to voice their opinions. By providing a platform for people to share their voice, participants felt as though a communication channel was created, leading to better understanding and a sense of community. Overall, users engaged with the InstaBooth and created new memories based on what they learned from others or how they felt about sharing their thoughts.

To support this argument, it is valuable to discuss what aspects of the InstaBooth worked well in helping to attract the attention of participants. When asking the community representative from the Heart of Pomona committee why he wanted to bring the InstaBooth to Pomona, he said:

> Because it created a presence that would not have been created if there were two people sitting at a card table and handing out sheets of paper. It's an interactive thing. I think people have been first of all captivated by the look and feel and shape and intrigue about what it is, and the second thing is that once they engage with it, their minds are extended.
>
> (Community representative, Pomona)

Another participant echoes these thoughts, though also refers to the emotional aspects of the InstaBooth:

> It probably made you a little bit more thoughtful about what you were saying or writing, not just filling out a survey and circling a response. I guess it provoked a little bit more emotion than just doing a straight survey.
>
> (Kylie, Pomona)

When Kylie was asked to explain what inspired the emotion, she said it was the visual aspects of the InstaBooth, such as the interactive map of the town where people could indicate the places that needed more love. This allowed her

165

to visualize her town and think about what was placed where and why, which caused her to analyse the questions in more depth.

The InstaBooth's design integrated digital and tangible materials to construct a 'creative catalyst' (Ogawa et al. 2012: 58), which promoted a collective creative experience for participants through processes of drawing, writing and making, while questioning the experience of place. This approach was intended to attract the involvement of all people regardless of their access to technology or ability to read or write. The interviews demonstrate that this aspect of the design facilitated a sense of creativity and authenticity from a range of users.

In our project, we integrated concepts from media architecture and urban informatics to create a situated community engagement tool that encouraged interaction from a broad spectrum of society. Understanding what the InstaBooth meant to participants and what motivated their use of it will inform future design research in this area but also provides a better understanding of the impact that examining place through a creative approach can have on a community. The InstaBooth was a physical disruption in public space and it was by enabling the creative citizens (Hargreaves and Hartley 2016) to express themselves freely that the InstaBooth acted on the three dimensions of engagement within Manzo and Perkins's framework (2006): cognitive, affective and behavioural. When this type of engagement is possible and people feel empowered over their conditions, research indicates that they have greater ability to create change and take action within their communities (Kemmis 1990; Manzo and Perkins 2006).

Conclusion

This chapter explored how the InstaBooth affected people's experience of place. The interview excerpts assist us in responding to the research question: How does the InstaBooth, a DIY/DIWO media architecture design intervention, impact on place? From the analysis of 28 semi-structured interviews with InstaBooth participants, the findings reveal three key aspects of the InstaBooth in terms of its impact on place: it generated situated knowledge; it created spaces for thinking and learning, instilling creativity; and it increased a sense of community.

By offering a mechanism for people to express themselves, the InstaBooth, a DIY/DIWO prototype of media architecture, is a valuable tool assisting citizens in communicating issues of concern and thoughts on the future of the place in which they live. The ability to share their ideas through different media prompted creativity and provided a space for thinking and learning. For some participants, the process of interacting with the InstaBooth evoked emotions and facilitated connections between participants, the booth and the location. Therefore, we argue that the InstaBooth provided a valuable experience for its users, shifting from a media architecture space to a memorable place. The InstaBooth created a positive impact within the context of its deployments by assisting local citizens to establish a sense of community through a situated engagement tool that promoted creativity and expression.

The people in Brisbane and Pomona have felt as though they have minimal outlets for expression and are removed from decision-making processes. By combining an architectural structure with varied media and the theories of participation and urban informatics, it is possible to provide new communication channels that enable creative citizens to explore notions of place. Future research will continue to explore how such community engagement tools operate in different cultural and social contexts.

REFERENCES

Altman, I. and Low, S. (1992), *Place Attachment, Human Behavior, and Environment: Advances in Theory and Research* (vol. 12), New York: Plenum Press.

Arefi, M. (2004), 'The pedagogy of the American city: Revisiting the concepts of place, non-place, and placelessness', *Urban Design International*, 9:3, pp. 103–17.

Bodker, S. and Pekkola, S. (2010), 'A short review to the past and present of participatory design', *Scandinavian Journal of Information Systems*, 22:1, pp. 45–48.

Braun, V. and Clarke, V. (2006), 'Using thematic analysis in psychology', *Qualitative Research in Psychology*, 3:2, pp. 7–101.

Brynskov, M., Dalsgaard, P. and Halskov, K. (2013), 'Understanding media architecture (better): One space, three cases', in *Proceedings of the* Workshop of Interactive City Lighting, New York: ACM.

Caldwell, G. and Foth, M. (2014), 'DIY media architecture: Open and participatory approaches to community engagement', in P. Dalsgaard and A. Fatah gen Schieck (eds), Proceedings of the 2nd Media Architecture Biennale Conference: World Cities, New York: Association for Computing Machinery, pp. 1–10.

Caldwell, G. and Foth, M. (2017), 'DIY / DIWO media architecture: The InstaBooth', in A. Wiethoff and H. Hussmann (eds), *Media Architecture: Using Information and Media as Construction Material, Age of Access?* Grundfragen der Informationsgesellschaft 8. Berlin: Walter de Gruyter GmbH, pp. 61–80.

Caldwell, G., Guaralda, M., Donovan, J. and Rittenbruch, M. (2016), 'The InstaBooth: Making common ground for media architectural design', P. Dalsgaard and A. Fatah gen Schieck (eds), *Proceedings of the 3rd Media Architecture Biennale Conference: World Cities*, New York: Association for Computing Machinery, pp. 1–8.

Carmona, M., Heath, T., Oc, T. and Tiesdell, S. (2010), *Public Places – Urban Spaces: The Dimensions of Urban Design*, Abingdon: Routledge.

Douglas, G. C. C. (2014), 'DIY urban design: Inequality, privilege, and creative transgression in the help-yourself city', Ph.D. thesis, Chicago: University of Chicago.

Dow, S., Ju, W. and Mackay, W. (2013), 'Projection, place and point-of-view in research through design', in S. Price, C. Jewitt and B. Brown (eds), *The SAGE Handbook of Digital Technology Research*, London: Sage, pp. 266–85.

Foth, M., Choi, J.H. -J. and Satchell, C. (2011), 'Urban informatics', *ACM Conference on Computer Supported Cooperative Work, Hangzhou*, 19–23 March.

Francisco, S. (2007), 'The way we do things around here: Specification versus craft culture in the history of building', *American Behavioral Scientist*, 50:7, pp. 970–88.

Frayling, C. (1993), 'Research in art and design', *Royal College of Art Research Papers*, 1:1, pp. 1–5.

Fredericks, J., Caldwell, G. and Tomitsch, M. (2016), 'Middle-out design: Collaborative community engagement in urban HCI', in C. Parker (ed.), *Proceedings of the 28th Australian Conference on Computer–Human Interaction.* New York: Association for Computing Machinery, pp. 200–04.

Galletta, A. (2013), *Mastering the Semi-Structured Interview and Beyond: From Research Design to Analysis and Publication*, New York: NYU Press.

Garrett, M. (2012), 'DIWO (do it with others): Artistic co-creation as a decentralized method of peer empowerment in today's multitude', http://Marcgarrett.org/2014/02/12/Diwo-Do-It-with-Others-Artistic-Co-Creation-as-a-Decentralized-Meth Od-of-Peer-Empowerment-in-Todays-Multitude. Accessed 14 September 2016.

Gauntlett, D. (2007), *Creative Explorations: New Approaches to Identities and Audiences*, Abingdon: Routledge.

Geertz, C. (1992), 'Local knowledge and its limits', *Yale Journal of Criticism*, 5:2, pp. 129–35.

Guaralda, M., Mayere, S., Caldwell, G., Donovan, J. and Rittenbruch, M. (2019), 'The InstaBooth: An interactive methodology for community involvement and place-making', Journal of Place Management and Development, 12:2, pp. 209–26.

Haeusler, M. (2017), 'From allopoietic content to autopoietic content for media architecture through a better understanding of architectural typologies', *Media Architecture: Using Information and Media as Construction Material*, 8, pp. 25–26.

Hargreaves, I. and Hartley, J. (2016), *The Creative Citizen Unbound: How Social Media and DIY Culture Contribute to Democracy, Communities and the Creative Economy*, Bristol: Policy Press.

Harrison, S. and Dourish, P. (1996), 'Re-place-ing space: The roles of place and space in collaborative systems', *CSCW*, 96, pp. 67–76.

Iveson, K. (2013), 'Cities within the city: Do-it-yourself urbanism and the right to the city', *International Journal of Urban and Regional Research*, 37:3, pp. 941–56.

Jackson, J. B. (1994), *A Sense of Place, a Sense of Time*, New Haven, CT: Yale University Press.

Johnstone, S., Caldwell, G. and Rittenbruch, M. (2015), 'Defining the InstaBooth: facilitating debate and content creation from situated users', in K. S. Willis, A. Aurigi, G. Corino and M. Phillips (eds), *Proceedings of the 5th Media City International Conference and Exhibition*. Plymouth: School of Architecture, Design and Environment and i-DAT, Plymouth University, pp. 187–205.

Kemmis, D. (1990), *Community and the Politics of Place*, Norman: University of Oklahoma Press.

Manzo, L. and Perkins, D. (2006), 'Finding common ground: The importance of place attachment to community participation and planning', *CPL Bibliography*, 20:4, pp. 335–50.

Massey, D. (1994), *Space, Place, and Gender*, Minneapolis: University of Minnesota Press.

Muller, M. (2003), 'Participatory design: The third space in HCI', *Human–Computer Interaction: Development Process*, 4235, pp. 165–85.

Muller, M. and Kuhn, S. (1993), 'Participatory design', *Communication of the ACM*, 36:6, pp. 24–28.

Ogawa, H., Mara, M., Lindinger, C., Gardiner, M., Haring, R., Stolarsky, D., Ogawa, E. and Hörtner, H. (2012), 'Shadowgram: A case study for social fabrication through interactive fabrication in public spaces', *Sixth International Conference on Tangible, Embedded and Embodied Interaction*, Ontario, 19–22 February.

Perkins, D. and Long, A. (2002), 'Neighborhood sense of community and social capital', in A. T. Fisher, C. C. Sonn and B. J. Bishop (eds), *Psychological Sense of Community*, Boston: Springer, pp. 291–318.

Pretty, G. H., Chipuer, H. M. and Bramston, . (2003), 'Sense of place amongst adolescents and adults in two rural Australian towns: The discriminating features of place attachment, sense of community and place dependence in relation to place identity', *Journal of Environmental Psychology*, 23:3, pp. 273–87.

Ratto, M. and Boler, M. (2014), *DIY Citizenship: Critical Making and Social Media*, Cambridge, MA: MIT Press.

Sanders, E. B. N. and Stappers, P. J. (2008), 'Co-creation and the new landscapes of design', *Co-Design*, 4:1, pp. 5–18.

Trancik, R. (1986), *Finding Lost Space: Theories of Urban Design*, Hoboken, NJ: John Wiley & Sons.

Tuan, Y.-F. (1974), *Topophilia*, Englewood Cliffs: Prentice-Hall.

Tuan, Y.-F. (1977), *Space and Place: The Perspective of Experience*, Minneapolis: University of Minnesota Press.

Vaismoradi, M., Turunen, H. and Bondas, T. (2013), 'Content analysis and thematic analysis: Implications for conducting a qualitative descriptive study', *Nursing and Health Sciences*, 15:3, pp. 398–405.

York Cornwell, E. and Behler, R. L. (2015), 'Urbanism, neighborhood context, and social networks', *City and Community*, 14:3, pp. 311–35.

8

Narratives, Inequalities and Civic Participation
A Case for 'More-Than-Technological' Approaches to Smart City Development

Carla Maria Kayanan, University College Dublin
Niamh Moore-Cherry, University College Dublin
Alma Clavin, University College Dublin

> Cities have the capability of providing something for everybody,
> only because, and only when, they are created by everybody.
> (Jacobs 1961: 238)

Introduction

In 2019, the International Institute for Management and Development (IMD) ranked Dublin 30 out of 102 cities in their Smart City Index (Smart City Observatory 2019). This 'average' ranking, as reported by the *Irish Times*, was primarily driven by a gap between the priorities of municipal authorities and those of the citizens (Taylor 2019). Despite the billions of Euros invested to develop, brand and promote Smart Dublin, in the handful of reputable smart city indexes, Dublin's position consistently ranks as average.[1]

Rankings drive how the market engages with cities through investment decision-making. In contrast with earlier smart city indices, these contemporary smart city rankings reveal an intentional shift away from the purely technological utopian futures celebrated at the onset of smart city efforts spearheaded by Cisco, IBM and Siemens (Greenfield 2013; Townsend 2013). Today's indices recognize the importance of residents in co-creating urban futures and contributing to shaping their surrounding environment. While these rankings have become more progressive in terms of how they assess 'smart', some local authorities have not yet caught up. A conceptualization of smart cities beyond the technical emphasizes the need for good city governance to be accompanied by empowered city leaders, smart or 'intelligent citizens' and investors, as well as appropriate technological platforms (Moir et al. 2014). A truly smart city is one that is not just technology enhanced but one that is shaped by the support for and inclusion of a diversity of 'intelligences'.

This chapter draws on three current projects in Dublin (Ireland) to investigate the relationship between civic participation/engagement and smart city projects and narratives (Figure 8.1). The first, Smart Docklands, is a top-down 'first-generation' smart city project focused in the recently regenerated Docklands. In this project, multinational tech companies play a significant governance role with limited engagement of the publics who live and work in the district. The other two projects presented (A Playful City and Mapping Green Dublin) do not have the global recognition or visibility of Smart Docklands, yet they engage communities more inclusively and highlight the importance of non-technological forms of intelligence in the contemporary urban environment. All three projects demonstrate the power and potential of a diversity of intelligences in influencing policy and the material environment. However, A Playful City and Mapping Green Dublin deliberately recognize and embrace the significance of civic capacity and knowledge in creating inclusive visions of the future city. They are positioned in direct contrast to the Smart Docklands experience to demonstrate the potential of 'bottom-up' or 'hybrid' approaches to the smart city.

This work contributes to the growing literature critiquing top-down smart city strategies as vehicles for neo-liberal urban development (Hollands 2008). Simultaneously, it responds to calls for case studies that demonstrate nuances in smart city applications (Shelton et al. 2015). By demonstrating current narrowly defined conceptions of what constitutes 'smart' in the Irish case, this chapter argues for a more robust conceptualization of the smart city and its attendant policies. Importantly, it forefronts the potential of Dublin's citizens and residents in the process of imagining and enacting better urban futures.

The Dublin context

Similar to many western capital cities, over the last two decades Dublin has experienced significant population increase and accompanying urban development. Although Dublin has historically been a relatively compact city, beginning in the mid twentieth century, suburbanization and the dispersal of housing and employment to the outer rings became a key feature. The resultant disinvestment created social and economic problems by the mid 1980s and led to a focus on

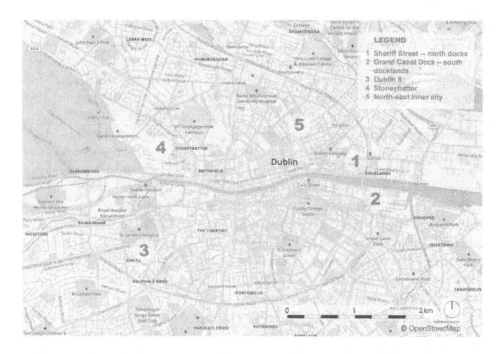

FIGURE 8.1: Inner-city Dublin. Authors, 2020.

inner-urban regeneration (Williams et al. 2010). These transitions particularly affected lower-income Dublin neighbourhoods housing blue-collar workers, first through the shifting of industrial activity to the periphery of the city and the loss of port employment, and later through property-led urban regeneration resulting in gentrification and escalating costs of living (Moore 2008; Williams and MacLaran 2003) throughout the 1990s.

A low corporate tax regime, a housing and construction boom, strong export market, deregulated markets and the growth of the service sector spurned what is commonly referred to as the Celtic Tiger period (Breathnach 1998). In this period, Dublin underwent accelerated development. The renewed interest in the inner-city meant that over the last 30 years, Dublin City has transformed dramatically through property-led urban regeneration programmes (MacLaren and Kelly 2014; Williams and MacLaran 2003). Large-scale regeneration projects in Docklands, Temple Bar and smaller but highly impactful infill developments have been under-pinned by the sectoral transformation of the economy (Moore 2008). In 2008, the global financial crisis and ensuing austerity temporarily halted and deeply impacted development activity (Fraser et al. 2013). However, from 2015 onwards the increasingly internationalized and financialized nature of the urban property market retriggered development activity (Aalbers 2020). For many, Dublin has become a more exclusionary city (van Lanen 2020) where 'smart city' narratives have little resonance. This is particularly the case in neighbourhoods where 'top-down' smart narratives exist cheek by jowl with some of the most long-term disadvantaged communities, such as in the Dublin Docklands.

Case study 1: Smart Docklands

Dublin Docklands encompasses land on both sides of the River Liffey, east of the Central Business District, in an area formerly dominated by maritime and industrial activity (Figure 8.2). Since the late 1980s, the redevelopment of the Docklands has been shaped by neo-liberal approaches to urban development (Coletta et al. 2018; MacLaran and Kelly 2014; Moore 2008). Though the 2008 global financial recession temporarily halted construction, the designation of a strategic development zone (SDZ) in 2012 on the Docklands to fast track development reignited large-scale construction and soaring real estate prices (Kayanan et al. 2018). Deliberate efforts continue to regenerate existing brownfield sites into an innovation district for university research labs, research centres, global tech companies, tech talent and the infrastructure amenable to 'corporate' smart city applications requiring orderly, sanitized and easily programmable spaces to thrive (Datta 2015).

Of the three case studies discussed in this chapter, Smart Docklands most closely resembles the initial wave of smart city strategies advanced by tech corporations and is based on digital, technology-driven, solution-oriented, futuristic visions (Greenfield 2013; Kitchin 2014; Townsend 2013). Smart Docklands is one of three smart districts under the Smart Dublin banner, an initiative of the four Dublin local authorities to engage with smart technology providers, researchers and residents to solve challenges and improve city life. It mobilizes future visions to create an urban imaginary focused primarily on projecting and promoting Dublin as a node in a globally connected network. Materially, the area has become a test bed for smart city technology and the deployment of prototyping solutions to address urban challenges, primarily driven by the tech sector.

The geography of the Docklands and the ability to build from scratch, given that much of the Docklands was previously brownfield land, played a pivotal role in the top-down application of Smart Docklands (Figure 8.3). Equipping new construction with low-power wide-area networks (LWPAN), conducive to installing tracking sensors, was easier and less expensive than retrofitting older buildings. The presence of global companies situated in the Docklands, such as Facebook, Google and Accenture, provided a pathway for multinational companies to exert

FIGURE 8.2: Construction of the Dublin Docklands. Photo by authors, 2019.

influence over the strategy as stakeholders and as business partners. Even beyond its geography, the governance and financing of Smart Docklands suggest its global rather than local remit. In 2018, through €70,000 grant funding from European Union's URBACT Smart Impact project, Smart Dublin formally launched Smart Docklands. This brought together a consortium of actors, including government representatives and global tech companies Google, Cisco, Huawai, AT&T, Intel and Vodafone. Today, Dublin City Council finances Smart Docklands through collaborations with global companies who benefit from the existing infrastructure and user-generated data captured through sensor technology.

These global efforts to develop the Docklands into a place to prototype prod-ucts before scaling them up to global markets are a type of investment. As such, the outcomes of these partnerships have a global reach. For example, in 2018, Softbank, a Japanese-based company, was given permission to test bed an internet of things (IoT) network – a system of interrelated and communicating computer devices that form the basis for big data analytics – in the Docklands. Softbank's contract, their first investment outside of Japan, is itself a prototype to scale operations to the rest of Europe (O'Brien 2018a). Another company, Dense Air, is using Docklands as a testbed for 5G. The research conducted by Dense Air in the Docklands informed 5G roll-outs in Australia, New Zealand and Portugal. The company benefits from the Docklands existing infrastructure and existing mobile data records. Without these resources, testing 5G would be cost prohibitive for Dense Air (Dense Air 2019). Small locally based start-ups also benefit. The start-up See.Sense, an intelligent lighting system for bicycles, depended on the urban fabric and Docklands commuters as 'ideal guinea pigs to trial her own invention' (Andrews 2019: n.pag.). Smart Docklands has also been used as a test bed for new forms of urban development and governance (Smart Docklands 2019). These projects demonstrate a collective understanding of the Docklands as an urban laboratory to prototype innovations and this logic informs its evolution. In 2018, a group of chief technology officers representing cities across the globe met in Dublin to develop the framework for Smart Districts (O'Brien

FIGURE 8.3: Bigbelly smart bin. Photo by authors, 2019.

2018b). That Smart Docklands contributes to policy formation and business best practices demonstrates the global scale of interaction and influence, as well as the likely probability that Smart Docklands will remain a highly top-down, closely monitored and tightly controlled project.

Although driven by tech companies and investors working with the municipal authorities, Smart Docklands does not operate entirely absent of citizen and/or resident engagement. Throughout the course of its roll-out, Smart Docklands managers conducted stakeholder workshops with residents of the Docklands to learn their perspectives on local problems and challenges in their neighbourhood. In addition, not all Smart Docklands projects have an immediate global scope. Some, such as the use of sensors to monitor lifebuoy thefts and rainfall and smart bins that send electronic signals when they are at capacity, remain focused on targeting local issues.

However, by and large, the geography, governance structure and growth potential informs the future imaginary of the Docklands in a way that refrains from incorporating visions of the residents and legitimately accepting and engaging them as 'smart citizens' (Cardullo and Kitchin 2018). Furthermore, given the socio-economic profile of many of the longer-term residents in the wider docklands area, Smart Docklands is a physical manifestation of a sharp digital divide that exists in the city where material inequalities are now compounded by virtual inequalities. Poor access to broadband and higher education is a disadvantage in both contributing opinions for the planning process, as well as for a clear understanding of privacy implications that are part of urban laboratory realities (Heaphy 2018).

Case study 2: A Playful City

Our second case study is A Playful City, a not-for-profit organization comprising a team with backgrounds in architecture, design, urban studies, community engagement through co-creation, law, marketing and teaching, drawn together because of their shared passion for making a difference in the city of Dublin. The goal of A Playful City is to build solidarity and enhance social cohesion. This is done through empowering sometimes silenced groups and visions for the city by developing places where people of all ages, cultures and abilities can freely mix and develop ties that have traditionally been the bond within our cities. The domain of the adult, cities rarely focus on the role or agency of children in their shaping and priority-making. In many cases, children, and other groups that possess lower levels of social and cultural capital, are actively excluded (Russell et al. 2017). A Playful City has deliberately focused on mainstreaming the place and role of the child and young people in urban design and implementation, in order to harness their creative potential and forge intergenerational relationships where knowledges, practices and the realities of urban living across time are shared, valued and incorporated into the design of living environments.

The context for the project

As outlined earlier in the chapter, the impact of the global financial crisis on the property development and banking sector adversely impacted Dublin. The collapse of the construction industry brought about the stalling of property markets, opening up a window of opportunity to rethink urban life and city development. While not without its critiques (Rosol 2012), this was exemplified by the emergence and ubiquitous nature of temporary, tactical and do-it-yourself (DIY) urbanisms (Bishop and Williams 2012; Pagano 2014). The latent potential of civic society to reshape the urban environment became apparent across many European and North America cities, with some local authority practitioners open to embracing a more informal, networked and creative approach to urban governance and development than heretofore (Moore-Cherry and McCarthy 2016). Yet as the economy bounced back, urban development policies and practices once again became largely predetermined by urban planners within narrow parameters defined by the state and dominant, often corporate, actors (Cardullo and Kitchin 2018). Within this context, the voice of children, young people and those with lower levels of social capital become marginalized despite their potential to contribute (Russell et al. 2017). A Playful City was founded to challenge the exclusionary nature of post-austerity urban landscapes and decision-making, and to demonstrate the potential for, and power of, more creative civic engagement to enhance the city. Given its trajectory of development outlined earlier, the north docklands became a target for A Playful City.

How does A Playful City work?

A Playful City takes a design-led approach to co-creating playful spaces for all ages, and using playful techniques to build community engagement. The goal is to reclaim the city for all generations through tactical, planned interventions in consultation with key stakeholders. The project demonstrates the potential of low-tech interventions to create new visions of urban living and open up the possibilities of alternative uses and framings of urban public spaces, such as streets and under-utilized green spaces such as grass strips alongside roads and other infrastructure.

In contrast with the Smart Dockland's high-tech urban laboratory, A Playful City has used low-tech, open design charrettes to engage children and adults, and to playfully gather local perspectives and views on the type of city that local residents want. In the north docklands, in the wake of profound change, significant social polarization has emerged between new 'gentrifiers' – both residential and commercial – and longer-term residents. Part of A Playful City's goal of working with a diversity of communities was to reclaim the streets for local people through play and begin to bridge divides. Hubspot, a key employer within the tech industry, was brought on board as a partner. Hubspot employees became volunteers at some community events in recognition of their corporate social responsibility to the area within which they have become embedded. This speaks to an awareness of that broader conceptualization of the smart city as one that is about more than just technology and sensors, but rather is inclusive of sensory experiences and the lived experience and needs.

A Playful City commissioned a very simple engagement tool to be used as a mobile, pop-up device to capture citizen voices and views, later named the Spiel Mobile (Figure 8.4). Designed by one of the project partners, Sean Harrington Architects, with financial support from the Bank of Ireland, the device can be moved between neighbourhoods. When opened out, the Spiel Mobile has a blackboard and space to pin ideas, thoughts and suggestions accessible to all ages and backgrounds.

One of the most dynamic projects emerging from the Spiel Mobile's open consultation processes was A Playful Street. Working with communities and the local police, this temporary road closure provided a safe environment (from traffic, criminality and antisocial behaviour) for children to play outdoors on the street for a morning or afternoon on nominated days. Temporally limited, this approach acted as a prototype for what a car-free city could look like and achieve. Although primarily focused on supporting children to play and on building intergenerational solidarity, the taking back of the street from car-based traffic and other activities encouraged people of all ages and abilities to come out of their homes and rediscover the potential of the city streets for social interaction, akin to the innovative ways urban space was used during the initial COVID-19 lockdowns. This simple and tactical intervention was constructed to enable children to do what they do best, supported by older residents and to build community cohesion. A key element of success aimed at harnessing civic capacity and sustaining the project was to hand over control at the outset to local groups and leaders, and support them with stewarding and organizing. A Playful City provided the inspiration and know-how to get started, but the approach was founded on enabling local community groups such as residents associations to take control, and providing a brokerage role.

Arising from suggestions gathered through the Spiel Mobile, another idea was to animate an under-utilized grass strip (euphemistically termed a linear park)

FIGURE 8.4: The Spiel Mobile consultation device. Photo by authors, 2018.

adjacent to Spencer Dock on the Royal Canal. Following community consult-ations and a design hackathon in Spring 2018, the Zig-Zag was installed as a playful public seating area. It responded to a demand, captured through com-munity consultations and surveys, among the young people of the area for a colourful, welcoming and interesting space to hang out in a part of the city that has become dominated by commercial buildings and demonstrates the poten-tial simplicity of smart interventions in an ever-changing city. Drawing on the project management literature (Doran 1981), SMART in this case refers to the setting and achievement of community-developed goals that are Specific, Meas-urable, Achievable, Relevant and Time-bound. Broadening definitions of smart city-ness, beyond simple technology, and through this type of lens, opens up the space for more grass-roots-led and inclusive approaches to urban development and community-building, an increasingly important component of progressive smart city rankings. This tactical approach to reimagining new possibilities for urban space opens up conversations with residents and other stakeholders on what a more progressive city might look like but also achieves the broader aims of urban strategy-making.

Case study 3: Mapping Green Dublin

Our third case study is the Mapping Green Dublin project (www. mappinggreendublin.com), funded by the Irish Environmental Protection Agency (EPA), with the goal of co-creating a greening strategy from the bottom up with a particular Dublin community – Dublin 8. In the recent past, a number of local design-led greening strategies, with associated public consultations, have been carried out in various parts of the inner city by Dublin City Council. These include plans for the Liberties (Dublin City Council 2015); Stoneybatter and North East Dublin, the latter two are currently ongoing. Mapping Green Dublin aims to create a different urban greening imaginary, focused on the particularities of the Dublin 8 locality, while acknowledging the larger patterns and associated pressures of urban life in Dublin as a global city. The project recognizes and values a diversity of knowledges of the city and aims to empower those who use the city on a daily basis for living and work to voice their needs, desires and imaginaries of a good urban future to the relevant authorities.

The first phase of the community-led Mapping Green Dublin project mapped the span and territories of trees and green spaces in Dublin city to deliberately make Dublin's green resources publicly visible. This provided an evidence base to articulate the unequal distribution of trees and green space across the city and the relative disadvantage of some communities in order to inspire, motivate and inform the crucial engagement of grass-roots activists and residents. The second phase of mapping involved recognizing and unveiling the histories and vulnerabilities of the local area in question, revealing knowledges and intelligences that give rise to a deeper, more locally relevant greening strategy (Anguelovski 2015; Anguelovski et al. 2019). Recent studies in environmental policy research identifies that justice still remains a 'blind spot' in ecosystem services mapping (Langemeyer and Connolly 2020) and authors from various disciplines have scrutinized the gentrifying effects of the new or improved provision of urban parks and green spaces (Anguelovski et al. 2019; Rice et al. 2020; Rigolon and Christensen 2019; Tubridy 2020). There is an increasing acknowledgement that not only might the effects of urban greening on health be different for different populations, but also that the health effects of different modes of urban greening might vary by socio-economic status, levels of civic engagement or other sociocultural norms or by green space size, type or quality (Cole et al. 2017). For urban greening to be truly smart and strategic requires an acknowledgement of these issues and a plan to unpack more just pathways to greening for the community.

Engaging a greening community

In alignment with the recent work on smart cities that recognizes the importance of municipal plans aligning with citizen needs and priorities, the civic engagement approach in Mapping Green Dublin is grounded, situated and experimental in nature, first attempting to listen to the community and carry out careful observations (Jacobs 1961) to gain insights into the everyday use of public green spaces. The project's twitter account (@DublinGreening) is an effective way to engage in media 'urban social listening' (Hollander et al. 2016) and creates a virtual space for further social engagement and information sharing. Although much more simple and everyday technologies than those traditionally associated with smart city applications, they can be important tools for democratizing the city.

For at least twenty years, media depictions of parts of Dublin 8 have presented it as a marginalized community with high levels of crime and an associated poor-quality built environment. Dublin 8 has one Local Area Plan (LAP),[2] which only covers the area closest to the city centre (Figure 8.1). This Liberties plan was created in 2009, extended in 2014 and expired in May 2020. A recent report commissioned by the Department of Housing, Planning and Local Government (Nolan 2019) about the area (Kilmainham and Inchicore) details local concerns about the visible appearance of the environment, the lack of green space, persistent intergenerational social problems and a sense of being left behind in terms of social and infrastructural development. At the same time, there are reports of a Dublin 'docklands style' development for the area (Quinlan 2019) with associated gentrifying effects. Previous research has provided critical insight into the spatial inequalities of this kind of development (Bissett 2009; Hearne and Redmond 2014; MacLaran and Kelly 2014). Local resistance and academic critique has been operationalized in the form of a rights-based approach to regeneration in one particular social housing estate (Hearne 2014), but tensions remain between residents and the local authority, often founded in the perception of a local democratic deficit in the area.

Such local context is significant in creating a community-based greening strategy that engages on a strategic level with local actors outside of Dublin City Council governance arrangements and acknowledges the critiques of public participation practices (Brudell and Attuyer 2014; Collins et al. 2005; Cooke and Kothari 2001). Notwithstanding the general problems with global rankings and indices that strive to benchmark and manage urban development through 'indicators', today's smart city indices increasingly recognize and value residents' activity in co-creating urban futures and contributing to shaping their environment. The Mapping Green Dublin project, while primarily about urban greening, provides a model for how Dublin might engage in more bottom-up knowledge acquisition and sharing, and become more progressively smart.

Three key ways the project mobilizes a deeper and more inclusive approach to community greening that activates interest for all users are as follows:

1. *Mapping and re-mapping*: engagement with the tree and green space data for the entire city and more focused analysis on the study area provides both a greening context and recognition of greening inequalities that exists. These maps are made available online and presented at community events. During the engagement process further mapping needs have been unveiled (e.g. pollution maps, maps of public land and access, maps of vacant spaces). In this way the mapping process is iterative in nature, mapping community assets and those aspects of the environment that concerns them and remapping these with the help of the community. Citizen science, specifically using the digital CURIO[3] tree app is critical to empowering the community to learn about and contribute to knowledge-building about private and public trees (Figure 5).

2. *Deep mapping*: deep-mapping workshops unpacked various pathways to greening in the area at a variety of scales, first with those groups and individuals already involved in local greening and social inclusion concerns. Then all users of green space (i.e. those who lived/worked/moved through the area) were invited to engage in a one-day event in a community location. The event included an arts workshop for families and children focusing on their favourite trees in Dublin 8; an open mapping workshop adapting participatory workshop techniques (Chambers 2002, 2006), here individuals and groups mapped the greening strengths, opportunities and deficits in the area. Finally, participants engaged in a 'lunch dialogue' where the experience of communal dining was combined with structured, facilitated conversation. These workshops created an opportunity to map out desires for, and expectations of, a community greening strategy, how this can be achieved, at what scale and what actors need to be involved.

3. *The hyper local level*: PLOTS is a subproject developed to digitally (using MyMaps[4]) or physically plot (by hand) how people move (walk/run/cycle) in their immediate locality (#2kmfromhome). This micro-geographical mapping exercise links people to their immediate environment, encouraging all users to consider the quality of their neighbourhood. Geographically localized analysis of people's experience of green space has been particularly relevant in high-density locations under COVID-19 restrictions. Recent research on how one's immediate environment impacts on mental health (Houlden et al. 2019) has become more important in the context of temporary 2 km (and subsequent 5 km) mobility restrictions implemented in spring/summer 2020 as a COVID-19 containment measure.

FIGURE 8.5: Deep-mapping exercise in Dublin 8. Courtesy of Jason Sheridan.

These various and scalar local knowledges are mapped on to the initial tree and green space data, to inform a deeper, multilayered greening plan with strategic, appropriate and relevant objectives emerging. How this data and associated civic engagement can culminate in greening actions on the ground is of interest. Many high-profile parks and green public attractions (e.g. see Friedrich [2019] on the New York high line) have been critiqued for their inequality of access and gentrification effects. Actions emerging from civic engagement, whether tangible or intangible, smart/high-tech innovative nature-based solutions[5] or lower-tech community gardening initiatives are evaluated for their social impact. A newly informed design-based prototyping workshop with the community forum incorporating the values of reflexivity and positionality to iterate roles and methods in community-based design (Schiffer 2020) ensures a regrounding of insights to produce a more just series of actions to feed into the community greening strategy. This design activism approach (Fuad-Luke 2009; Julier 2013: Thorpe 2012) examines how, why and where design can create a more positive impact to address objectives and aspirations related to inclusion and sustainability. The approach may go some way to reveal the real value and meanings of community design and design thinking (Julier 2017) in a neo-liberal smart city design context. The scalability of process and of the tools and technology used may be significant in the diffusion of a more critical and participative type of enquiry into greening policy and provision in other parts of Dublin and other cities but also challenges how current 'smart city' thinking and planning is undertaken.

Discussion

Dublin is a rapidly transforming and complex city where a diversity of narratives coexist but where particular narratives of the 'future' or 'successful city' centred on high technology and globality dominate. Smart Docklands is a particular kind of narrative, one that is attractive to policy-makers and municipal authorities as it suggests urban advancement, positions Dublin within a particular international framing and is easily controlled. However, the narrow articulation and understanding of 'smartness' is a limitation.

Broadening the conception of smartness to embrace the intelligent setting and achievement of specific, measurable and relevant objectives for the city that harnesses the diversity of knowledges at multiple scales, our three case studies demonstrate the potential for merging top-down approaches with the support of community-led and grass-roots engagements. Each of our three cases demonstrate different narratives of the city. Smart Docklands focuses on the effective deployment of smart technologies and data to address infrastructural and technical challenges, with citizen engagement as a comparatively low priority. A Playful City has brokered engagement between local residents and policy-makers and high-tech firms to develop innovative, low-tech solutions to address challenges related to a sense of belonging, sense of place, community cohesion and intergenerational solidarity – a critical element in sustainable and inclusive urban place-making. Mapping Green Dublin uses big data and a range of social media and other technologies such as mapping software to inspire citizen science in support of just city goals, while also linking into a European-wide network that is emerging around communities of practice and community-based coalitions for gathering information and data (Anguelovski et al. 2016).

Comparison of the three cases reveals a number of themes that assist in understanding how the various urban narratives and associated visions are constructed in each case study. Across the projects, citizens have different degrees of influence and power to shape their everyday geographies and environments. This in turn shapes the perceptions of residents of, and influences their engagement with, the planning and policy processes. The diversity of interpretation is linked to the political economies of specific places (Karvonen et al. 2019). From this perspective, Smart Docklands exemplifies critiques of centralized planning and governance control from above (Castells 1996; Scott 1999). The development of the Docklands, from as far back as the 1980s, has always been top down (MacLaran and Kelly 2014; Moore 2008), operating on a calculable spatial logic that depends on control from above to trigger profit (Datta 2015; Rebentisch et al. 2020). Capitalizing on the gridded layout of the Docklands and smart-supporting infrastructure, Smart Docklands cultivates an outwardly facing image of the Docklands as global 'living laboratory' and test bed where the landscape, residents, users and infrastructure are commodities for sale (Evans and Karvonen 2012; Karvonen and van Heur 2014). Dublin residents are taught to read the space of the Docklands as an up-and-coming business district where future innovations are meant to take hold and where smart city technologies can be prototyped on the bodies that move within that space. This image, one that flattens and homogenizes individual experiences and future imaginaries for the sake of deriving a superficially calculable whole (Dalton et al. 2020), impacts decision-making, development, prioritization and governance of the space.

On the other hand, A Playful City and Mapping Green Dublin demonstrate the potential for a new way of reading the city and its potentials, or, in the language of Scott (1999), a legibility that teaches people how to intervene in the process of shaping their surroundings. In both these cases, citizen/residents, whether through play or through deep and iterative engagement, embody the central role in deriving change, albeit in very different ways. Mapping Green Dublin remains situated (and invested) at the neighbourhood scale. At no point is the knowledge generated through Mapping Green Dublin removed from local context. By taking the voices of the residents and creating tools for them that are in turn given back to them, co-created knowledge is not abstracted to higher scales inaccessible to residents. The dynamic process of how a community-led greening plan can be created is, however, transferable. The creation of a greening network and the ambition to create a community greening forum shapes a type of knowledge about how to operate in the space and develops a community of practice. It demonstrates a rebuilding of trust (Anguelovski 2013) between citizens and policy stakeholders and confidence in citizens' imaginaries of their neighbourhoods and their ability to effect change. Through a slow and incremental co-creation process, unlike the Smart Docklands project that is dependent on constant innovation, speed and rapid return on invest-ments, citizens become contributors invested in more progressive and just urban futures. Similarly, although A Playful City has a very different temporal framing, punctuating urban space for short tactical bursts of activity, it materially demon-strates to local communities what an alternative urban future might look like and the strategic negotiations required to achieve it.

In examining how each of the three cases frame urban problems and gen-erate solutions, the role of place and community is differentially understood and embraced. Although the desire to be smart is difficult to reject – 'what city does not want to be smart or intelligent?' (Hollands 2008: 304) – how 'smartness' is made manifest should be problematized to incorporate other 'smart' place-based intelligences that are grounded in local knowledges with associated aesthetics particular to that locale and community vision. Drawing on the work of Deleuze and Guattari (1987), due to trends toward globalization and virtual realities, such real-world places are often seen as obsolete, favouring unpredictable flows and movements, generating centreless networks that mostly ignore boundaries or containments (Kogl 2007). Due to its perceived rigid, unchanging stasis, place itself is often questioned as a site for political action (Seamon 2014), but unless life becomes entirely virtual and non-material as a result of digital technologies, places will remain an integral part of being human and being place based. Grass-roots participation in the design of cities, such as through the Dublin 8 greening forum, will remain relevant and could potentially become important in the context of post-COVID cities and the increased attention being paid to interrogating the relationship between the pandemic, pre-existing inequalities and urban responses.

The narratives, forms and structures of regulation that exist in the city have real implications for the social experience of places, including who is included and who is excluded. According to Stevens (2009: 371), public spaces are often viewed as 'broken' and citizens are believed to be responsible for its ruination – that certain kinds of orderly appearance invariably mean higher aesthetic quality or an overall increase in quality of life, remains untested. Untamed physical, sometimes dis-orderly urban disruptions/disturbances (Allen et al. 2015; Lydon et al. 2015) to the usual aesthetic of urban spaces and places such as those created for A Playful City and community-led growing initiatives that have emerged in Dublin 8, may nurture transformative, dynamic, inclusive and participative modes of urban engagement. Such practices may give people the freedom to think more critically and expan-sively about how they live their everyday urban lives and interact with others. However, these aesthetics and urban punctuations stand in direct contrast to the control and orderliness that traditional smart city narratives strive to create and uphold. The Smart Docklands initiative focuses almost entirely on technological or digital transformation and innovation in the service of efficiency, investment and economic development. But as urban liveability becomes a critical issue in driving investment and residential choice, how to reconcile these top-down approaches with more grass-roots-led initiatives – effectively plugging the gap between muni-cipal authorities, policy-makers and communities – will become the key challenge.

Concluding thoughts

Since the 1990s 'turn to community', the planning and policy professions have become more cognisant of the need to engage citizens with urban issues

(Allmendinger 2002; Sager 2005). How this is achieved is context-specific but in Dublin this has often been done through formalized and relatively weak public consultation channels that have been subject to much critique (Brudell and Attuyer 2014; McGuirk 2000; Moore 2008). The dominant narratives in the city have been based on strongly neo-liberal approaches to urban development and, since 2014, on a particular version of financialized urbanism (Aalbers 2020; Byrne 2016). The idea of the smart city has become caught up in these narratives with the city increasingly commodified as a market-focused test bed or laboratory for new technologies (Cardullo and Kitchin 2018). Although some private companies pushing smart city strategies have developed a citizen-centric rhetoric, this has generally not focused on longer-term urban residents or disadvantaged urban communities.

This chapter has illustrated the narrowness of the smart city ideal as it is grounded in the context of Dublin. Focused on narratives of order, control and the deployment of individualized data for some abstracted greater good (Hollands 2008), like other forms of neo-liberalized urbanism, it can be exclusionary and ignore the complexity of real urban living. We call for a broader conceptualization of the smart city that recognizes the value of multiple and diverse intelligences, that privileges lived experience and place-based knowledges and that becomes comfortable with slower, more iterative and longer-run approaches to urban development in order for different imaginaries to evolve, be heard and inscribed (Goodman et al. 2020). Returning to the words of Jacobs (1961), only when cities are 'created by everybody' will they achieve their full potential as a smart city 2.0 and realize their potential as more just and inclusive places.

NOTES

1. IESE Cities in Motion Index 2019 ranks Dublin 37 out of 174. The study, conducted by the University of Navarra Business School's Global Center for Globalization and Strategy, factors in human capital, social cohesion, economy, environment, governance, urban planning, international outreach, technology, mobility and transportation (IESE 2019). Easypark's Smart City Index ranks Dublin 69 out of 100 for 2019 (Easypark 2019). Their methodology includes measures in transport and mobility, sustainability, governance, innovation economy, digitization, cyber security, living standard and expert perception.

2. A Local Area Plan (LAP) is A LAP is a legal or statutory document prepared in accordance with Part II, Section 20 of the Planning and Development Acts 2000–13. The making of a LAP is the responsibility of the elected members of the City Council (councillors) who can decide to adopt, amend or reject a LAP based on the issues raised during the public consultation. This process is carried out with the assistance of the local community, stakeholders and interested bodies.

3. See https://www.curio.xyz/.

4. See https://www.google.com/maps/d/u/0/.
5. The European Union's definition of nature-based solutions (NBS) states that these solutions are inspired and supported by nature, which are cost-effective, simultaneously provide environmental, social and economic benefits and help build resilience (see https://ec.europa.eu/research/environment/index.cfm?pg=nbs).

REFERENCES

Aalbers, M. (2020), 'Financial geography III: The financialization of the city', *Progress in Human Geography*, 44:3, pp. 595–607.

Allen, A., Lampis, A. and Swilling, M. (2015), 'Untamed urbanisms: Enacting productive disruptions', in A. Allen, A. Lampis and M. Swilling (eds), *Untamed Urbanisms*, London: Taylor Francis, pp. 296–317.

Allmendinger, P. (2002), 'Towards a post-positivist typology of planning theory', *Planning Theory*, 1:1, pp. 77–99.

Andrews, J. (2019), 'Dublin's Docklands becomes a centre for innovation', *Cities Today*, 17 April, https://cities-today.com/dublins-docklands-becomes-a-centre-for-innovation/. Accessed 29 April 2020.

Anguelovski, I. (2013), 'New directions in urban environmental justice: Rebuilding community, addressing trauma, and remaking place', *Journal of Planning Education and Research*, 33:2, pp. 160–75.

Anguelovski, I. (2015), 'Tactical developments for achieving just and sustainable neighborhoods: The role of community-based coalitions and bottom-to-bottom networks in street, technical, and funder activism', *Environment and Planning C: Government and Policy*, 33:4, pp. 703–25.

Anguelovski, I., Argüelles, L., Baró, F., Cole, H. V. S., Connolly, J. J. T, García, M., Loveless, S., Pérez del Pulgar, C., Shokry, G., Trebic, T. and Wood, E. (2016), *Green Trajectories: Municipal Policy Trends and Strategies for Greening in Europe, Canada and United States (1990–2016)*, Barcelona: Barcelona Laboratory for Urban Environmental Justice and Sustainability, http://www.bcnuej.org/wp-content/uploads/2018/06/Green-Trajectories.pdf. Accessed 26 March 2021.

Anguelovski, I., Connolly, J. J. T., Garcia-Lamarca, M., Cole, H. and Pearsall, H. (2019), 'New scholarly pathways on green gentrification: What does the urban "green turn" mean and where is it going?' *Progress in Human Geography*, 43:6, pp. 1064–86.

Bishop, P. and Williams, L. (2012), *The Temporary City*, London: Routledge.

Bissett, J. (2009), *Regeneration: Public Good or Private Profit?* Dublin: Tasc at New Island.

Breathnach, P. (1998), 'Exploring the "Celtic Tiger" phenomenon: Causes and consequences of Ireland's economic miracle', *European Urban and Regional Studies*, 5:4, pp. 305–16.

Brudell, P. and Attuyer, K. (2014), 'The collapse of PPPs: Prospects for social housing regeneration after the crash', in A. MacLaren and S. Kelly (eds), *Neoliberal Urban Policy and the Transformation of the City – Reshaping Dublin*, Basingstoke: Palgrave Macmillan, pp. 203–19.

Byrne, M. (2016), ' "Asset price urbanism" and financialization after the crisis: Ireland's National Asset Management Agency', *International Journal of Urban and Regional Research*, 40:1, pp. 31–45.

Cardullo, P. and Kitchin, R. (2018), 'Smart urbanism and smart citizenship: The neoliberal logic of "citizen-focused" smart cities in Europe', *Environment and Planning C: Politics and Space 2*, 37:5, pp. 813–30.

Castells, M. (1996), *The Rise of the Network Society*, vol. 1, *The Information Age: Economy, Society, and Culture*, Oxford: Blackwell.

Chambers, R. (2002), *Participatory Workshops: A Sourcebook of 21 Sets of Ideas and Activities*, London: Earthscan Publications.

Chambers, R. (2006), 'Participatory mapping and Geographic Information Systems: Whose map? Who is empowered and who disempowered? Who gains and who oses?', *Electronic Journal of Information Systems in Developing Countries*, 25:1, pp. 1–11.

Cole, H. V. S., Garcia Lamarca, M., Connolly, J. J. T and Anguelovski, I. (2017), ' "Are green cities healthy and equitable?" Unpacking the relationship between health, green space and gentrification', *Journal of Epidemiology and Community Health*, 71:11, pp. 1118–21.

Coletta, C., Heaphy, L. and Kitchin, R. (2018), 'Actually-existing smart Dublin: Exploring smart city development in history and context', in A. Karvonen, F. Cugurullo and F. Caprotti (eds), *Inside Smart Cities: Place, Politics and Urban Innovation*, London: Routledge, pp. 85–101.

Collins, E., Kearins, K. and Roper, J. (2005), 'The risks of relying on stakeholder engagement for the achievement of sustainability', *Electronic Journal of Radical Organisation Theory*, 9:1, pp. 81–101.

Cooke, B. and Kothari, U. (eds) (2001), *Participation: The New Tyranny?* London: Zed Books.

Dalton, C., Wilmott, C., Fraser, E. and Thatcher, J. (2020), ' "Smart" discourses, the limits of representation, and new regimes of spatial data', *Annals of the American Association of Geographers*, 110:2, pp. 485–96.

Datta, A. (2015), 'The smart entrepreneurial city: Dholera and 100 other utopias in India', in S. Marvin, A. Luque-Ayala and C. McFarlane (eds), *Smart Urbanism: Utopian Vision or False Dawn?* London: Routledge, pp. 52–70.

Dense Air (2019), 'Unlocking 5G for a connected city', white paper, 9 October, Slough: Dense Air, https://denseair.net/whitepaper-unlocking-5g-for-a-connected-city. Accessed 28 April 2020.

Deleuze, G. and Guattari, F. (1987), *A Thousand Plateaus: Capitalism and Schizophrenia*, Minneapolis: University of Minnesota Press.

Doran, G. T. (1981), 'There's a S.M.A.R.T. way to write management's goals and objectives', *Management Review*, 70:11, pp. 35–36.

Dublin City Council (2015), *The Liberties Greening Strategy*, Dublin: Dublin City Council, https://www.dublincity.ie/residential/parks/strategies-and-policies/greening-strategies/liberties-greening-strategy. Accessed 1 May 2020.

EasyPark (2019), *Smart Cities Index 2019*, https://www.easyparkgroup.com/smart-cities-index/. Accessed 15 April 2020.

Evans, J. and Karvonen, A. (2012), 'Living laboratories for sustainability: exploring the politics and epistemology of urban transition', in *Cities and Low Carbon Transitions*, London: Routledge, pp. 126–41.

Fraser, A., Murphy, E. and Kelly, S. (2013), 'Deepening neoliberalism via austerity and "reform": The case of Ireland', *Human Geography*, 6, pp. 38–53.

Friedrich, M. (2019), 'How landscape urbanism is making gentrification look like fun', *Washington Post*, 19 November, https://www.washingtonpost.com/outlook/2019/11/19/how-landscape-urbanism-is-making-gentrification-look-like-fun/. Accessed 19 November 2019.

Fuad-Luke, A. (2009), *Design Activism: Beautiful Strangeness for a Sustainable World*, London: Earthscan.

Goodman, N., Zwick, A., Spicer, Z. and Carlsen, N. (2020), 'Public engagement in smart city development: Lessons from communities in Canada's smart city challenge', *Canadian Geographer/Le Géographe canadien*, 64:1, pp. 1–17.

Greenfield, A. (2013), *Against the Smart City*, London: Verso.

Heaphy, L. (2018), 'Interfaces and divisions in the Dublin Docklands "Smart District"', working paper, Maynooth: Maynooth University, pp. 1–27. Available at: https://osf.io/preprints/socarxiv/z2afc.

Hearne, R. (2014), 'Achieving a right to the city in practice: Reflections on community struggles in Dublin', *Human Geography*, 7:3, pp. 14–25.

Hearne, R. and Redmond, D. (2014), 'The collapse of PPPs: Prospects for social housing regeneration after the crash', in A. MacLaran and S. Kelly (eds), *Neoliberal Urban Policy and the Transformation of the City – Reshaping Dublin*, Basingstoke: Palgrave Macmillan, pp. 219–33.

Hollander, J. B., Graves, E., Resnski, H., Foster-Karim, C., Wiley, A. and Dibyendu, D. (2016), *Urban Social Listening*, London: Palgrave Macmillan.

Hollands, R. G. (2008), 'Will the real smart city please stand up? Intelligent, progressive or entrepreneurial?' *City*, 12:3, pp. 303–20.

Houlden, V., Porto de Albuquerque, J., Weich, S. and Jarvis, S. (2019), 'A spatial analysis of proximate greenspace and mental wellbeing in London', *Applied Geography*, 109, p. 102036.

IESE (2019), *IESE Cities in Motion Index 2019*, Barcelona: Business School, University of Navarra, http://www.iberglobal.com/files/2019-1/cities_in_motion_2019.pdf. Accessed 16 April 2020.

Jacobs, J. (1961), *The Death and Life of Great American Cities*, New York: Vintage.

Julier, G. (2013), 'From design culture to design activism', *Design and Culture*, 5:2, pp. 215–36.

Julier, G. (2017), *Economies of Design*, Thousand Oaks, CA: Sage.

Karvonen, A., Cugurullo, F. and Caprotti, F. (eds) (2019), *Inside Smart Cities: Place, Politics and Urban Innovation*, London: Routledge.

Karvonen, A. and van Heur, B. (2014), 'Urban laboratories: Experiments in reworking cities', *International Journal of Urban and Regional Research*, 382, pp. 379–92.

Kayanan, C. M., Eichenmüller, C. and Chambers, J. (2018), 'Silicon slipways and slippery slopes: Techno-rationality and the reinvigoration of neoliberal logics in the Dublin Docklands', *Space and Polity*, 22:1, pp. 50–66.

Kitchin, R. (2014), 'The real-time city? Big data and smart urbanism', *GeoJournal*, 79:1, pp. 1–14.

Kogl, A. (2007), *Strange Places: The Political Potentials and Perils of Everyday Spaces*, New York: Lexington Books.

Langemeyer, J. and Connolly, J. J. T. (2020), 'Weaving notions of justice into urban ecosystem services research and practice', *Environmental Science & Policy*, 109, pp. 1–14.

Lydon, M., Garcia, A. and Duany, A. (2015), *Tactical Urbanism: Short-Term Action for Long-Term Change*, Washington, DC: Island Press.

McGuirk, P. M. (2000), 'Power and policy networks in urban governance: Local government and property-led regeneration in Dublin', *Urban Studies*, 37:4, pp. 651–72.

MacLaran, A. (1993), *Dublin: The Shaping of a Capital*, London: Bellhaven Press.

MacLaran, A. and Kelly, S. (eds) (2014), *Neoliberal Urban Policy and the Transformation of the City: Reshaping Dublin*, Basingstoke: Palgrave Macmillan.

Moir, E., Moonen, T. and Clark, G. (2014), *What Are Future Cities? Origins, Meanings and Uses*, https://www.gov.uk/government/publications/future-cities-origins-meanings-and-uses. Accessed 27 June 2020.

Moore, N. (2008), *Dublin Docklands Reinvented: The Post-Industrial Regeneration of a European City Quarter*, Dublin: Four Courts Press.

Moore-Cherry, N. and McCarthy, L. (2016), 'Debating temporary uses for vacant urban sites: Insights for practice from a stakeholder workshop', *Planning Practice and Research*, 31:3, pp. 347–57.

Nolan, J. (2019), *Building a Sustainable Community: Report on Scoping Exercise Inchicore-Kilmainham*, Dublin: Department of Housing, Planning and Local Government, https://www.housing.gov.ie/planning/development-plans/building-sustainable-community-report-scoping-exercise-inchicore. Accessed 27 April 2020.

O'Brien, C. (2018a), 'SoftBank joins Dublin City Council's Smart City programme', *Irish Times*, 26 June, https://www.irishtimes.com/business/technology/softbank-joins-dublin-city-council-s-smart-city-programme-1.3544301. Accessed 1 May 2020.

O'Brien, C. (2018b), 'Tech leaders discuss new "smart districts" for Dublin', *Irish Times*, 15 February, https://www.irishtimes.com/business/technology/tech-leaders-discuss-new-smart-districts-for-dublin-1.3392405?mode=print&ot=example.AjaxPageLayout.ot. Accessed 1 May 2020.

Pagano, C. B. (2014), 'DIY urbanism: Property and process in grassroots city building', *Marquette Law Review*, 97:2, pp. 335–89.

Quinlan, R. (2019), 'Dublin 8 revival: Liberties area set for docklands-style makeover', *Irish Times*, 29 August.

Rebentisch, H., Thompson, C., Côté-Roy, L. and Moser, S. (2020), 'Unicorn planning: Lessons from the rise and fall of an American "smart" mega-development', *Cities*, 101, p. 102686.

Rice, J. L., Cohen, D., Long, J. and Jurjevich, J. R. (2020), 'Contradictions of the climate-friendly city: New perspectives on eco-gentrification and housing justice', *International Journal of Urban and Regional Research*, 44:1, pp. 145–65.

Rigolon, A. and Christensen, J. (2019), *Greening without Gentrification: Learning from Parks-Related Anti-Displacement Strategies Nationwide*, Los Angeles, CA: Institute of the Environment and Sustainability, https://www.ioes.ucla.edu/project/prads/. Accessed 14 April 2020..

Rosol, M. (2012), 'Community volunteering as neoliberal strategy? Green space production in Berlin', *Antipode*, 44:1, pp. 239–57.

Russell, P., Scott, M. and Redmond, D. (2017), 'Active citizenship: Resident associations, social capital and collective action', in M. Scott and N. Moore-Cherry (eds), *Renewing Urban Communities: Environment, Citizenship and Sustainability in Ireland*, London: Routledge, pp. 213–34.

Sager, T. (2005), 'Planning through inclusive dialogue: No escape from social choice dilemmas', *Economic Affairs*, 25:4, pp. 32–35.

Schiffer, A. (2020), 'Issues of power and representation: Adapting positionality and reflexivity in community-based design', *International Journal of Art & Design Education*, 39:2, pp. 418–29.

Scott, J. C. (1999), *Seeing like a State: How Certain Schemes to Improve the Human Condition Have Failed*, London: Yale University Press.

Seamon, D. (2014), 'Lived emplacement and the locality of being: A return to humanistic geography?', in S. C. Aitken and G. Valentine (eds), *Approaches to Human Geography: Philosophies, Theories, People and Practices*, London: Sage, pp. 35–48.

Shelton, T., Zook, M. and Wiig, A. (2015), 'The "actually existing smart city"', *Cambridge Journal of Regions Economy and Society*, 8:1, pp. 13–25.

Smart City Observatory (2019), *Smart City Index*, Switzerland and Singapore: IMD World Competitiveness Center, https://www.imd.org/smart-city-observatory/smart-city-index/. Accessed 14 April 2020.

Stevens, Q. (2009), ' "Broken" public spaces in theory and in practice', *Town Planning Review*, 80:4–5, pp. 371–92.

Taylor, C. (2019), 'Dublin ranks average in listing of the smartest cities globally', *Irish Times*, 3 October.

Thorpe, A. (2012), *Architecture and Design Versus Consumerism: How Design Activism Confronts Growth*, Abingdon: Earthscan.

Townsend, A. M. (2013), *Smart Cities: Big Data, Civic Hackers, and the Quest for a New Utopia*, New York: W. W. Norton and Co.

Tubridy, D. (2020), 'Green climate change adaptation and the politics of designing ecological infrastructures', *Geoforum*, 113, pp. 133–45.

Smart Docklands (2019), 'Unleash the power of 3D data for Dublin!' http://smartdocklands. ie/3d-hack/. Accessed 28 April 2020.

van Lanen, S. (2020), 'Exclusion and sense of displacement under austerity: Experiences from young adults in Ballymun, Dublin', *ACME: An International Journal for Critical Geographies*, 19:1, pp. 352–63.

Williams, B. and MacLaran, A. (2003), 'Dublin: Property development and planning in an entrepreneurial city', in A. MacLaren (ed.), *Making Space: Property Development and Urban Planning*, London: Hodder Arnold, pp. 148–71.

Williams, B., Walsh, C. and Boyle, I. (2010), 'The development of the functional urban region of Dublin: Implications for regional development markets and planning', *Journal of Irish Urban Studies*, 7:9, pp. 5–30.

SECTION 3

SPATIAL HUMANISM

9

Building Participatory City 2.0
Folksonomy, Taxonomy, Hyperhumanism

*Carl Smith, Learning Technology Research Centre (LTRC) and
Ravensbourne University London*
Fred Garnett, London Knowledge Lab
Manuel Laranja, University of Lisbon

Introduction

Current debates concerning how cities might develop in the twenty-first century tend to be focused entirely around the smart city ethos, with wired streets and internet of things connectivity. Several writers, such as Jacobs ([1962] 2011), Jerram (2011), Landry (2008) and Sennett ([1970] 2008), have argued that the twentieth-century city was shaped by the rise of popular culture and its consequent impact on identity, social behaviours and neighbourhood developments. From a twenty-first-century perspective we see these popular culture initiatives as being based on participatory behaviours and we wish to argue for digitally enabled participatory cities that are 'social cities not smart cities'. The authors have been involved in various projects that have been building twenty-first-century city neighbourhoods, often in city regeneration areas, where citizen initiatives have created original ways of thinking about and designing for the city that offer an alternative playbook of new popular culture, which we are calling a 'folksonomy of the participatory city'. From this folksonomy we argue for the need to think about an alternative taxonomy for the emerging networked city that arises from citizen behaviours not smart city protocols. We take the five-layer model of networked business e-maturity, developed by MIT, and rework it as a five-layer model for the networked city, designed to enable the adoption of citizen-centric behaviours such as those documented within our folksonomy. However, we don't think that an alternative model of the digitally enabled twenty-first-century participatory city will be adopted simply because it is in some way 'better' or more 'citizen-centric' than smart city models. What we currently face in the next phase of development of the city after its century of being responsive to popular culture is a debate about the values that drive city developments. As Jerram (2011) and Minton (2012) both argue, in the late twentieth century, city developments moved out of the hands of planners and were turned over to the 'market'. The technocentric smart city, or 'no-touch' cities, as Eric Schmidt argues for as a result of the COVID-19 pandemic, are corporate-driven proposals for the twenty-first-century city, which are based on globalized free-market thinking (cited in Klein 2020). Reflecting on our folksonomy of citizen initiatives and our citizen-centric taxonomy of a possible networked city we finally argue for a values-based approach to 'rights to the city' based on 'hyperhumanism', which is a design approach (to technology use) enabling the human to emerge from developing technology platforms. The authors attempt to broaden current debates about city futures by creating a fresh 'development framework' to help inform our thinking about the paths we might choose.

In this chapter the three authors look backwards, to identify a possible folksonomy of citizen-centric behaviours emerging in the twenty-first century; then sideways, at a possible current taxonomy of the city for developing an inclusive networked society; and also forwards, to suggest how a hyperhumanist approach to the range of citizen initiatives can be incorporated into a new values-based approach to a dynamic 'context engineering' – what we are calling the 'participatory city' at a time when technocentric smart city approaches are currently the only ones under serious consideration by academics, mayors and policy-makers across the globe.

Folksonomy

Initially we look at a range of citizen-initiated practices concerning localism in the digital economy across Europe that have taken place in Bordeaux (France), Lewisham (London, England), Bilbao (Pays Basque, Spain), Lisboa (Portugal) and Pula (Croatia). These were brought together in the Origin of Spaces Erasmus+ project (2014–17), which created an information resource for community activists wanting to transform the localities where they lived, in opposition to the smart city with its 'top-down' municipality-driven modelling. These citizen practices were documented in the online #oosEU Toolbox. The toolbox identified five critical, dynamic, public–civic, themes: local partnerships, participatory governance, multidisciplinary co-working, social entrepreneurship and ecological transitions.

Taxonomy

From this folksonomy, and earlier work on creating a citizen-centric taxonomy of the city (Laranja 2018) based, to some extent, on the networked organization e-maturity model developed at the MIT Sloan School in the 1990s (Scott Morton 1991), we will look at how a 'development framework' (Ecclesfield 2020) for networked cities could offer a design heuristic incorporate continuing, and yet historic, citizen behaviours. We think that any such networked city taxonomy needs to be dynamically updated, incorporating fresh folksonomy elements that update social design guidelines and so further enable local, transformative citizen-centric practices

Hyperhumanism

The future is as contested a space as the past, perhaps in cities now more than ever, and while 'smart cities' are compelling as both metaphor and toolkit for municipal planners we will examine alternative metaphors, through hyperhumanism allied with our expertise and experience in 'context engineering'. While 'smart city' technology is concerned with e-enabling the municipality around a 'real-time City Hall' (or digital panopticon) we wish to decentralize the use of social technologies and remove the proprietary drive that currently underlies the deployment of smart city technology. For us, hyperhumanism is an alternative metaphor used to highlight a person-centric vision of citywide social technologies, with 'context engineering' providing the conceptual framing tools by which an alternative approach to building citywide digital infrastructures can be developed.

Towards a folksonomy of the city

Social cities not smart cities (cities for people not technocrats)

In *Designing Disorder* (Sennett and Sendra 2020), a proposal for an 'open city', Richard Sennett talks of the city as being a place of 'self-expression and social engagement'. In this follow up to his *The Uses of Disorder* ([1970] 2008) – which also absorbed reflections captured in *Buildings and Dwellings* (2018) – he builds on his earlier, simpler idea of the city as a place where individual personal identities can be built, to a now much broader of view of cities as social places where *communities also emerge from social engagement*. This is the very idea that Jane Jacobs ([1962] 2011) wrote about in *The Death and Life of Great American Cities* in 1962 as she took on urban planner Robert Moses who was redesigning New York City as a city made safe for cars.

However, Sennett (2018: 15) also cautions that 'the city, while being an exemplary theatre for self-expression and social engagement, is also a site of complex networks of dominance'. While Jane Jacobs is now recognized as an early theorist of the social city, it was actually Robert Moses who won the battle of making cities gridlocked with pollution. In 2020, intensified by the social distancing of the COVID-19 pandemic, people in cities faced the same battle all over again, namely that of social behaviours in the city being determined by urban planners; however, this time it was based on the idea of 'smart cities' promoted by the new technology elites rather than General Motors. Eric Schmidt of Google, arguably the twenty-first-century Robert Moses, is now desperate to make cities safe for technology, this time polluted by digital disruption rather than the exhausts of internal-combustion engines. Along with digital co-conspirators such as Bill Gates and Andrew Cuomo, the governor of New York (yet again), the untouchable digital 'robber barons' are planning to inflict a 'no-touch' city (Klein 2020) upon us. As smartphones have already enforced digital 'social distancing' while our 'personalized search' (Pariser 2012) addicts us to our information appliances, it is but a short step to these no-touch cities where we accept the decontextualized virtual information beamed down to us from advertising sites (as prefigured in Spielberg's 2002 film *Minority Report*), rather than the localized knowledge we gain from engaging in the kind of local, street-level human interactions Jacobs was arguing for 60 years ago and that Sennett reaffirms the social value of yet again right now.

Voluntary community in context or virtual communities decontextualized?

In the early 1980s Yoneji Masuda (1990), arguably the first theorist of the twenty-first-century digital economy, talked of future 'mass-knowledge creation' societies being based, in part, on 'voluntary' community. His theoretical position aligned well with the people-first social thinking of both Sennett and Jacobs. However, ever since Howard Rheingold (1993) talked of 'virtual' communities emerging from the continuing evolution of personal computing, the mediation of digital technologies within cities has been more shaped by virtual communities (driven by advertising ever since Google transmuted page rank search into personalized search in 2008). This tension between self-organized 'voluntary' communities, such as those we can see in the Origin of Spaces project discussed later in the chapter, and the decontextualized virtual communities described by Rheingold, is at the heart of the difference between the citizen-centric, value-driven, social cities we are advocating here, and the no-touch, advertising-driven, smart cities that Siemens, IBM, Cisco and Intel are selling to us (Greenfield 2015); now joined by Google and Microsoft in the 'no-touch' 'Smart City 2.0' that has emerged in the COVID-19 pandemic. A discussion concerning the smart city and the participatory city is also a fight over the metaphors with which we will describe, or perhaps limit, our emerging city infrastructures. As Korzybski

(1933) has said, 'the map is not the territory', but, whereas smart city planners believe only in the maps that they draw and the data it produces, the participatory city relies on citizen actions on the ground for it to give meanings to the territory. To paraphrase René Magritte in *The Treachery of Images* (2017): 'a no-touch city is not a city'.

This chapter

In this chapter we are looking towards a folksonomy of the city in three dimensions: first, in terms of alternative historical practice, the coinage of the limiting metaphors by which we allow our thoughts of the city to be shackled; second, in terms of a framing 'development framework' approach to taxonomy (Ecclesfield 2020), by which our thoughts of the emerging digital city can be shaped and shared; and, third, in terms of offering future thoughts that have not been hijacked by the technological determinism of those talking about the technological singularity, through the use of the emerging concept of hyperhumanism.

In *Streetlife*, Leif Jerram (2011) argued that despite a degree of success from formal urban planning in the years of rebuilding cities following the Second World War it created a problem of overly controlling every aspect of the social life of people living in cities. Town planning produces 'order, perfect knowledge of the citizenry by the state, everything in its place' (Jerram 2011: 317). And this social control was not attenuated by the work of what might be called 'advocacy planners' where the interests of the inhabitants of city neighbourhoods could be formally represented back to municipalities within the planning process. Planners were experts not representatives and Jerram's book is concerned to articulate an alternative vision of how 'spaces and places dominated [the] transformation' of human society during the twentieth century and his focus is on identifying popular culture, rather than 'great men' or nation states, as creating the key 'spaces and places' where people meet to both 'produce and consume culture' and so transformed the character in cities (Jerram 2011: 317). The popular Scottish comedian Billy Connolly (2019: 9) captured this nexus of city and popular culture when he described his art as follows:

> I love losing my way. I love getting lost in cities and small towns and all kinds of places, wandering off down long and winding streets and wee lanes and exploring the area, turning corners and seeing what's there. And I love getting lost in my stories for the same reason. It's how I discover things, how I learn things, how I imagine things.

Planning excludes this kind of spontaneous cultural life.

Our work begins by looking at a number of spaces and places in Europe, drawn together in the Origin of Spaces project, which are driven by a fresh, twenty-first-century understanding of popular culture where people 'represent the world to themselves and each other'.

The Origin of Spaces, City 2.0 and folksonomy of the city

The Origin of Spaces European Union (EU) Erasmus+ project (#oosEU), which looked at how abandoned city places could be repurposed for the emerging digital economy (2014–17), also discovered, in practice, what Sennett ([1970] 2008) describes as 'communities also emerge from social engagement'. The project discovered *communities emerging from the social engagement* of key actors and 'trusted intermediaries' within their communities in abandoned areas in the European cities of Lisboa, Bordeaux, Bilbao, Pula (Croatia) and, to some extent London (all with critical waterside locations). The purpose of the project was to build a 'toolbox' containing critical insights into how community-driven regeneration had been achieved based on five themes, self-identified by the key actors and developed collaboratively by the project team around the organizing theme of 'co-creating co-working spaces'.

As someone who taught on the social impact of information technology and a history of technology from 1984 to 2000, Fred Garnett has a key insight in his definition of technology as being 'order imposed on nature'. As part of the Learner-Generated Contexts Research Group (2006–10) he has also written on how to develop both 'learner-generated' and 'citizen-generated contexts' within cities. The Ambient Learning City project in Manchester (MOSI-ALONG 2011) was designed to create new 'beyond the classroom' learning contexts using techniques developed in the 'open context model of learning' (Luckin et al. 2010). This allowed for learning to be designed for any context, not just within educational institutions.

Designing 'context-responsive' learning was more complicated than expected because the classroom, as well as being a defined physical space, is also a metaphor for learning and so embodies many hidden qualities, such as time, length, pace, level, group, purpose, process, pedagogy and more. In sum, education institutions provide metaphors for learning. Designing context-responsive learning processes requires rethinking the metaphors that help frame our learning because the chosen metaphor, traditionally the classroom, helps to enable the learning process by reducing the number of contingent elements the learner needs to focus on. Consequently, in order to turn the city of Manchester into a multi-context learning environment, we needed to design a new enabling metaphor for 'open context learning' to inspire the self-organization of learners. 'Cabinets of curiosities' was the chosen metaphor as the project was working with the Museum of Science and Industry (MOSI) and museums were originally personal cabinets of curiosities, as can still be seen in the Wellcome Institute in London. In the United Kingdom this changed in 1860 as the Museums Act formalized the heritage role of museums and introduced professional curators and structured taxonomies. Subsequently the subjective complexities of collections made by individuals collapsed into the singular metaphor of curation by objective experts: from folksonomy to taxonomy. The MOSI-ALONG project had an objective of creating 'participative curatorial strategies' for the emerging digital age where professional curators (in museums) shared their expertise and taxonomic knowledge, with the individual 'CityZens' of Manchester who wished to develop the folksonomies of their individual collections of objects telling stories about their personal economic history of Manchester; using what Nina Simon (2010) calls 'object-centred sociality'.

Furthermore, as Ambient Learning City was also a project for working with digital technologies, a new process model for social media learning across the city had to be designed, in order to minimize social inclusion. This was done with the 'aggregate then curate' model; arguably this can be seen as a hybrid process based on an organizing folksonomy of choice shaped by a structuring taxonomy within a process that was actively facilitated by trained library workers (in Manchester).

The successes, or the learning, that came from Ambient Learning City were captured in the 2012 presentation 'Social Cities of Tomorrow', and are listed below. This work was prepared for the conference of the same name organized by 'Pakhuis de Zwijger', a next generation cultural community centre in a regeneration area in Amsterdam, very similar to the five participant projects in #oosEU.

Social Cities of Tomorrow: Conclusions

- New metaphors that help reframe thinking about cities;
- new social relationships, both within and across the city;
- object-centred sociality (participants share stories using personal objects);
- participative curatorial strategies (the community-wide sharing of professional expertise – as in 'advocacy planning');
- aggregate then curate (social media participation model that enables transformative participation);
- post-institutional thinking as dynamic context engineering beyond the institution;
- participatory cities that enable active citizenship not smart city halls.

This summative presentation was developed just before the smart city concept emerged and in terms of creating participatory cities this requires us to ask fresh questions concerning both (a) existing institutions and (b) the social relations and power structures of democracy as revealed practically in urban contexts. We think our subsequent arguments concerning the #oosEU creative practices folksonomy provide a way of addressing the institutional issues and that our networked city taxonomy provides a way of addressing the cross-city issues of the social relations and power structures of a modern city that wishes to be democratic first and e-enabled second.

Ambient Learning City (MOSI-ALONG) and a folksonomy of emerging 'participatory practice'

The Ambient Learning City project discovered that 'cities have multiple ambient contexts which we can both allow for and support, if we *design for appropri-ation* by our citizens' (Garnet and Whitworth 2015: n.pag., original emphasis). We would argue that #oosEU exemplifies what can be achieved when spaces are 'appropriated' by the citizens who live there, whereas smart cities are about extending the control of the existing municipal power elites using proprietary technologies.

At present, cities are based on institutional public spaces so we need to allow new personal public stories to be (re)written in new digital public spaces as was achieved with Urban Tapestries in Brighton by Proboscis and is currently being destroyed by CCTV and artificial intelligence (AI) in London's Kings Cross. Digi-tization in cities needs to support non-proprietary collaborative uses of social media as fora for context-responsive debates enabling the context shaping of neighbourhoods by the citizens of those neighbourhoods.

The Origin of Spaces: Towards a folksonomy of the city

The Origin of Spaces Erasmus+ project looked at innovations in digital workspaces in four cities across Europe – Barcelona, Bilbao, Lisboa and Pula (Croatia) – with a fifth city, London (represented by the London Borough of Lewisham), committed to taking the learning from the project and then applying it to local projects, as it did with the award-winning co-working space Place: Ladywell. The purpose of the project was to build a toolkit to help people in other cities across Europe create people-centric, collaborative spaces located in urban regeneration areas where the emerging digital economy could be built, but based on a shared sense of commu-nity derived from existing communities. This sense of community would not only be within the new 'spaces' but also as a part of the locality.

Consequently, the project was concerned to build an open-access online resource – the Origin of Spaces 'toolbox'. The toolbox was concerned to capture and share emerging best practice around five self-identified headline themes, which were identified by the partners at the bid-writing stage and that are already widely known and understood. For example, the concept of being a 'social entrepreneur' is well understood and so, within the toolbox, a link is provided to an existing social entrepreneur toolkit produced by Unlimited in London. However, the developmental process of the project was one of 'co-creating' the toolbox, which began with all partners being involved in 'transnational' visits to other partners, and within that process a toolbox requirements guidelines workshop was held in which each partner's work can also be presented as a developmental element for anyone wishing to create an economically functioning and culturally diverse neighbourhood as part of a 'participatory city'.

The Origin of Spaces: 'Folksonomy'

While the full dimensions of this work are presented within the toolbox (Origin of Spaces Toolbox n.d.), we provide a summative description of key elements of the #oosEU folksonomy here:

1. *Local partnerships (Bilbao):* identified that you need a 'core of local people interested in change and local impact' and that the 'different synergies by neighbourhood frame local partnerships' where the regeneration of former industrial spaces create opportunities for cultural life and work.
2. *Participatory governance (Pula):* saw the 'team-building' of running ROJC (the community centre in Pula, named after Karl Rojc) as part of an 'urban transformation process' based on the shared 'public management of industrial heritage' and that local governance was part of a 'transition from situated action to modus operandi'.
3. *Multidisciplinary co-working (Lisboa):* saw their place as a 'community of projects, ideas, co-workers and visitors' based on a 'dedicated project analysis enabling autonomy and self-organization' and talked of the 'social design' of the project enabling emergent, 'new social business practices'.
4. *Social entrepreneurs (London):* drawing on the practice of the earlier 'citizens connect' project of enabling active citizenship within the borough of Lewisham, this highlighted 'social change using entrepreneurial skills', a process described as 'risk-taking, learning from mistakes, self-confidence, determination, the ability to adapt'
5. *Ecological transitions (Bordeaux):* Darwin saw all social change as also requiring environmental sustainability where places are 'designed as an

ecosystem' with 'shared values' based on 'ecological transitions' to a 'collaborative development' of a 'measured mind and action set' for all participants to become pro-actively 'green' in their everyday workplace behaviours.

All the #oosEU projects saw the 'regeneration of former industrial spaces creating opportunities for cultural life' and, unlike smart city municipalities, the projects weren't based on a toxic combination of 'property development' and the reductive plug and play ethos of the digital gig economy. They were about breathing social and cultural life back into their host communities while returning economic development to abandoned city areas. A more detailed discussion of the elements of this folksonomy is available on the Origin of Spaces Blog (n.d.) and in Garnett (2015).

Sharing participatory city practices after #oosEU

Third places and urban regeneration

The #oosEU toolbox was developed as the first aggregation of citizen-centric behaviours (in this sense a shared folksonomy) in creating culturally driven economic regeneration practices in the time of the emerging digital economy. As such it exists as a heuristic to inform municipalities of fresh approaches to regeneration differing from the 'property-owning democracy' model that has driven, say, the economic development of London (Minton 2017) since the marketization and privatization of the economy in the 1980s, which Jerram (2011) identifies as the key economic driver of European cities in the last quarter of the twentieth century. However, following the build of the #oosEU toolbox there were further discussions concerning how this work might be further conceptualized, refined and shared, both as a model of digital 'third places' (Garnett 2016a) and as a taxonomy of developing the networked city as we describe here. A key element of CoWorkLisboa, the co-working hub within LxFactory, is the idea of 'multidisciplinary co-working', which means working as an individual within a digital workspace while also being a part of the social conversations that characterize 'third places' from which new projects can emerge collaboratively. In just this way, further discussions were held on how to better conceptualize the toolbox 'folksonomy' of emerging economic and cultural practice within the now emerging 'smart city' concept. Subsequent to discussions with both the City of Lisbon smart city team and the City of Bristol medium-size city project (Smith 2014), a way was identified of building a taxonomy of 'networked city' development that enables grass-roots 'advocacy planning' (as captured by the #oosEU folksonomy) to inform the development of the participatory twenty-first-century city (Laranja 2018).

How to make City 2.0 participatory: A five-step model

While working on the Origin of Spaces project, both Laranja and Garnett sat down and tried to determine how the elements being identified in these regeneration projects could help develop the digital futures of the city as a 'networked city' of neighbourhoods rather than a smart city. This section outlines a five-stage development model of how to move the creation of techno-centred cities driven by local authorities and their specialized tech suppliers to a distributed bottom-up model, developed from grass-roots. We see these citywide ecosystems as work, living and learning environments that are co-created by citizens and local authorities and align current trends towards a more participatory society.

The proposed model draws from our experience at the Erasmus+ initiative Origin of Spaces project (2014–2017), which has been researching how new multi-disciplinary co-working hubs operate and how they can be used to support new economic and social needs.

After the unemployment crisis in 2008, a growing dissatisfaction with traditional work-life styles combined with growing concerns with mobility and sustainability, contributed to rapid growth of freelance and temporary work located in new urban workplaces (*The Economist* 2014; Florida 2002; Storper and Venables 2004).

These relatively new urban workplaces appear to have specific characteristics, such as being physically compact, transit accessible, internet enabled, offering a mixed use of office, leisure, cultural and retail activities and in some cases combining avant-garde architecture with re-reuse of obsolete buildings (Katz and Wagner 2014). In their activities they mix arts and culture with software programming, digital marketing, freelance consultancy, etc. (Whitt 1987). To a certain extent, these new workplaces usually operate on a flat organizational architecture. For example, Project Darwin in Bordeaux is run collectively by the 'Darwiniennes' and is based on practices that promote an ecological culture through participatory governance, rather than top-down administration. Much the same way the project RojcNet at Pula Croatia was created through a wide participatory governance process.

These urban 'places' for work, living and learning resemble what Ray Oldenburg (1999) identified as 'third places'. Today, many different terms for these 'places' can be found, such as clusters, districts, zones, precincts, parks, creative quarters, co-working hubs, etc. (Bell and Jayne 2004; Cinti 2008).

Based on the experiences of five different 'places' in five different locations, four of which are what Oldenburg (1999: n.pag.) calls 'great good places' in the 'heart of [our] communities' namely ZAWP in Bilbao, Project Darwin in Bordeaux, LxFactory in Lisbon and RojcNet in Pula, we propose a City 2.0 framework for participatory development of these kinds of places and their community ecosystems. The fifth #oosEU partner, Capture Arts (London), was tasked to brief how the London Borough of Lewisham might use the lessons provided by the existing 'great good places'. In order that the recommendations were not merely anecdotal. Some of the project partners developed an outline taxonomy to help shape the folksonomy characteristics identified within the project and discussed above. In line with the Sloan School e-maturity model of the five stages of development of the 'networked' business organization, a five-stage 'development framework' was created as a way of guiding municipal policy with a framework populated with detailed examples of community-based practice. The proposed framework has the following five steps.

Step 1: Setting a 'place' – gathering the resources

Often these places originate from the initiative of individual citizens or private promoters that identify areas or buildings in the city that could be put to a different use. Hence, at step 1, public or private promoters of these new urban 'places' are usually focused on finding a location and on the physical characteristics of the places and how they may fit their purpose. There are many different types of places, but in general, they may be reduced to three kinds. First, they may be based on a real estate approach. This is about an entrepreneur or a private real estate operator that wants to rehabilitate or rebuild parts of the city in order to get an economic return. Second, there are places the purpose of which is not just economic but they believe in creating a community among people that live and/or work in that area/building. Normally, these places are not just a physical 'place'. They aspire to create a 'cognitive space' supporting their local community. There is an important distinction between 'places' and 'spaces'. According to Grandadam et al. (2013), 'places' correspond to how the physical elements (rooms, buildings, quarters, corridors, valleys, etc.) are configured and furnished. 'Spaces' should be understood as 'cognitive spaces', 'spaces of socialization' enabling collective and individual self-determined learning, favouring collaborative practices, community development and relationships based on cognitive proximity and common understandings. As we will argue in the next steps, while places are local, spaces extend beyond the local physical place and may be associated with global communities located at different places around the world. Finally, a third model for these new urban places corresponds to those cases where, based on a community with physical and cognitive proximity, there is also the ambition to develop a new philosophy of life. In our cases, while the LxFactory in Lisbon departed from a private real estate 'place' project and slowly evolved to a 'community' space, driven by its local CoWorkLisboa, places like ZAWP, Darwin and Rojc were created already with the initial ambition of becoming community spaces with specific lifestyles.

Step 2: Attracting, promoting collaboration and building a community ecosystem

A second step in our development model is related to how the promoters are able to attract the right individuals and organizations to the space and promote internal linkages. In certain cases, such as LxFactory for example, we observed some kind of 'social engineering' (i.e. the careful management of a few key first people to come into the place). At the beginning in 2008, founders of LxFactory (the name 'LxFactory' is itself a tribute to Andy Warhol's New York art space The Factory) made selective invitations to projects and companies and negotiated special conditions for their relocations from other parts of the city. These first flagship projects were invited because of their potential to become the genesis of a micro ecosystem that needed to grow in the right directions. Also, because their reputation would signal to the outside the existence of this 'new place' downtown in Alcântara, at local and at international level, lending credibility to the new place and helping to attract other workers, organizations and projects.

For example 'Ler Devagar' (a new innovative bookshop concept) already with an international reputation, came to the LxFactory as one of the first tenants. Other important anchors were Café da Fábrica (a family coffee shop), Act (an acting school), Balneário (architects, illustrators, designers, seamstress and modeller), bike recycling, Xuz (Portuguese shoe brand – clogs and wooden-soled shoes), etc. Other 'anchor' projects on a second wave, such as 'Kiss the Cook', 'Cantina', 'Lara Seixo Rodrigues' and others were instrumental in consolidating a dynamic underground of arts, cultural and leisure activities promoted by talented people

Individual people inside the place, playing the role of gatekeepers, can be fundamental nodes helping to build the internal network and attracting others inside the place. For example, Lara, an architect with a passion for street arts, came to an LxFactory event in 2007. She 'felt like home' and saw in LxFactory a place for street artists to work and connect. She did not want to let the 'black and white' culture to spread and wanted to improve public spaces – 'get rid of the wall culture' – so she proposed to paint the LxFactory walls. More than blending in the local 'LxFactory community', Lara is one good example of how a particular person can play an important role in building a local community. Lara was also instrumental as a 'relationships builder'; she shared a lot of information with other place workers and is responsible for numerous street artworks and events.

Another key person is Fernando. Fernando is a design professor at the European University School of Design. Together with Ana, he came to LxFactory in 2010 to establish the first co-working place in Lisbon – CoWorkLisboa. Occupying the fourth floor of the central building, CoWorkLisboa started with an initial group of 25 co-workers that helped to build the identity of the space. Fernando likes to be known as the person that helps to incorporate newcomers on the daily routines and rituals of the co-workers' community. He prefers not to set any strong legal contracts with the co-workers, but rather to stimulate trust and reinforce the sense of a true community. Fernando believes that the only way to grow a community of co-workers is by establishing one-to-one relationships, and although he doesn't want to occupy a formal role as a mentor of these relationships, he does recognize that, informally and unintentionally, he ends up providing most of this support.

At CoWorkLisboa, although co-working rules are not written, nor self-imposed by any form, co-workers feel an environment of creativity, strong collaboration and experimentation of new ideas. Co-workers recognize that there is a 'climate of open share of information, creativity and celebration'. No matter how complicated your problem may be, there is a sense that you can always find someone that can help you. Co-workers see CoWorkLisboa as a space where it is easy for people to socialize and integrate and where there is great tolerance to different backgrounds. Also, it is a space where they can freely expose their ideas to each other, 'receiving positive feedback'. Beyond CoWorkLisboa, smaller communities present at LxFactory also appear to play an important role. For example, the presence of bloggers and associated community activities (e.g. LIAM – Like a Man, a blog for men over 40 – and 'Correr na Cidade' – people who share their passion for running) also appear to play an important role in promoting networking inside and outside LxFactory.

Step 3: Building a community

At step 3, when the place is already growing and some linkages between local organizations and individuals already exist, there is a need for further engagement in building a local community. However, building a community is much more than just collaboration and linkages between organizations and individuals. Activating a sense of community appears to be related to how the place/space owners/managers promote internal animation activities through events of low structure and impermanence, similar to the so-called creative scenes referred to in the Warhol economy (Currid 2007). These include organizing or sponsoring events of all kinds in order to further promote linkages and the fundamental values in association with internal events, such as organization of lunch floors, Ignite Portugal, pitches at CoWorkLisboa and others where people inside the LxFactory quarter would meet, which have an important role in building a community. Other places such as Project Darwin and Rojc also animate their spaces by organizing events that help local people to get together and share their projects.

According to Grandadam et al. (2013) internal events that effectively join creative freelance individual workers with technical staff working in large organizations are essential to animate to so-called middle ground where tacit knowledge of diverse origins is translated, possibly leading lead to collaboration projects (including both short- and longer-term projects).

Step 4: Extend to the city – connect your space community to other city space(s)

Step 4 is about connecting communities and ecosystems across the city (online and offline). At this stage the participatory nature of the initiative is well developed and therefore there is no need for centralized public administration/regulation. As in the earlier steps, often the role of the city council was to facilitate helping citizen participation to emerge and enable shared best practices to be shared.

However, as in step 3, organization of events appears to be the key mechanism by which different places across the city connect to each other. For example, the organization of events opened to the outside, such as international conferences and/or the open days at LxFactory, structured as a combination of art exhibitions, workshops, demonstrations, live events, etc., was greatly recognized as helping to create visibility across the whole city, connecting an extensive network of artists, tech developers, designers, theorists, etc. These events not only appear to contribute to create a local 'cognitive space', but they are also instrumental in further attracting people and in refreshing local knowledge co-creation, avoiding a community closed in on itself.

Step 5: Connecting citywide ecosystems to other cities

Finally, step 5 is about connecting the city community ecosystems beyond the boundaries of the city to other cities and other countries (i.e. entering a global network of community ecosystems).

We hope this proposed framework can help smart city developments to become human-centred, not technology-centred. Our suggestion is that the smart city concept cannot be only associated with physical rehabilitation of older buildings and quarters combined with fancy technology. In addition, simply joining at the same place artists, projects and freelance workers from different areas does not necessarily form a local ecosystem. There is a need to develop mechanisms that contribute to activating a self-determined participatory ecosystem community, enabling new lifestyles of work, life and leisure. These mechanisms need to be based in human-centred values relevant to the twenty-first century and to that end we now examine hyperhumanism.

Hyperhumanism

Today there is an increasing understanding that, more than ever, technology is not necessarily working for us and that it could be perceived as intentionally being designed to work against us. Through the use of current technology citizens have fallen prey to the corporate-driven digital feed that directs their behaviour. We are populating and occupying our minds almost entirely with input from this feed, it holds our attention and suffocates our perceptual bandwidth, making us prisoners of the digital panopticon. As a result, we have largely become passive consumers and have forgotten that technology could instead be used to develop the real world. As we have seen above in the discussions on the practical folksonomies of the Origin of Spaces project and in the alternative conceptual modelling of the networked city as a five-layer model, this need not be the case.

It is ironic that many technology developers in the 1990s assumed that they were creating new technology in order to free up time for citizens to spend in more meaningful ways. Instead, that very same technology has enslaved us into an illusory world. Transhumanism forces us to become utterly dependent on technology, subverting our ability to develop the skills for ourselves. 'We do not want to wear technology; we want to become technology' is fundamentally a transhumanist trait. In contrast, hyperhumanism utilizes technology as a catalyst for developing our own innate human abilities. Transhumanism is problematic because of its heavy reliance on technology, the individual ego and corporate-driven agendas make it hard for humans to implement it collectively (so as to be used productively for community driven goals). The healing of the land and the purification of the human spirit is the same process (Fukuoka 2009).

Values of hyperhumanism

1. Use technology to undo the damage caused by poorly designed technology (technology as a design problem).
2. Reclaim our attention by becoming conscious of what we pay attention to.
3. Recognize that technology is not working for us but is actually being intentionally designed to work against us. However, it is clear that humanity

has to decide to use tech for good and avoid becoming ever-more dependent.

4. To enhance perception at scale:
   (a) from within and about yourself;
   (b) about your surroundings;
   (c) about your relations.
5. Focus on combining our innate human abilities (community, empathy, compassion, imagination, kindness) with the carefully designed use of technology (where it acts primarily as a stimulus to reveal our own untapped abilities, potential and resources).
6. While also thriving on an individual growth basis, its social structure is based on diminishing human needs as much as possible in order to help others achieve the resources needed for achieving such a state.
7. Provide ways to use technology that helps us to liberate ourselves from the all-consuming feed and scroll rot.
8. We cannot grow effectively using the current technology standards and inadequate protocols for human cognitive and emotional growth.
9. The use of technologies and techniques that act as scaffolding for a short period in order to allow the development of skill that you can then exercise yourself once the scaffolding is removed.
10. The need to stop human downgrading and value human flourishing: the Center for Humane Technology has developed a model involving the redesigning of technology to protect the vulnerabilities of human nature while supporting the social fabric. Some 2 billion people are immersed in social platforms designed with the goal of not just getting our attention, but getting us addicted to getting attention from others. This is an extractive attention economy. By exploiting human weaknesses, tech is taking control of society and human history. Technology has been downgrading our well-being, while upgrading machines (Harris 2019).

According to the Center for Humane Technology there are three ways to catalyse the development of this humane technology:

• humane social systems;
• humane AI, not overpowering AI;
• humane regenerative incentives, instead of extraction.

Crucially the model concludes that if we design our systems to protect humans then we can not only avoid downgrading humans, but actually achieve an upgrade in human capacity.

11. The design of a way of becoming, not just creating crutches with technology but actually facilitating the evolution of human capability (Willis 2006).
12. Technology does not mean tools of science fiction but tools that will allow us to get to know ourselves better, through the use of feedback loops that will in turn allow us to enter and practise different states of awareness.
13. In any technological development, either in terms of hardware, software or philosophy there is always the ever-present danger of the double-edged sword; the hidden trap between the proper use of a tool and the risk of becoming subservient to the tool and the philosophy behind the tool itself (which is often the case with transhumanism). Indeed, it is the misguided use of technology that has taken us to our current state of unconsciousness driven by the hijacking of our attention versus embodied presence, curiosity and choice.
14. As much as hyperhumanism is a movement towards the future, it is also a fundamental return to our roots, while also applying the learning from our modern understandings of neuroscience.

As Viktor Frankl, celebrated Austrian psychiatrist and Holocaust survivor states: 'Everything can be taken from a man but one thing: the last of the human freedoms – to choose one's attitude in any given set of circumstances, to choose one's own way' (Frankl 1963: n.pag.).

Internet of fungus

Humans of the past were much more intimate with their ecosystems, and if we are to survive the climate changes before us, we must reacquaint ourselves with the more-than-human life that lives beyond the concrete and computers that define modernity.

The 'internet of fungus', is an intricate underground information network where plants and fungi communicate with each other through a mass of threadlike strands, known as mycelium, that are spread over great distances. Plants and fungi depend on each other for survival through mutually beneficial relationships. This fungal network provides plants with nutrients like phosphorus and carbon nitrogen and with defence-related chemicals that protect against disease in a process known as 'priming'. Meanwhile, plants provide fungi with food. The exchange takes place via the fungi's mycelia strands (Medina 2014).

Nature works in circles, and we can apply this principle of recomposition to the economy to make *circular economies*. Instead of converting natural resources into landfill waste, products can be designed so as to be upcycled as much as possible, creating value out of every reincarnation of natural resources we can find.

This is the fungal way of resource management, for it turns otherwise dead and useless products back into the fertile soil from which can grow multitudes of brilliant forms. It is the only guarantee against the resource depletion that the future has in store for us.

Context engineering

We are moving from a content-based economy to a context-based economy. Context engineering is the investigation of the ethical combination of analogue and digital technologies to enhance human and societal capacities. Context engineering provides the ability, within one field of view, to be both in the world and to see yourself in it, the power of looking through and occupying your own field of vision (Gibson and Gibson 1994).

Context engineering will give us new abilities, control over our senses and the ability to develop new forms of perception. Human–computer interaction (HCI) that relies predominantly on vision alone or the engagement of a limited range of senses can cause individual – and, by implication, societal – dissonance, creating a diminished rather than an augmented reality.

The core problem is how to (re)design a workable balance between digital and analogue modes of interaction. Without thoughtful design, digital interventions are simply distracting people away from meaningful engagement with the learning opportunities and social situations that they are actually designed to augment.

Hans Monderman's shared space traffic system emphasizes the difference between the smart cities ethos and that of context engineering – the shared space traffic system was designed and implemented in many places from the 1980s onwards and involved controlling all the signage and formal 'rules' at intersections, instead of relying on active human interaction.

Web 2.0: From rhizomatic learner to rhizomatic citizen

O'Reilly (2005: n.pag.) defined Web 2.0 as a being based on an 'architecture of participation' in which 'users must be treated as co-developers', arguing that the current instantiation of the internet was becoming based on a dynamic co-creation process instead of just a few people in the back office. As a consequence of the affordances of twenty-first-century 'read/write web' that supports 'prosumer' behaviours (Tapscott 2006) a number of educational theorists have created 'post web 2.0 models of learning' such as 'connectivism' (Seimens 2006), connective massive open online courses (cMOOCs), as well as the open context model of learning (Luckin et al. 2010), all of which offer more personal agency to learners. Cormier (2008) also talked of 'rhizomatic learning' being enabled by

Web 2.0, taking his cue from the earlier work of Deleuze (Deleuze et al. 2013) on 'the rhizomatic layers of belonging'. This collaborative, self-determined learning behaviour was also a design feature of the WikiQuals project (Garnett 2016b), in part derived from Stewart Hase's work on heutagogy (Hase and Kenyon 2013). As the UK Advance HE Knowledge Hub (n.d.: n.pag.) defines it, 'rhizomatic learning uses the botanical metaphor of the rhizome to describe the complex and often messy nature of learning'.

Cormier ran the only course, actually a cMOOC, on rhizomatic learning in 2014, which was entitled 'Rhizomatic Learning: The Community Is the Curriculum'. The WikiQuals project uses the motto 'We Are Rhizomatic', based on the belief that, rhizomatically, the learner 'owns' (or defines) their learning and that learning is a co-creation process. We can, perhaps, extend these fungus-based metaphors of co-creation and think of the rhizomatic citizen being involved in co-creating City 2.0 through the full exercise of their 'self-expression and social engagement', as Sennett describes it (Sennett and Sendra 2020).

If Web 2.0 is the 'participative web' as it is based on a social architecture of participation, then we can talk about City 2.0 being a participatory city and so requiring a framework for citizen-centric participation. In which case in order to oppose the smart city we need to be able to co-create a participatory City 2.0 where the 'rhizomatic citizen' defines creatively what their city is 'from the inside out'. This is what we have tried to do here by identifying an open-ended and dynamic folksonomy of the emerging creative practice demonstrated by citizens in regeneration neighbourhoods in cities across Europe. We believe that this dynamic co-creation approach to a citizen-centric city populated by 'rhizomatic citizens' reflects the values we have identified here in hyperhumanism.

Afterword

While this chapter builds on much earlier work by the authors, and draws on a wider range of references than previously, it is not a summative statement of our ideas. Rather this a formative expression of how we might draw on a folksonomy of emerging citizen practice – only partly articulated here – and design new dynamic taxonomies that can further enable that practice in ways that can be recognized by 'community animateurs' (Schuler 2008), local and national government officials, as well as city planners. As, in the end, these choices are about values, we offer hyperhumanism as a model of how citizen-centric approaches to the city can be integrated into the networked city at a time when the digital economy, and digital corporations, are the key drivers of socio-technical change. We look forward to working with interested cities to develop these ideas dynamically with local communities.

REFERENCES

Bell, D. and Jayne, M. (2004), 'Afterword: Thinking in quarters', in D. Bell and M. Jayne (eds), *City of Quarters: Urban Villages in the Contemporary City*, Aldershot: Ashgate, pp. 249–56.

Cinti, T. (2008), 'Cultural districts and clusters: The state of the art', in P. Cooke and L. Lazzeretti (eds), *Creative Cities, Cultural Clusters and Local Economic Development*, Cheltenham: Edward Elgar, pp. 70–92.

Connolly, B. (2019), *Tall Tales and Wee Stories*, London: Two Roads.

Cormier, D. (2008), 'Rhizomatic education: Community as curriculum', *Innovate: Journal of Online Education*, 4:5, n.pag., https://core.ac.uk/download/pdf/51073522.pdf. Accessed 17 July 2021.

Currid, E. (2007), *The Warhol Economy: How Fashion Art and Music Drive New York City*, New York: Princeton University Press.

Deleuze, G., Guattari, F. and Massumi, B. (2013), *A Thousand Plateaus: Capitalism and Schizophrenia*, London: Bloomsbury.

Ecclesfield, N. (2020), *Digital Learning: Architectures of Participation*, Hershey, PA: IGI Global.

The Economist (2014), 'A Cambrian moment', 18 January, https://www.economist.com/sites/default/files/20140118_tech_startups.pdf. Accessed 16 July 2021.

Florida, R. (2002), *The Rise of the Creative Class*, New York: Basic Books.

Frankl, V. E. (1963), 'Man's search for meaning: An introduction to logotherapy', *American Journal of Orthopsychiatry*, 58, pp. 552–61.

Fukuoka, M. (2009), *The One-Straw Revolution: An Introduction to Natural Farming*, New York: New York Review of Books.

Garnett, F. (2015), '#oosEU toolbox resource analysis', https://www.slideshare.net/fredgarnett/ooseu-toolbox-resource-analysis-origin-of-spaces-project. Accessed 1 July 2020.

Garnett, F. (2016a), 'Third Places and City 2.0, Pula', https://www.slideshare.net/fredgarnett/third-places-and-city-20. Accessed 1 July 2020.

Garnett, F. (2016b), 'WikiQuals and personalised learning', https://www.slideshare.net/fredgarnett/wikiquals-and-personalised-learning. Accessed 1 July 2020.

Garnett, F. and Whitworth, D. (2015), 'Aggregate then curate', www.slideshare.net/fredgarnett/aggregate-then-curate. Accessed 26 April 2021.

Gibson, E. J. and Gibson, E. J. (1994), 'The perceived self', in E. J. Gibson, *Ontogenesis of the Perceived Self*, Cambridge, UK: Cambridge University Press, pp. 25–42.

Grandadam, D., Cohendet, P. and Simon, L. (2013), 'Places, spaces and the dynamics of creativity: The video game industry in Montreal', *Regional Studies*, 47:10, pp. 1701–14.

Greenfield, A. (2013), *Against the Smart City*, New York: Do Projects.

Harris, T (2019), 'Technology is downgrading humanity: Let's reverse that trend now', https://humanetech.com/. Accessed 5 April 2020.

Hase, S. and Kenyon, C. (2013), *Self-Determined Learning: Heutagogy in Action*, London, Bloomsbury.

Jacobs, J. ([1962] 2011), *The Death and Life of Great American Cities*, New York: Random House.

Jerram, L. (2011), *Streetlife: The Untold History of Europe's Twentieth Century*, Oxford: Oxford University Press.

Katz, B. and Wagner, J. (2014), *The Rise of Innovation Districts: A New Geography of Innovation in America*, Washington, DC: Brookings Institute, Metropolitan Policy Program.

Klein, N. (2020), 'Screen new deal', *The Intercept*, 8 May.

Korzybski, A. (1933), *Science and Sanity: An Introduction to Non-Aristotelian Systems and General Semantics*, New York: International Non-Aristotelian Library.

Landry, C. (2008), *The Creative City: A Toolkit for Urban Innovators*, London, Routledge.

Laranja, M. (2018), *Collaborative Places as Catalysts and Intermediators of Innovation in Cities*, Beijing: RSA.

Luckin, R., Clark, W., Garnett, F., Whitworth, A., Akass, J., Cook, J., Day, P., Ecclesfield, N., Hamilton, T. and Robertson, J. (2010), 'Learner-generated contexts: A framework to support the effective use of technology for learning', in M. J. W. Lee (ed.), *Web 2.0-Based E-Learning: Applying Social Informatics for Tertiary Teaching*, Hershey, PA: IGI Global, pp. 70–84.

Magritte, R. (2017), *The Treachery of Images*, Paris: Museum of Modern Art.

Masuda, Y. (1990), *Managing in the Information Society*, London: Blackwell.

Medina, D. (2014), 'Plants have an internet of fungus, and they're hacking each other', https://qz.com/318847/plants-have-an-internet-of-fungus-and-theyre-hacking-each-other/. Accessed 12 June 2020.

Minton, A. (2012), *Ground Control: Fear and Happiness in the 21st Century*, London: Penguin.

Minton, A. (2017), *Big Capital: Who Is London For?* London: Penguin.

Oldenburg, R. (1999), *The Great Good Place: Cafes, Coffee Shops, Bookstores, Bars, Hair Salons, and Other Hangouts at the Heart of a Community*, Cambridge, MA: Da Capo Press.

O'Reilly, T. (2005), 'What is Web 2.0?' www.oreilly.com/pub/a/web2/archive/what-is-web-20.html. Accessed 29 April 2021.

Origin of Spaces Blog (n.d.), https://thirdplaceeu.wordpress.com/. Accessed 1 July 2020.

Origin of Spaces Toolbox (n.d.), http://toolbox.originofspaces.com/. Accessed 1 July 2020.

Pariser, E. (2012), *The Filter Bubble*, London: Penguin

Rheingold, H. (1993), *The Virtual Community: Homesteading On The Electronic Frontier*, New York: Basic Books

Schuler, D. (2008), *Liberating Voices: A Pattern Language for Communication*, Cambridge, MA: MIT Press.

Scott Morton, M. S. (ed.) (1991) *The Corporation of the 1990s: Information Technology and Organizational Transformation*, New York: Oxford University Press.

Sennett, R. ([1970] 2008), *The Uses of Disorder: Personal Identity and City Life*, New Haven, CT: Yale University Press.

Sennett, R. (2018), *Building and Dwelling: Ethics for the City*, London: Allen Lane.

Sennett, R. and Sendra, P. (2020), *Designing Disorder: Experiments and Disruptions in the City*, London: Verso Books.

Siemens, G. (2005), 'Connectivism: A learning theory for the digital age', International Journal of Instructional Technology and Distance Learning, 2:1, n.pag., www.itdl.org/. Accessed 29 April 2021.

Simon, N. (2010), The Participatory Museum, Santa Cruz, CA: Museum 2.0.

Smith, C. (2014), 'Context engineering hybrid spaces for perceptual augmentation', *Electronic Visualisation and the Arts (EVA)*, 8–10 July, London: British Computer Society.

Spielberg, S. (2002), *The Minority Report*, Los Angeles, CA: 20th Century Fox.

Storper, M. and Venables, A. J. (2004), 'Buzz: Face-to-face contact and the urban economy', *Journal of Economic Geography*, 4:4, pp. 351–70.

Tapscott, D (2006), *Wikinomics: How Mass Collaboration Changes Everything*, New York: Portfolio.

UK Advance HE Knowledge Hub (n.d.), 'Rhizomatic learning', https://www.advance-he.ac.uk/knowledge-hub/rhizomatic-learning-0. Accessed 29 March 2021.

Whitt, J. A. (1987), 'Mozart in the metropolis. The arts coalition and the urban growth machine', *Urban Affairs Quarterly*, 23:1, pp. 15–36.

Willis, A. M. (2006), 'Ontological designing', *Design Philosophy Papers*, 4:2, pp. 69–92.

10

Psychogeography
Reimagining and Re-Enchanting
the Smart City

*Adrian Sledmere,
University of the Arts, London*

Introduction

I begin this chapter with a very brief outline of what is meant by the smart city. My aim here is to treat the smart city as a starting point, something that is integral to the assumptions and imperatives upon which our ideas of the modern city are based. To do this means subjecting urban regeneration, as it is defined and justified by ideas of the smart city, to a different type of critique. In his work on visual culture, Jenks (1995: 144) argues that that 'dominant views and appropriations of space have become taken for granted and have, in turn, enabled routine human organisation and governmentality'. He also talks about a lack of 'critical theoreticity' in the social sciences together with a need to explore 'alternative geographies' (Jenks 1995: 144). With this in mind, I want to ask whether or not psychogeography can be used to provide a timely critical intervention in relation to the smart city. There is a strongly political edge to this project, which involves being able to somehow reimagine what a city might look like in the face of powerful neo-liberal forces that have come to condition every facet of our existence. Here, I will show how philosophical currents dating back to surrealism and the situationist movement have been used to critique both the urban space and its inequalities.

The smart city

The smart city embraces a number of intersecting areas and prerogatives; these form an important background to the discussion of a specific locale that I am

220

looking to develop here. Many of these have resulted with the advent of digital technology and the emergence of big data. There is not space to catalogue all of these in detail or deal with the many ramifications of new technologies here. Therefore, I want to offer a wide-ranging discussion that locates the notion of 'smart' within a set of broader structural forces. Here, I take the position that we increasingly inhabit a world of particulars: new technologies, concepts and ideas that have entered our orbit so quickly that they have become naturalized. Philosopher Graham Harman (2005: 268) notes:

> For the most part, we deal with objects by taking them for granted, by silently relying on them as we direct our attention elsewhere. At any given moment, we invisibly make use of numerous tables, computers, blood cells and steel girders, not to mention atmospheric oxygen and the rotation of the earth. By and large, we live in a world in which things withdraw from awareness, silently enabling our more explicit deeds.

At a philosophical level, and drawing upon Heidegger's distinction between objects and things, this is to acknowledge that 'things are what they are by virtue of their relation to everything else' (Rorty 2005: 274). Adam Greenfield (2017: 48) has suggested that this need for a critique of things becomes even more urgent at the broader level of the smart city, 'a place where the instrumentation of the urban fabric, and of all the people moving through the city, is driven by the desire to achieve a more efficient use of space, energy and other resources'. With this in mind, we would do well not to presume that 'smart' is, of itself, efficacious but rather that the way in which it relates to other phenomena, in often complex ways, requires proper scrutiny. My contention here is that a psychogeographic approach can help generate much-needed alternative perspectives on 'smart'. I want to explore this possibility via a subjective account of a specific locale close to my home in South London: Burgess Park. There are several reasons for providing this topographical focus. First, I want to ask, in practical and subjective terms, how this urban environment impacts upon the individual (me). Second, I want to suggest that it serves as a metonym: the particularities of its ongoing evolution as an urban space can speak more broadly to the modernity, environment and neo-liberalism in which it is embedded. By offering a subjective account I want to adopt a Sinclairian strategy that has to do with reclaiming 'place'. Here, by foregrounding the notion of cultural memory I too hope to 'counter the "vampiric logic" of neo-liberalism' (Martin 2015: 149) and to interrogate the ways in which 'smart' might be viewed as complicit rather than neutral in political terms.

221

Psychogeography

One of the main purposes of this chapter is to ask how psychogeography might offer a set of critical tools with which to interrogate the emergence of the smart city. I will argue here that a particular style of writing and approach to the city has emerged across the twentieth century, which deals specifically with modernity and offers a voice that is both timely and critical in relation to our built environment.

Psychogeography finds many of its antecedents in key debates within philosophy. Here we could even go as far back as Plato and Aristotle in order to trace the possibility of an ideal realm beyond the reach of our senses, which we have yet to connect with or have lost touch with. Indeed, this notion of the ideal was later integral to the work of Hegel (Hopkins 2004: 105), Kant (noumenal), Schopenhauer (the world as will and representation) and Nietzsche. The latter's *Birth of Tragedy* (Nietzsche 2000) suggested precisely that a world of primal energies and irrational impulses (Dionysian) had been lost in the world of art via a Socratean quest to sanitize it: art had come to mean contemplating life rather than truly participating in it. Here, following Plato, was an allusion to the possibility of transcendence and oneness. The dualism referenced here has continued to play out at the level of culture, a kind of dialectic between science/positivism and something more mystical/animistic/occulted; forces or aspects of our existence that cannot be so systematically explained. I want to suggest here that psychogeography forms part of this dialectic, a timely foil to both the rational and the scientific.

Surrealism

Before moving on to consider modern psychogeography I want to talk about two of its chief tributaries: surrealism and, its predecessor, dadaism. Surrealism is characterized by the assertion that there is a kind of greater reality to which we do not routinely have access. Here, there is a sense of the 'noumenal', which extends not only to the inner psychic life of each of us but also into the 'concrete' world of objects (Young 1995: 191). The precise nature of this world, to which we do not have access, is referenced by the surrealists in variety of ways: the marvellous, the eternal, the infinite, the inconceivable, the heavenly, the transcendent. All of these allude to a form of secular mysticism and the possibility of energies and intuitions not routinely available to us. At the same time, and by implication, it seeks to criticize our blind faith in systems of knowledge that claim to explain everything. The pursuit of the marvellous alluded to here becomes increasingly difficult in an age where science can account for so much phenomena in the outside world. There is even a sense in which the marvellous has been displaced, that it now resides in the particular: the affordances of all the gadgetry and technology that we now use on a daily basis. As such, all of our amazement and wonder is potentially subsumed within a digital world that is both personal but also transparent, subject to total scrutiny.

Surrealism concerns itself then with the way in which the effects of the marvellous have become lost to us; there is clearly a comparison to be made with romanticism's response to enlightenment ideas of logic, rationality and secularity (although the surrealists were anti-romanticism) and, most strongly, the more pietistic strains of Christianity. Nietzsche's *Birth of Tragedy* concerned itself too with the ways in which a culture might be divested of its access to primal energies; his ideas formed an important tributary for the surrealists. He symbolized this dynamic via the contrasting contradictory qualities of particular Greek gods: Apollo and Dionysus. Similarly, and central to the surrealists, was a metaphysical quest for transcendence, a state of self-realization where such contradictions would ultimately cease to exist (Hopkins 2004: 105). The very barriers to this concern the way in which we interact with the concrete: the hard logic and rationality of science. Again, and like romanticism, surrealism meant the search for 'a force that would break the cold, clinical fetters of rationalism and instrumental approaches to knowledge' (Negus and Pickering 2004: 7). Here lay the belief that the order with which we had been conditioned to perceive the outside world could only be countered by embracing disorder. Imposed order, symbolized by Nietzsche in the form of Apollo (the god of order and beauty), could be disrupted via orgiastic drunken rites where 'the effort, in brief, was to stun the rational faculties and the moral inhibitions, to break down the boundaries between selves, until, at the climactic moment, the god himself made himself present to his celebrants' (Danto 1981: 19). The surrealists didn't, to the best of my knowledge, engage in such practices, although there were clearly parallels.

While the relationship with psychoanalysis is not always straightforward, there was a sense for the surrealists in which the marvellous resided beneath the level of consciousness but it could be glimpsed in terms of the collision between wish and reality that took place in dreams. The thinking here was that dreams often produced surreal imagery as certain wishes failed to successfully emerge into consciousness: unspoken desire would necessarily become distorted. Such a collision between conflicting psychic impulses offered a certain primacy to ideas of disorder/hazard/chance/contingent. As Aragon (1987: 217) was to write:

Reality is the apparent absence of contradiction. The marvellous is the eruption of contradiction within the real. Love is a state of confusion between the real and the marvellous. In this state, the contradictions of being seem really essential to being.

Wherever the marvellous is dispossessed, the abstract moves in.

The deliberate pursuit of these would be a strategic means of unlocking or feeling the effects of the marvellous as part of the ultimate quest for transcendence, a way in, a means of reconnecting. To open the doors of perception meant deliberately unsettling those ideas and practices that had become normalized. From this account of the surrealists emerges an important pursuit of psychogeography that I think can best be described as a sense of wonderment. This could be found variously in the mind, through love, but also in the common place: 'In everything base there is some quality of the marvellous which puts me in the mood for pleasure' (Aragon 1987: 50).

As a final note on the surrealists, it is also important to mention that many of its leading figures were progressive city dwellers, natural heirs to Charles Baudelaire's idea of the modern artist as *flâneur* (Hopkins 2004: 60). Louis Aragon's *Paris Peasant* (1987) in many ways is a proto-psychogeographic piece. Its focus upon two Paris locations prefigures much of the later psychogeographic writing. Here, a poetic resonance derives from the elegance and seediness of a Parisian arcade. The commentary is both rich in personal material and detail, which sketches out the full spectrum of human activity from cafes to a *'maison de tolerance'*, which Aragon clearly knew well. Ultimately, it was destroyed as part of Haussmann's reforms and the creation of wide boulevards; a rebuke to the medieval, organic and disordered city topography that had been blamed for facilitating civil insurrection. Perhaps of critical importance here is more literary/imaginative than scientific; it is the sense of wonder that the built environment can confer upon us if, that is, we are open to looking beyond its harsh utilitarian surfaces. It also serves as warning that the rationalization of city spaces, in any era, can also be tied up with ideas of surveillance and control.

The situationists

The notion of psychogeography begins to take shape more formally with the emergence of the Situationist International. The situationists drew inspiration from the ideas of the surrealists, not least the 'sense of a world hidden beneath the commercial banality of the city' (Jordan 2016: n.pag.). While a critical perspective had been important to the surrealists, the situationists more formally embraced a revisionist Marxism, situating themselves as part of a critical tradition that has in its sights the dislocating and alienating effects of both modern life and capitalism. Guy Debord (2005), a key figure in the movement, wrote about the 'society of the spectacle'. Such a society had normalized a set of surface appearances that informed all social life and from which it was difficult to achieve any kind of critical distance (Jenks 1995). However, he also acknowledged the possibility that our environment can impact upon us in very real but also subjective ways: 'Psychogeography could set for itself the study of the precise laws and specific effects of the geographical environment, consciously organized or not, on the emotions and behavior of individuals' (Debord, cited in Coverley 2010: 88–89).

Such ideas about the city raise the question of agency: what an individual can do to overcome or resist its strictures and structures and their effects upon consciousness. Here, the idea of walking occupies a privileged position in the psychogeographic strategic arsenal. This is to attribute far greater significance to the activity than simply getting from A to B or just going for a stroll. Continuing the work of the surrealists, Debord developed the idea of 'the derive' by deliberately introducing the notion of chance or disorder into the urban activity of walking. Derives, he wrote, involved 'playfulconstructive behavior and awareness of psychogeographical effects, and are thus quite different from the classic notions of journey or stroll' (Debord 2006: 62). This was a deliberate assault on the rationality of the Cartesian prescription to 'always walk in as straight a line as possible' (Descartes 1998: 14). There was also something mildly shamanistic or spiritual about this process: getting in touch with and penetrating one's environment in a way not normally possible. In a sense then, employing such tactics was deemed a deliberate strategy to reclaim lost individuality and to frustrate the very rationality of the urban. This meant mapping it in an entirely different way with reference to a fresh set of coordinates. In essence then, walking is about looking to uncover something else; this can only be achieved by traversing the cityscape in a disinterested way. It also hints at a kind of connectivity or totality between walker and landscape that a normal map cannot capture. As Jenks (1995: 154) notes:

> The city begins, without fantasy or exaggeration, to take on the characteristics of a map of the mind. The legend of such a mental map highlights projections and repressions in the form of 'go' and 'no-go' space. These positive and negative locational responses claim, in their turn, as deep a symbolic significance in the orientation of space as do the binary moral arbiters of 'purity' and 'danger' or the 'sacred' and the 'profane' in relation to the organisation of conduct. Such an understanding propels the *flâneur* towards an investigation of the exclusions and invitations that the city (as indeed the state of [post] modernity) seems to present.

To explore the city then in this way alludes to a covalence or unity between city and mind. The city mirrors the contradictions of the human psyche together with the way in which we symbolically order our lives. Within such a reading or mapping, the city is always much more than just a set of coordinates. There are similarities here with the way in which structuralism alludes to 'myth' in a very

Freudian way in terms of the unconscious mind, as a working out of conflicts in the human psyche.

This significance of walking is worth developing with reference to the work of Michel de Certeau. He argued that the city, in a Foucauldian sense, was complicit as part of a wider set of disciplinary power structures or a micro-physics of power to which the individual is subjected. For de Certeau, walking became an act of protest, a creative means of shrugging off the effects of spaces that were designed to impose power upon, scrutinize and contain the individual. As Jordan (2016: n.pag.) notes:

> De Certeau was explicit in understanding his 'itineraries' as transgressive forays across what he saw as an oppressive and hegemonic 'urbanistic system'. The city was an extension of socio-cultural power structures, a vast system for the regulation of its citizens. The walk was therefore an opportunity to create a 'network of an antidiscipline', de Certeau stating that his book was merely showcasing the tactical, and makeshift creativity of groups or individuals already caught in the nets of 'discipline'.

De Certeau explains this idea via his distinction between voyeur and walker. Within this dichotomy, and with particular reference to New York, the city offers contrasting experiences. Here, height becomes reminiscent of Fritz Lang's 1927 film *Metropolis*, where control over the city is exercised over a mass of workers by a small elite who live high above street level. Walking in this context, in contrast to voyeurism,

> emphasises the democratic importance of the street-level perspective to be gained from walking the city and reconnecting with individual life. In the light of this distinction it is clear how the simple act of walking can take on a subversive hue, abolishing the distancing and voyeuristic perspective of those who view the city from above. For the totalising gaze of the voyeur, who sees the city as a homogenous whole, encompasses an anonymous urban space that sees no place for individual or separate identities and which erases or suppresses the personal and the local.
>
> (Coverley 2012: 32–33)

Like Debord, de Certeau sees walking as both productive and performative. Pushing this metaphor even further, he suggests that the city was analogous to speech (de Certeau 1984: 98). Rebecca Solnit (2001: 347–48) develops this point, warning that 'if the city is a language spoken by walkers, then a post-pedestrian city not only has fallen silent but risks becoming a dead language, one whose colloquial phrases, jokes, and curses will vanish, even if its formal grammar survives'.

226

These different views of the city are linked by the idea that the human environment and subjectivities are dialogic. If speech in this context becomes constrained then its limitation is caused by particular imperatives that condition the modern age: 'The rationalist grid, so favored by modernist urban planners, enforced an instrumental rationality that was based on increasing both productivity and consumption. Creativity and individuality were replaced by and for the capitalist state' (Shortell and Brown 2014: 4).

In his discussion of globalization Zygmunt Bauman (1998) suggests that the two stages of modernity (modernity and then postmodernity) are both characterized by production and consumption. However, consumption in this latter context 'is linked not only to a global system of production, but also is the result of time-compressing technology' (Shortell and Brown 2014: 4). Rather presciently Baumann (1998: 81–82) remarks:

> That all consumption takes time is in fact the bane of consumer society – and a major worry for the merchandisers of consumer goods. There is a natural resonance between the spectacular career of the 'now', brought about by time-compressing technology, and the logic of consumer-oriented economy.

He goes on to suggest that 'the needed time-reduction is best achieved if consumers cannot hold their attention or focus their desire on any object for long; if they are impatient, impetuous and restive, and above all easily excitable and equally easily losing interest' (Bauman 1998: 81–82). These observations generate questions about how the modern city might be different and, in particular, the ways in which the imperatives of a consumer society in turn impact on the way the urban environment is planned and inhabited. Indeed, when we factor in how data, the product of continuous surveillance, is now a commodity, sold precisely with a view to providing in-depth predictions about our routes and routines, we begin to understand why Google introduced the term 'for-profit city' (Zuboff 2019: 435). As Han (2017: 21) notes, 'persons are being positivized into things, which can be quantified, measured and steered'. It is for this reason that walking holds such significance in modern psychogeography.

Psychogeography (Iain Sinclair)

Most modern psychogeographic writing is concerned with place, history, walking and the possibility of presences that cannot always be rationally accounted for. In what follows I attempt to give the reader a brief sketch of what has become a broad field and that for some writers has become too generalized. When I first interviewed him back in 2013, Iain Sinclair was keen to emphasize that the subversive, anti-capitalist nature of the psychogeographic movement had partially been lost: 'There is a hardcore term of essential meaning which has now dissolved into a generic thing that has to do with pretty much anything to do with walking, cities, concepts of geography/space' (Sinclair 2013: n.pag.). In a later exchange of e-mails he remarked that he was weary of the demands of the 'burgeoning field of psychogeography which seems to have moved from a lazy mainstream brand to an academic discipline. When, if it goes anywhere, it should try to reclaim its subversive roots' (Sinclair 2020: n.pag.). With this in mind, my own overview seeks to focus upon the subversive potential of psychogeography. This is a recurring theme that goes back as far as William Blake. As Coverley (2010: 41, 42) notes:

> Blake remaps the city as he walks its streets but, if the city is to be rebuilt as Jerusalem, then it must first be destroyed and his poems abound with apocalyptic imagery that is shaped, not merely by an anti-rationalism and anti-materialism, but also by a strong sense of political radicalism that stands in opposition to authority of every kind.

Sinclair's work forms part of this legacy; a through-line connecting Blake, Baudelaire, Surrealism, the situationists and modern psychogeography. His work foregrounds particular elements that might be used to critically remap the city and mitigate against the tyranny of rationality. This contributes to a strongly political critique of the contemporary London landscape based at least in part on the idea that it is the city's imperfections that go to triggering the form of 'possession' that he describes in what follows. His work makes many references to the ways in which commercial imperatives have exerted a topographical pull on the landscape. In what follows I want to briefly locate Sinclair within the tradition of psychogeographic writing before offering my own personalized vision of Burgess Park.

More walking

As I have already indicated above, walking has been a critical element to the situationists and psychogeography. For Sinclair too, this is an essential part of his writing process. In an interview with the *Fortean Times* in 2001, Sinclair described the method of his historio-psychological approach to documenting London:

> The way I work, it's largely coming from place, my system has always been to meditate on certain areas or structures, then to visit them and walk about until I get into some kind of slightly mediumistic contact with the story. If it's going to work you

find that your intuitions are usually pretty good [...] It is a form of mild possession when it works and the care comes in revising it. But certainly that's how it operates.

(Sinclair 2001: n.pag.)

This emphasis on walking suggests a kind of active dialogue or compact with the past, via the retelling and curation of stories and history: 'Only when we walk with no agenda does the past return' (Sinclair 2018a: 44). It also stresses the defining nature of the environment we make to live in and how our relationship with it is contingent, organic and mutually constitutive:

I had my own defensive magic in place, the routine of walking unresolved problems out into the city, eavesdropping on random incidents, forcing connections, and carrying annotations and photographs back to the house in which I had lived for fifty years. If we are to sustain a relationship with the buildings that precede us, we must solicit their tolerance of our intrusion. Structures ripped down leave a cloud of active dust. New builds are hungry for narrative. When that equation falters, we sicken, and search for scapegoats among the developers and architects. But the buildings and their interior spaces, bedrooms, corridors, kitchens, become evolving self-portraits, visions of how we see our better selves. Working or resting, we shape who we are, and are shaped, in exchange, by the walls that contain us. Some of the older tribes on this earth, indigenous peoples able to convert time into space, flow with the seasons, with their seminal rivers. Shelters are made and abandoned. Ancestors are always in attendance.

(Sinclair 2019: 25)

Buildings then offer powerful reminders of the lives of those who have gone before, they signify absence, disappearance, but most importantly they confer narrative upon place. The advertisements for new blocks of flats that appear online often attempt to tap into the energy that Sinclair alludes to, the 'active dust' of the past. In some instances, especially converted buildings, like the ex-headquarters of the London Fire Brigade or the gas holders at Kings Cross, the city's industrial past becomes integrated into the lived experience of these dwellings, creating a version of Auge's 'non-place'. However, two-bedroom flats in these blocks are beyond the reach of most Londoners forming part of a broader global narrative of exclusivity. As Jonathan Raban (2008) notes:

The densely populated inner-urban honeycomb – what Henry James, writing of London, once called 'the most complete compendium in the world' – has become so expensively reconstructed, so tarted up, that only people with a merchant banker's income will soon be able to live there, outside of the steadily diminishing supply of low-rent public housing.

The irrational

Sinclair's work has been described as 'occult psychogeography' and it is useful to unpack this term a little and consider why his alternative perception of the city might be of importance. The above quotation suggests that architecture is both defining and ephemeral; buildings remind us of the lives of those who have inhabited them (the ancestors), that we are merely passing through spaces and structures that will easily outlive us. Underlying this is a collective presence made visible by traces of the past, which reveal that which is hidden. This occult dimension is expressed using a vocabulary of analogous terms that allude to a kind of unseen historical continuity – spectral, haunting, ghosts and revenants. As Bond (2005: 17–18) remarks, 'Sinclair's interest in occultism, for instance, indicates his concern with the irrationality which is buried away in the nooks and crannies'. It is precisely this contingent aspect of the city that requires a particular methodology in order to reveal its secrets. As Wolfreys (1998: 140) notes, the 'psychogeography which Sinclair traces raises spectres which are always already there, revenants of the city, endlessly recalled through walking, memory and writing'. This goes some way to explaining Sinclair's role as shaman or medium: connecting with place by means of a particular, immersive process. Such a methodology responds to a city where the irrational rationality of capitalism necessitates what Adorno had identified critically as an occultism, 'a second mythology or reborn animism' (Bond 2005: 18). This is not a literal reference to headless Tudors or floating white sheets, but rather an openness to particular presences and forces that do not normally register as part of the city experience. In this context, 'to be haunted by a phantom is to remember something you've never lived through; for memory is the past which has never taken the form of presence' (Derrida cited in Wolfreys 1998: 149). Haunting here then is a reference to the effect of all those elements (histories, stories, forgotten lives) that can be uncovered via a psychogeographic mode of enquiry. The significance of this type of experience resides in its potential to disrupt or provide contradictory experiences of the city. As Wolfrey (1998: 139) notes: 'Ghosts return to disturb the idea of structure. To understand the city is to acknowledge a form of haunting, its being-spectral'. Here, a focus upon 'occultist irrationality' in Sinclair's work enables him to marshal these processes as part of an anti-capitalist critique. So, there is an added significance to Sinclair's interaction with the city, one that seeks to criticize the political or structural forces involved in reshaping the landscape but with reference to the past.

For Sinclair, the landscape of modern utopianism is largely to be strenuously resisted, especially the notion of 'the grand project'; most famously the 2012 Olympic site at Stratford. Registering that resistance can involve negotiating space in different ways. In *Ghost Milk* (2011), Sinclair documents his own history of Stratford Park, stalking the blue exclusionary fence that surrounded the Olympic site; trespassing when possible. A slightly different tactic involves the remapping and reimagining of space. This is not to glibly accept the stark logic of the map with its accuracy and measured certainty. Rather, it involves writing one's own shapes and structures on to the map in order to tease out the occult. In *Lights Out for the Territory* (2003), Sinclair imposes a triangle on London comprising the coordinates of Charlton, Chingford Mount and Abney Park. The territory is not read using a map but rather by collecting graffiti en route. In an earlier work (*Lud Heat*) Sinclair (2012) uses the locations of Hawksmoor London churches, imposing two triangles into the form of a pentagram on to a map of London. This is an attempt to uncover something more psychic, providing a resonance with a lingering doubt over the architect's rumoured occult sympathies. Bond (2005) remarks that these, perhaps playful, surrealistic gestures can be understood as a sacralization of place or a means of reenchanting the landscape. When I interviewed him in 2013 I asked Sinclair about the significance of triangulation:

ME: What is the essence of the triangulation?
SINCLAIR: I don't know that there is any logical explanation [...] it's a subjective
            feeling, putting shapes on to maps [...] I mentioned the triangle,
            shaping triangular things to make a narrative between three points.
            The point of *Lights Out for the Territory* was a decision to actually
            walk it, in that version of psychogeography rather than, as earlier,
            perhaps just looking at maps and working things out: physically to
            do these things and in that case was recording lines of graffiti, begin-
            ning to feel that you could read the city by how the graffiti changed,
            which it dramatically did over the course of that geography.

A complementary tactic to walking, triangulation forms part of Sinclair's process; a means of accessing the city's occult energies and facilitating an alternative interpretive framework.

A *changing* London

Important to this chapter, and psychogeography more generally, is a sense that London has changed in the current era; that history speaks to a certain continuity, unity or defining essence that is under threat. Other writers have expressed a similar sentiment:

In journeying about the capital, of London's rich antiquity, it is possible, surely, to believe that we have, in quite recent times, entered a phase which is completely new. The history is there, hidden like the lost rivers, but in all effective senses it has been obliterated by what London in the last half century has done to itself.

(Wilson 2005: 9)

Andrew Wilson (2005) further develops this point with reference to another aspect of London's uniqueness. Here, he talks about the first great historian of London, John Stow (1525–1605), remarking that 'he saw London as being steadily wrecked by overpopulation, overbuilding, and the greed of developers, city men, and speculators' (Wilson 2005: 27). The suggestion here is that history evidences an ongoing tension between a planned and an unplanned London: 'one of the characteristics of London has always been its degree of architectural anarchy, the fact that it has never submitted itself to a single overall plan or planner' (Wilson 2005: 35). Wilson's remarks are useful here as they allude to a sense of disorder and that London's specialness is routed in a history that has been characteristically organic and contingent. Plans to submit London to some kind of rational order or unique vision (as in say Paris or Vienna) are deemed to have failed here. Such a landscape is critical to the psychogeographic approach; it is resistant to rationalization and the threat that this poses to the layers of history that do and should define it. In the same way that surrealists sought to uncover the marvellous, there is a sense that urban life too offers a way in or passage to something magical and occulted. Such an idea has remained important to psychogeography. In relation to this, Coverley (2010: 18) notes the influence of author Arthur Machen:

Machen [Arthur] extends De Quincey's role as urban wanderer, his explorations of the city's outer limits positioning him as a direct influence upon contemporary psychogeographers such as Iain Sinclair. Machen once again seeks out the strange and otherworldly within our midst – a single street, event or object capable of transforming the most mundane surroundings into something strange or sinister, revealing that point of access, called the Northwest Passage by De Quincey, which provides an unexpected shortcut to the magical realm behind our own.

Having lived in London for close to 40 years I too have witnessed a shift. To cycle and walk the city on a regular basis (as I do) is to be surprised by the ferocity of the processes at work. Here, the city has become 'planned' in the sense that it is guided and shaped by the jealous and relentless logic of global capitalism, most notably in relation to housing. As Atkinson (2020: 2) notes:

The psychology, economy, politics and deeper operating system of the city are run more and more for money, its reason for being in many ways forgotten and its vision of the future indifferent to the plight of many of its residents.

Sinclair recognizes a dynamic at work that has taken the indigenous population unawares with a kind of tragic irony. Here, he suggests that the cityscape can be read through its graffiti:

The world is turning fast: new-build canalside towers are purchased by Chinese investors while nice middle-income English couples become boat people in a parody of crowded, deck-to-deck Asian harbours and rivers. A new white stencil among the wall-tats on the towpath: SHOREDITCH IS THE REVENGE OF FU MANCHU.
(Sinclair 2018a: 31)

This is a vision of a London where the tables of British imperialism have been turned, where intergenerational injustice means that youngsters can no longer afford bricks and mortar and are forced to explore alternatives like the growing number of canal boats. Sinclair goes on to suggest that certain capital cities, most notably London, have become suburbs of the world: 'London is a suburb of everywhere: Mexico City, Istanbul, Athens. The same malls', a place within which we become transformed 'into dumb tourists in our own midden' (Sinclair 2018a: 13). In this global landscape,

one city is another city; all the places of a fugitive life and career are a single cancerous cell. London is like that now, more a part of other expanded conurbations than of England: the real aliens are in Sunderland, Hull, Stoke-on-Trent [...] London was everywhere, but it had lost its soul.
(Sinclair 2018a: 6–7)

These 'alpha cities' (Atkinson 2020: 1) are homogenous and home to a global elite; a form of *Lebensraum* where space is set aside for those that can afford it. As Sinclair (2018a: 8) notes:

Our cities are becoming electrified iceberg liners, islands from which the underclass can be excluded; liners serviced by zero-hour contracted serfs. In time, the floating cities will be the only safe places in which to patrol the world's oceans. Sealife: perpetual tourism. With cinemas, gyms, theatres, private hospitals and cycle lanes.

Globalization, mobility and the international division of labour have then created an accompanying concierge class that, increasingly cannot afford to live in the centre of town.

233

Such an analysis might easily invoke a form of lazy bigotry, but it is important to recognize here that Sinclair's suburban analogy (or metonym) signals something more profound than nationality; it is a global capitalist class defined in terms of money, not necessarily racial or ethnic superiority, which is transforming London and the way it looks. In this way, London has become what Atkinson has described as an 'alpha city': 'Taken as a whole, this city, alongside a handful of others globally, is a key node in a global economy founded upon endless cycles of extraction and growth' (Atkinson 2020: 3).

My London (the emergence of non-places)

Drawing on my own experience and, as part of a psychogeographic commentary, I want to argue that what has disappeared from many parts of London is a sense of imperfection and, via this, a sense of the marvellous. We might even think of this in terms of seediness, the essential grit that helps form the gothic underside of any city. There is a particular dynamic at work here: after many years of mapping the strange and wonderful in London I repeatedly discover that the most seedy and gothic of London's sights eventually receive a makeover. Liz Wilson, in her book *The Sphinx and the City* (1991), references Claude Levi-Strauss's assertion that beauty in Latin American cities was a product of their wildness: 'extremes of wealth and poverty, of enjoyment and misery, made an essential contribution to this perception of the city. It was just those things that were shoddy and awful about city life that constituted its seduction, its peculiar beauty' (Wilson 1991: 5). Years after Jonathan Raban had published *Soft City* (1974), he reflected: 'My London was far seedier than it is now – an immense honeycomb of relatively inexpensive flats and bedsits, mostly contained by the perimeter of the Circle Line' (Raban 2008: n.pag.). It is precisely those aspects of ordinariness, disorder and imperfection that form the essence of psychogeographic enquiry.

A set of particular areas in London speak powerfully to a kind of flattening out: Covent Garden, the Thames/Canary Wharf, the South Bank, the Olympic site, Spitalfields, Borough Market, Brick Lane, Camden Market, Shoreditch, Arnold Circus, Bermondsey Street, Stoke Newington. I'm suggesting here that these have become 'non-places'. I use Auge's term with a degree of licence here: the spaces he cites are airports and shopping malls, places no longer characterized as 'anthropological' (Auge 2008). Non-places, he suggests, are disconnected with identity; all that remains is some gesture to the past: a name perhaps, often prominently displayed historical photographs. They do not integrate what precedes them: instead these are listed, classified, promoted to the status of 'places of memory' and assigned to a circumscribed and specific position' (Auge 2008: 63) (Figure 10.1).

Like Auge's non-place, the areas I list above impose a kind of transience upon us – our licence to be there rests upon the understanding that we are passing through or there to consume. A visit to Camden Lock shows much of the original architecture to still be intact: the remnants of a goods yard, stables and its gin industry. However, what has often happened here is a kind of hollowing out of the buildings: empty signifiers stripped of their historical intestines. The real identity of London's 'markets' and other sites is consigned to 'memory': the unappealing offal, grime, shit and industry safely gone, often moved out of the town centre to be replaced by sanitized consumer-facing retail units. In this way, Borough Market, once a source of food for its locale, has been destroyed by the supermarket; now it is a reinvented 'Borough Market' an integral part of the tourist industry. Spitalfields market, which when I worked in Artillery Lane in the mid 1980s stank of rotting fruit and veg (like the original Covent Garden Market), has long gone. What replaces it are expensive boutiques and a flawless ambience of niceness: every detail is clearly worked out, every need anticipated. Sinclair (2018a: 179) captures this in typical style:

FIGURE 10.1: Temporary display window at Mountview Academy of Theatre Arts, Peckham, referencing the erstwhile Grand Surrey canal.

One afternoon I walked to Whitechapel to see if Stephen had been visiting his office. But Whitechapel was no longer there. The whole sweep on the south side of the Spitalfields Market, apart from a tragic façade propped up as a mocking quotation, was gone. Dust. Grit. You could taste it in your mouth all the way back to Hanbury Street. And without the brewery to wash away the hurt. Heritage tourists, style scavengers and city overspill occupied the narrow pavements in puddles of noise and whelping chatter. The concrete slab of the multi-storey car park built over the site of the final Ripper murder in White's Row was a nightmare eddy of oil and filth. But this view across the open ground, towards Hawksmoor's Christ Church, had not been available in generations. And would soon be obliterated by the latest thrust of aspirational towers. Already the field of rubble was enclosed with a green fence suitable for CGI promises and upbeat slogans. Toynbee Hall was part of the outwash, a pit, a destructive upgrade.

Here, the Truman brewery no longer produces beer – the smell of malt and hops has gone; Brick Lane is infused with the aroma of every possible kind of food the world has to offer mixed in with the acrid whiff of skunk. All of these areas have been recolonized by 'beards, the barista shamen, vegan pubs and discriminating archaeologists of vinyl' (Sinclair 2019:113). A seedy multi-storey car park has been flattened offering a temporary tantalizing glimpse of Hawksmoor's church while the dosshouse opposite it on White's Row has been converted into prime student accommodation.

A slightly more literal rendition of non-place can be seen in Sinclair's account of taking a swim at London's 'Shard'. Here, Auge's idea that identity must be rigorously performed and checked is made clear:

> I swam at the golden hour. There were softly-spoken barriers and checkpoints at every stage of my ascent towards the high pool. You come off the street, away from the fumes of stalled buses, the repressed waves of anger and frustration, and into this otherness of uniformed security that is both courteous and judgemental. You are bowed through to the metal cabinet where inappropriate baggage is checked for explosives. At the reception desk, thirty-four floors up, you must present your passport. The right credit status, the digital information that moves you to the new level, is never accessible on screen. The induction process acts like a Zen filter, fine-tuning anxiety and inoculating the unwary before the next stage of enlightenment in this attempt at a Tibetan lamasery out of James Hilton's *Lost Horizon*. A copy of Hilton's 1933 romance, newly printed in Singapore and cased in a leather binder, is left beside every king-size bed.
>
> (Sinclair 2018a: 145)

The significance of this privileged and rarefied part of London resonates with Fritz Lang's *Metropolis* (1927) and H. G. Wells's 'Eloi' and 'Morlocks', a literal and spatial layering produced by the new global class system; buildings as lived metonyms for inequality. De Certeau's distinction between voyeur and walker is increasingly written into London's high-rise architecture. Here, Sinclair (2018a: 145) notes that of all the sites owned by Chinese investors (the majority of which remain empty), the Shard, 'with its easy access to the Thames and the major heritage sites', is a preferred location. In this version of London he boldly asserts that we are the tourists. As a final remark on this he jokingly ruminates on the possibility 'that hardcore Maoist cadres have chosen to destroy capitalism from the inside, by buying London and leaving it empty' (Sinclair 2018a: 145).

Burgess Park

Discovery

It was some twenty years ago that I stumbled upon Burgess Park. I say stumbled upon because I set great store by the idea of discovering things on my own terms. Such an approach acknowledges that the experience of place can be conditioned by the notion of chance rather than in terms of it being a destination. Looking to escape the confines of Camberwell, where I lived at the time, I would often walk from my home with no firm plan or route in mind; if something caught my eye in the distance I would walk towards it – a kind of gentle, unpressured 'derive'. I quickly found that certain areas would compel me to return. In this way I became intrigued by an irregular-shaped piece of greenery that appeared just off the Old Kent Road: Burgess Park. There was something unusual or quirky about the space that I couldn't put my finger on: the road I took (Trafalgar Avenue) bisected the park creating a separate strip of land that disappeared in the direction of Peckham town centre (see Figure 10.2). Tracing this odd corridor on a later walk took me under two elegant Victorian bridges before it terminated opposite Rye Lane and the erstwhile Jones and Higgins department store (see Figure 10.3).

I was later to learn that this was the waterless remains of the Peckham branch of the Grand Surrey canal. On a subsequent trip to Postman's Park in the city of London, a place where the unsung heroes of the city are celebrated, I discovered that 'Richard Farris, labourer, was drowned in attempting to save a poor girl who had thrown herself into the canal at Globe Bridge Peckham May 20, 1878' (Figures 10.4 and 10.5).

Typically, the long walk from Camberwell would end in a small cafe that formed part of Chumleigh Gardens; the lady who ran it was a jazz aficionado

FIGURE 10.2: Burgess Park – a psychogeographic map. Credit: Sinead McDonnell.

FIGURE 10.3: Faded glory of the Jones and Higgins department store.

FIGURE 10.4: Globe Bridge.

FIGURE 10.5: Tribute to Richard Farris, Postman's Park, London EC1.

would occasionally put on Sunday gigs. The walled gardens were an oasis, the perfect spot to take a book and laze away an afternoon. This small collection of almshouses, a female asylum originally, seemed somehow widowed in the large green expanse of the park. In 2006, and partly because the area appealed, I bought

239

a flat on the edge of the park on Sumner Road, which afforded me great views of the park and northwards across the city (Figure 10.6).

Having moved to Peckham I would regularly explore the park and began to learn more about its history. Walks home from work would involve deliberately choosing alternative routes across the space. From my north-facing balcony I would pick out local landmarks and see if I could locate them. Prominent local architecture, especially churches, become a source of wonder and fascination. I began to map these out: St George's on Wells Way (1824, Francis Bedford), St Peter's in Walworth (1823, John Soane), St Mark's, Camberwell (Norman Shaw, 1879), St James's in Bermondsey (1829, James Savage) and, further afield, St George's in the East (1729, Nicholas Hawksmoor) and St Anne's Poplar (1730, Nicholas Hawksmoor). Aside from walking, cycling would take me further afield, finding alternative passages out of London via the Grand Union canal, New River and River Lea.

Although I had no knowledge of psychogeography initially, my visits to certain places would produce a certain resonance; I would imagine this as some kind of atavistic energy, pretending that my current form was a reincarnation of sorts, a presence that embodied or referenced past lives. Rupert Sheldrake has written about the idea of morphic resonance, a term born out of what he describes as the science delusion: a disjuncture between science as a method of enquiry and methodology and then science as belief system, world-view or cosmology. It describes the possibility that knowledge and familiarity can be transferred diachronically

FIGURE 10.6: The author's home: Galleria Court, Peckham.

within different species in ways that scientifically cannot be explained: 'It need not be attenuated by either spatial or temporal separation between similar systems; it could be just as effective over 10,000 miles as over an inch, and over a century as over an hour' (Sheldrake 2009: 86). This is a concept that emerges from science, although I want to suggest here that it is consistent with a number of psychogeographic tropes: ley lines, lines of force, genius loci and spectrality. These all have to do with acknowledging the possibility of seemingly uncanny, gothic or irrational forces and connections that shape our conscious experience of place. While my perceptions may not be an example of morphic resonance they do signal a certain suspension of disbelief that is important to psychogeography. This concerns our subjective and emotional responses to the city environment: how it makes you feel, why certain areas can attract or fascinate at a visceral level. To explore this more fully requires an openness to place that embraces the unscientific; a range of concepts that deal with what might be unseen or occulted.

The ancestral connection

For me the appeal of Burgess Park was its 'otherness': it wasn't like most of its London counterparts. Yes, there was a lake, but no evidence of Victorian civic pride in the form of wrought iron bandstands or statues of prominent local figures; it seemed to comprise a myriad number of disconnected vistas. Many of the park's structures were unusual: there was a seemingly superfluous bridge over a central pathway, redundant roads and curbing (Figures 10.7 and 10.8).

These elements evinced a strange poetics: a certain level of disorder, chaos and irrationality, evidence of what Tim Charlesworth would mournfully refer to as 'the lost city of Burgess Park' (Friends of Burgess Park 2015). My exploration of the local area and its history coincided with another personal project: tracing my family ancestry. The two activities began to intersect in unexpected ways. If I explain to the reader that my name (Sledmere) is rare then the significance of what follows becomes clearer. The family derives originally from an eponymous village in Driffield in Yorkshire and latterly York. In the nineteenth century an exodus took place with one branch of the family (headed up by Thomas Sledmere) relocating to the East End of London and then drifting over to the more respectable North London. Extensive research in York suggested that the migration south was the product of a particular Victorian epoch of poverty that lasted from the 1840s to the 1870s, the result of an experiment in free-market economics known as the great transformation (Gray 1998: 5). On tracing the family lineage online I was surprised to learn that an Alfred Harry Sydney Sledmere had been married to Sarah at St Peter's (see above), his child Charlotte had been baptized at St George's

FIGURE 10.7: The bridge to 'nowhere'.

FIGURE 10.8: The bridge to 'nowhere' (from the path of the old canal).

and she had, in turn married at St Mark's. This discovery accentuated the magnetic pull that the area already exerted over me; there was a strange sense of connection, a confirmation of something more visceral generated by the thought of tracing my ancestor's footsteps; a morphic resonance possibly (Figures 10.9 and 10.10).

FIGURE 10.9: St George's Church.

These kinds of discovery are manna to the psychogeographer who seeks to bring together disparate elements as part of the effort to get in touch with an area. It provides Sinclair's 'active dust' a serendipitous moment of continuity between past and present. To seek out and discover these Sledmeres is to conjure up something spectral that helps provide 'an indissoluble marriage with place' (Sinclair 2003: 208). To develop this idea, I want to reference Derrida's (1994: 10) notion of hauntology. This draws upon Shakespeare's *Hamlet* where the presence of a ghost (Hamlet's father) evidences the way in which the natural order of things has been disrupted by the murder of his father, the king. Derrida uses Hamlet's assertion that 'the time is out of joint' (Shakespeare cited in Derrida 1994: 25) to signify 'the breaking down of delineations between past, present and future time' (Shaw 2018: 7). He then uses this to emphasize the spectral nature of Marx's work. The main thrust of this is to provoke a discussion about the failures of communism and how capitalism had emerged in a temporally inevitable way due to its perfectibility. This 'end of history' (Fukuyama 1992) orthodoxy presents several fixed ideological or ontological ideas to which Derrida aims to provide a fresh theoretical response. Derrida suggests that the logic of the spectre can function to disrupt all oppositions, between the sensible and the insensible, the visible and the invisible. It mounts a challenge to the 'now' and the notions of progress that attach to capitalism. Shaw (2018: 2) notes that 'hauntology gestures toward the "agency of the virtual", since the spectre is not of the here and now, yet is capable of exercising a spectral causality over the living'. The spectral in this context functions as

FIGURE 10.10: St Mark's Church.

a metaphor and describes a particular kind of encounter that can facilitate 'new ways of thinking about the past, present and future' (Shaw 2018: 5). Haunting then becomes a means of interrogating 'modern forms of dispossession, exploitation, repression, and their concrete impacts on the people most affected by them and on our shared conditions of living' (Gordon cited in Shaw 2018: 12–13).

Pursuing this hauntological motif, I want to suggest that Alfred, Sarah and Charlotte Sledmere are revenants: not alive certainly but also not completely dead. Having spent many hours online pouring over birth, marriage and death certificates the ancestral becomes spectral. Treading the same hallowed ground, imagining the lives of Alfred, Sarah and Charlotte is, I suggest, a form of haunting.

The information about these characters is there to be had but, in a very Derridean fashion, it is marginal, surfacing and returning only via the digital affordances of Ancestry.com. The narrative provided here is partial but evocative; like most of my female ancestors (dressmakers, glove sewers, seamstresses), Charlotte and Sarah work with their hands. Alfred, an ex-army policeman, disappears to the United States but Sarah describes herself as 'widowed' in the 1911 census; a compelling narrative emerges, a future project perhaps (see Figure 10.11). The little I can gather in my dialogue with these ghosts suggests a working-class existence, part of a healthy vibrant community. Here it is tempting to conclude that the park was born out of necessary post-war slum clearances. However, in his account of the space, Tim Charlesworth makes it quite clear that this was not the case (Charlesworth 2000a: 26–27). Moreover, comments on the 'I Grew Up in Peckham' Facebook page sound a notable lament concerning the loss of housing and forced migration out of the area. In hauntological terms there is a sense in which these narratives of displacement resonate with the more recent processes of gentrification that too have forced local working-class people out of the area.

Burgess Park: A brief history

The history of the park is unusual; unlike most London parks, which have been carefully planned, Burgess park is something of an afterthought. A glance at a

FIGURE 10.11: All that remains of Chumleigh Street (residence of Sarah and Charlotte Sledmere at the time of the 1911 census).

map from 1864 or aerial shots from the 1930s show the entire area to be covered with houses and streets; so what happened? By the end of the Second World War significant parts of the area had been destroyed by bombing and, as part of the Abercrombie plan (formulated in 1943), the decision was taken to create a large brownfield park – 'a St James of the south'. The post-war landscape of South London was, like much of London, heavily industrialized, with factories in close proximity to residences. The evolution of this landscape had been largely unplanned and organic. Burgess Park was no exception and included 'Sun Pat' peanuts and R. Whites Lemonade among its industries (Charlesworth 2000a: 21–22). The Abercrombie plan prioritized the idea of improving urban living via the creation of neighbourhood zones, which would include access to parks. Where necessary, overpopulation and slum living would be tackled by the building of new towns just outside of London and by moving industry away from the centre. Traces of Burgess Park's industrial past can be found in a variety of buildings and chimneys that still survive close by. The creation of the park addressed many of the prerogatives I have just described; a process of only very gradual, piecemeal change ensued for some years mainly due to a lack of funding. The recent master plan, and that I discuss below, addressed many of these perceived shortfalls.

From the outset, Burgess Park was considered an unsafe space (Charlesworth 2000b) – the unusual layout and lack of lighting rendered it a no-go area after dark. It is characteristic of psychogeographic writing to foreground this gothic underside of urban life often in conjunction with fictional representations that connect in some way with the area. In Daniel Barber's *Harry Brown* (2009), Michael Caine features as an ex-marine who looks to take on local crime in the 'Death Wish' vigilante tradition. The film's opening scene portrays a couple of drugged-up 'yoots' on a motorcycle exiting the Aylesbury Estate on to Burgess Park. For pleasure they terrorize and then shoot a mother taking her child across the park. The film references this and other wanton acts of cruelty in its portrayal of a dystopian South London estate. Later research online highlighted an uncanny resonance with real-life gangland activities in the area. In the 1960s, alongside the feared Kray twins, a South London crew had emerged in the form of the Richardson brothers Eddie and Charlie. Operating from Peckford Metals, a scrapyard in New Church street (see Figure 10.2), the gang, which included 'Mad' Frankie Fraser,[1] became notorious for torturing anyone who stood in their way. Victims were subjected to a variety of punishments including electric shocks, the removal of teeth with pliers and being nailed to the floor. Charlie Richardson was sent down for 25 years in 1966 after a jury was convinced that he had indeed tortured his victims (McVicar 2012). Peckford Scrap Metal is no longer there, in its place a dull block of modern flats. Nearby at 33 Addington square, Charlie and Eddie ran a private drinking club where they kept two dancing bears that escaped into Camberwell one night

(Friends of Burgess Park n.d.). It is hard to walk the parameter of the park and not imagine either the screams of the Richardsons' victims or the reaction of Camberwell residents at the medieval sight of a dancing bear.

Burgess Park and gentrification

Burgess Park forms part of a larger area that has and continues to exert an influence on the park's evolution. I want to suggest here that the characteristics of the park are entirely sympathetic to and reflective of changes to its immediate surroundings.[2] Inspired by the Ville Radieuse and Corbusian ideas of a modernist utopia, planners in London set out to transform the city as part of a radical housing initiative. From the early 1960s to the mid 1970s a variety of estates were built in the borough of Southwark, two of which border on to Burgess Park: the North Peckham Estate and the Aylesbury Estate. The former was considered a success initially although by the 1980s it had earned a reputation necessitating a substantial makeover in the 1990s. The Aylesbury Estate, like the nearby Heygate Estate in Elephant and Castle, is in the process of being redeveloped. Loretta Lees and Hannah White (2019) have argued that these evidence a broader set of neo-liberal imperatives. They have led to 'large-scale dispossessions due to the gentrification of council estates, what Elmer and Dening (2016) have called 'the London clearances' (Lees and White 2019). At the time of writing (2020), the Old Kent Road (on which is one of the main entrances to the park) is undergoing a planning consultation process that, if successful, will lead to a number of new high-rise blocks; initial plans referenced a block that was 44 storeys high. The model adopted here is one of allowing housing associations and private developers to assimilate responsibility for social housing by including a percentage of affordable homes. This in turn creates a tendency to build upwards in order to compensate for this condition. There appears to be little or no long-term considered assessment of the impact of such buildings. Julia Kollewe (2019: n.pag.) noted in *The Guardian* that 'there is no London-wide policy on tall buildings – councils decide whether they want them. Suburban Bromley has none, while Tower Hamlets, half the size, has plenty'. Moreover, council targets for the provision of new homes mean that there is considerable pressure on them to be supportive of such planning applications. Indeed, the relationship between council and large developers, like, Lendlease, has attracted considerable criticism (Novara Media 2013).

London often feels overcrowded although, in interviews with two Southwark councillors,[3] it was pointed out to me that its density is comparatively low: that of Paris is about twice that of London (CRBE n.d.). However, Londoners know, from their daily commute, that much of it is already beyond capacity in terms of pollution and lacks the requisite transport infrastructure to keep growing its population. It also overlooks both the historical lessons learned in the 1960s and 1970s about the efficacy of high-rise developments together with the need to build new towns. Amnesia in this regard is partly the product of the idea that increasing density and decreasing urban sprawl facilitate the possibility of the compact city. This is an idea often associated with Richard Rogers and laid out in his book/ manifesto, *Cities for a Small Planet* (1997). I mention this here, in part because, as Neuman (2005: 11) notes, 'recent attempts to halt sprawl and improve urban livability have been made by compact city, smart growth, healthy community, and new urbanist advocates'. Indeed, the notion of 'smart' is critical in arguing the case for compact cities that are justified on ideas of sustainability and other principles that underpin the 'smart growth movement'. These include mixed usage, a variety of transport options, inclusive housing options and collaboration with the communities concerned. Critical here is the notion of discrete communities with a strong identity and where most facilities (and possibly work) are within walking distance.

The orthodoxy or feasibility of compact cities is predicated upon ideas of sustainability, which are difficult to define and implement (Neuman 2005). While the notion of smart is integral to the Mayor of London's 2016 Plan this is something of a moving feast as different mayoral incumbents, serving varying political imperatives, produce different iterations of the plan. Previous versions, especially that delivered by Boris Johnson, have been criticized for their vagueness or 'lack of bite' (Holman 2010: 37). Here, there is a sense that the compact city and assumptions of sustainability that underpin it are by no means a given. It has been suggested that it 'is by no means clear that the compact city is the best or only way forward' (Jenks et al. 2005: 4). Neither is it a given that the compact city can achieve the kind of sustainability required. I mention this here largely because such a vision of the city relies on the notion of 'smart', a term that by no means offers a consistent or perfect vision. In his cautionary account of 'radical technologies' Adam Greenfield (2017: 55) warns against some of the assumptions that underpin the smart city and the idea it can be conditioned by 'perfect knowledge'. This is to suggest that whatever knowledge or mastery can be achieved under a heading of smart, 'there are and can be no Pareto-optimal solutions for any system as complex as a city' (Greenfield 2017: 55). Commenting on the all-important 'internet of things', he adds that many of its manifestations 'seem like an attempt to paper over the voids between us, or slap a quick technical patch on all the places where capital has left us unable to care for one another' (Greenfield 2017: 60).

Alongside doubts about the efficacy of the compact city exist concerns about fairness and equality in relation to the regeneration plans of which they form a part. The example of the Heygate and other estates in London tend to suggest that inclusivity in the form of affordable housing features strongly in the rhetoric of developers. However, critics are keen to accuse developers of profiteering while paying lip service to notions of equality when determining who can live on regenerated estates. Rather than automatically housing displaced residents from the Heygate Estate within the new development, the majority found themselves being decanted into other areas and even other parts of the country (Novara Media 2013, 2014). Southwark Council (2007) too seems complicit in terms of promoting exclusivity. Fred Manson, Southwark's former regeneration guru, famously declared that Elephant and Castle needed 'a better class of person' (Gann 2014). It was also hinted to me by Barratt Homes when purchasing my property that the council were looking to attract middle-class people into the area. While mixed-usage developments are intended to overcome potential ghettoization of city spaces, Niall Martin notes that neo-liberal urbanism tends towards the creation of two types of space. The first concerns shaping cities as global players that compete with their international counterparts for investment. The second are areas that are increasingly fragmented and populated by disenfranchised citizens and where public services suffer as money is redirected to entrepreneurial activities (Martin 2015: 145). Similarly, Atkinson (2020: 1–2) notes that 'the city's more or less unrivalled position has come about through its single-minded pursuit of the rich, creating seamless, open borders for capital while ignoring its working population and its poor'.

Burgess park: The revamp

In the time that I have lived in the area (fourteen years) the park has been revamped: a major re-landscaping that took place in 2010 and a series of other incremental changes. As I have already indicated, it is impossible to consider this in isolation from the wider efforts to regenerate the area. I want at this point to look briefly at some of the changes and imperatives that formed part of this initiative. Burgess Park received around £11 million as part of its regeneration (Crisp 2020: n.pag.) and, predictably, a period of planning and consultation preceded this. The wider rationale behind the changes was described in terms of 'Structure, Identity, and Programmatic Diversity' (LDA Design 2010). These headings covered an exhaustive list of imperatives, many of which were sensible and justifiable. More specifically:

- a park with a strong identity;
- a coherent park with a clear spatial structure;
- a park that links with its surroundings including the new structure of the Aylesbury Estate;
- a better used and more biodiverse lake;

FIGURE 10.12: Neate St, Burgess Park, in 2016.

- a sports hub that acts as a destination;
- a play hub that acts as a destination;
- a park that feels safe;
- a park for the future that is rooted in its past and in its communities;
- a robust and maintainable park.

The park's unusual evolution meant that it had some 42 entrances leading into what was considered to be an irrational space. Crossing the width of the park from north to south was deemed to be difficult and many of the original roads were still present in an uneven but pleasantly illogical configuration (2 km of curbing was ultimately removed from the park). The views into the park were deemed to be uninviting and the entrances not properly integrated into the surrounding areas. After a period of major disruption and some unexpected problems, the park was considered finished (Figures 10.12 and 10.13).

For my own part, I was struck by how the changes conflicted with my own dis-covery and enjoyment of the park. Its eccentricities and unexplained architecture had been described in the master plan as 'follies':

Burgess Park is the largest reclaimed park in Europe, and through its evolutionary process of being converted from a place of industry to a 51 hectare park, many of the significant buildings and follies have remained in the park. These buildings and follies include the listed St George's Church, impressive Bath House/Library, the

FIGURE 10.13: Neate St, Burgess Park, after the master plan makeover in 2020.

> listed Lime Kiln, Chumleigh Gardens and the historic Canal Bridge. (LDA Design
> 2010: n.pag.)

London, like all cities, is a kind of palimpsest, a text inscribing itself on itself. In this context there are no follies but rather a kind of unity where the past and its remnants possess a sacred character. As Sinclair notes in relation to Haggerston Park in Hackney:

> London is an organic entity, it's a kind of prescient being, the whole city is inter-
> linked: the material, the brick, the story of that brick and where it's come from in
> these columns, the grasses, the nature of the cobblestones, the memory of the park as
> being a gas and coke works, the bombs that fell here, the lives of the park keepers, the
> grass, the dog walkers, the joggers; all of this is making one complete organic thing.
> If you take out one element the whole thing trembles and loses some of its force.
>
> (Sinclair 2017: n.pag.)

Rather than being purposeless indulgences, funded by some aristocrat, these ghostly 'follies' were the clues for and starting point of a powerful narrative about the area, one that was in danger of being systematically effaced.

One of the striking characteristics of the above master plan list is the staggering amount of different prerogatives that it seeks to address – it is worth interrogating these a little. What a park may or may not be is arguably not fixed but the product of the social and historical conditions that prevail at the time it is conceived. As I have indicated in this chapter, my own ideas of what the park should be were borne out of the psychogeographic. That is a space which provides not only visual and ecological respite from the city but that is free from precisely those concepts that have a tendency to condition every other aspect of our lives. This is in turn connected with an imaginative rendering of the space: viewing it as an integral part of a totality comprising the various lives and histories that have shaped it.

Mine is then essentially a critical position, one that views each of the imperatives listed above as connected in some way with contemporary neo-liberal thinking. Although it does not use the word 'brand', the idea of a distinct identity for the park follows an instrumentalist or governmental logic whereby every facet of human life is rendered as part of a taxonomy of quantification and control: we must know exactly what it is and what it does. Without this it cannot merit any kind of funding (or justify the funding it has received): we must know if it is providing value for money. Moreover, and like commercial brands, it must have a purpose that, at the very least, offers the potential to evolve into areas with which it is not necessarily connected. When writing about the compact city, Richard Rogers (1997: 17) astutely observed that

> contemporary architecture and planning might be expected to express our common philosophical and social values. But in fact, most recent transformations of cities reflect society's commitment to the pursuit of personal wealth. Wealth has become an end in itself rather than a means of achieving broader social goals.

I want to suggest here that both the park and the area it is intended to service are all, in some way, the product of neo-liberal prerogatives; these shape not only the environment but increasingly the individual. Here, overpriced homes, investment bonds for foreign criminals and oligarchs will overlook a space that has increasingly been shaped by the ideas of individual fitness; a kind of stay-active hegemony that it is difficult to criticize. Gym-related equipment has been installed throughout the park (Figure 10.14). This common-sense transformation of park into an open-air gym seem natural enough, even smart.

However, the neanderthal grunts of rugby players and the sound of leather on willow remind me that sport is the ultimate embodiment of competition. As Chomsky notes in the documentary *Manufacturing Consent* (Achbar and Wintonick 1992): 'Sport [...] a way of building up irrational attitudes of submission to authority, and group cohesion behind leadership elements – in fact, it's training in irrational jingoism. That's also a feature of competitive sports.'

Burgess Park's acquisition of a branded identity is coterminous with an ideological shift that looks to transform everyone into a brand. Davies (2014: 22) refers

FIGURE 10.14: COVID-19 quarantined gym equipment.

to this as a form of 'economic imperialism', whereby techniques developed for the study of 'markets and commercial activity' can 'travel beyond their initial sphere of application' and be applied to the individual. Similarly, Couldry (2010: 13) talks about the way 'self-branding' now figures in marketing discourse, creating the sense in which each of us now functions as a commodity in relation to other competing individuals. Other critics have viewed this in terms of a necessary response to precarity and 'to the post-Fordist regime of flexible accumulation and neoliberal political practices' (Hearn 2008: 497). It is difficult to criticize the pursuit of individual health but the way in which Burgess Park has been increasingly given over to competitive sports speaks to the rigours of the human market place: the necessity of peak fitness in order to stay in the game. As Greenfield (2017: 15) notes, such a quest concerns the transformation of the individual 'into all-but-fungible production units, valued only in terms of what they offer the economy'. As philosopher Byung-Chul Han (2017: 21) notes: 'Today, everyone is an auto-exploiting labourer in his or her own enterprise. People are now master and slave in one.'

Currently there is little in the way of smart technology being deployed by Southwark Council in relation to the park. It might be argued here that smart in the context of individual fitness means that data can flow from many individual sites. Phones, fitbits, smart bracelets all address the common-sense desire to enjoy health. But, as Greenfield (2017: 35) cautions, 'against the backdrop of late capitalism, the rise of wearable biometric monitoring can only be understood as a disciplinary power traversing the body itself and all its flows'.

Conclusion

In addressing the notion of the smart city I have made the case for a psychogeographic approach. I began by providing an overview of the ideas and philosophy that have informed this field. My thinking here was to stress a number of tropes that help facilitate a modern critical reading of the smart city together with the political and social context in which it is embedded. The value of these is that they provide an alternative perspective upon what the ideal city space might look like, one that is not predominantly conditioned by technology, rationality and science. As per the surrealists, we might think of such a place as defined by the marvellous, the eternal, the infinite, the inconceivable, the heavenly and even the transcendent. And, also like the surrealists, we must be open to notions of disorder, irrationality, even the Dionysian. These function to delineate the city as a spiritual place, evidence of a possible 'continuum between the real and the supernatural or mythical' (Metzidakis 1996: 32). They also provide a cautionary and timely allusion to the possibility that perfect knowledge and mastery is unobtainable: we cannot know everything.

A psychogeographic approach facilitates the reimagining of a city without always invoking the forward-looking gaze provided by science or logic. As Iain Sinclair (2019: 71) puts it, 'holding out against the know-nothing, value-nothing futurism represented by Taylor Wimpey'. Imagining means factoring in the past; stressing the importance of the city as palimpsest, a kind of text inscribed upon multiple layers that represent the city's dense history. Here, history and spirit of place speak to a notion of unity; to silence the city's ghosts is to stifle our critical awareness of what is happening in the present.

In order to throw some of the above areas into relief I have given a critical account of a specific area: Burgess Park. The value of such an approach takes a number of different forms. First, it gives primacy to the individual and subjective accounts of the outside world. Such an approach might even be seen as a form of bricolage where the writer assembles a number of different signs, 'analyzing them and re-presenting them in another narrative that may operate against the grain of the dominant discourse that functions in a specific space' (Richardson 2017: 3). These elements have been gathered by walking, observing, photographing and bringing together my own narrative of the area. True to a psychogeographic approach, I have drawn upon the personal with the suggestion that voices from the past, ranging from my own ancestors to the Peckhamites who once lived in the area, are useful in offering a different and more inclusive perspective; it is precisely these that can be so systematically effaced in the rush to create a smart city.

I have also suggested that the smart city is underpinned by a number of assumptions that connect it in a very profound way with neo-liberalism; I make no apologies for using the term. Here there is a certain triumphalist discourse that attaches to science, defining it uncritically as a form of progress. And yet, the London I have been describing is rife with inequality. Traditional working-class areas, which Burgess Park and the surrounding area once were, are being developed in ways with which the smart city is complicit. A certain lip service is paid to inclusivity but the reality is a city where expensive real estate serves as an investment vehicle for foreign elites. The spectral voices of 1960s gangs like the Krays and the Richardsons remind us that crime is no longer the local affair it once was but is now global, its proceeds squirrelled away in safe, few-questions-asked investment havens like London. The resulting city space is deterritorialized, no longer anthropological, as the ties between people and place become weak-ened and altered. Flats lie empty while the original and inconvenient communi-ties are decanted elsewhere. In Neil Smith's *The New Urban Frontier Gentrifica-tion* (2005), he draws a useful parallel between 'frontiers' in the eighteenth- and nineteenth-century West and then in the late-twentieth-century inner city. Using the term 'revanchist' he suggests that the city can be thought of as territory that can be cast historically in a particular way (i.e. working-class neighbourhoods), only to be reclaimed by capital. He goes on to point out that 'economic expan-sion today no longer takes place purely via absolute geographical expansion but rather involves internal differentiation of already developed spaces' (Smith 2005: n.pag.). A similar point is made by Jonathan Raban (2008: n.pag.) via his concept of the soft city, where he remarks that in 'Dr Johnson's, Dickens's or my London – the rich lived cheek by jowl with the poor, a source of daily interest and entertainment to both parties'. The price of London property and a lack of genuinely affordable social housing increasingly suggest that this is no longer the case. If there is a frontier in this context it is driven by capital as it probably always has been. Moreover, this urban frontier must be thought of as a global one: 'gentrification is a thoroughly international phenomenon' (Smith 2005: xv), entirely consistent with the channelling of the world's wealth into the hands of a small global plutocracy.

The changes I am describing go against the grain of history, signalling a type of city that is qualitatively new. As Sinclair notes (2018b):

We've lost one kind of organic city that had existed for hundreds or thousands of years; it's really become something quite new and strange; in some ways interesting now but different [...] now it's clearly a world city rather than a British city and also very largely electronic, digital, fast synapse.

At the same time, he describes this as 'The Last London' (Sinclair 2018a), sug-gesting a certain resignation and a degree of powerlessness. Against a perceived

255

'endism' we need to think about a 'smart' version of the city that is not always technology led but more mindful of the fact that it is inhabited by individuals who often experience it in unique ways; rather like the psychogeographic reading I have offered in this chapter. Jonathan Raban, writing retrospectively about his seminal text, *The Soft City* (1974), had argued that the city was a place

> where every citizen created a route of his or her own through its potentially infinite labyrinth of streets, arranging the city around them to their own unique pattern. That was why it was soft, amenable to the play of each of its residents' imagination and personal usage.
>
> (Raban 2008: n.pag.)

Such a vision is perhaps less likely within the confines of a smart city, one that is carefully planned but increasingly determined by data and algorithms.

NOTES

1. Until his death, Fraser could regularly be seen walking his dog in Burgess Park; a visual testimony to the banality of evil.
2. In an interview with local councillor Barrie Hargroves he indicated that funding for a revamping of Burgess Park was at least in part contingent upon the regeneration of the nearby Aylesbury Estate.
3. Interview with Mayor of Southwark Barrie Hargrove 29 May 2020 and Councillor Richard Leeming 15 June 2020.

REFERENCES

Achbar, M. and Wintonick, P. (1992), *Manufacturing Consent*. Montreal: National Film Board of Canada, Necessary Illusions Productions.

Aragon, L. (1987), *Paris Peasant*, London: Picador Classics.

Atkinson, M. (2020), *Apha City: How the Super Rich Captured London*, Verso: London.

Auge, M. (2008), *Non–Places: An Introduction To Supermodernity*, London: Verso.

Barber, D. (2009), *Harry Brown*, London: Marv Partners in association with the UK Film Council, HanWay Films, Prescience and Framestore Features.

Bauman, Z. (1998), *Globalization: The Human Consequences*, Cambridge, UK: Polity Press.

Bond, R. (2005), *Iain Sinclair*, Cambridge, UK: Salt Publishing.

Calzada, I. (2019), 'Data spaces and democracy', *RSA Journal*, 2, n.pag., https://medium.com/rsa-journal/data-spaces-and-democracy-178054e9fc2b. Accessed 1 March 2020.

CBRE (n.d.), 'Density in cities', https://www.cbre.co.uk/research-and-reports/our-cities/density-in-cities. Accessed 1 March 2020.

Certeau, M. de (1984), *The Practice of Everyday Life*, Berkeley, CA: University of California Press.

Charlesworth, T. (2000a), *The Story of Burgess Park: From an Intriguing Past to a Bright Future*, London: Groundwork.

Charlesworth, T. (2000b), Telephone interview with the author, 19 May.

Couldry, N. (2010), *Why Voice Matters: Culture and Politics after Neoliberalism*, London: Sage.

Coverley, M. (2010), *Psychogeography*, Harpenden: Pocket Essentials.

Coverley, M. (2012), *The Art of Wandering: The Writer as Walker*, Harpenden: Oldcastle Books.

Crisp, S. (2020), 'Online interview', 9 June [Susan Crisp is a committee member of 'The Friends of Burgess Park'].

Danto, A. (1981), *The Transfiguration of the Commonplace*, Cambridge, MA: Harvard University Press.

Davies, W. (2014), *The Limits of Neoliberalism*, London: Sage.

Debord, G. (2005), *Society of the Spectacle*, London: Rebel Press.

Debord, D. (2006), 'Theory of the derive', in K. McNabb (ed.), *Situationist International Anthology*, Berkeley, CA: Bureau of Public Secrets, pp. 62–7.

Derrida, J. (1994), *Specters of Marx*, London: Routledge.

Descartes, R. (1998), *Discourse on Methods and Meditations on First Philosophy* (4th ed.), London: Hackett.

Elmer, S. and Dening, G. (2016), 'The London clearances', City, 20, pp. 271–77.

Friends of Burgess Park (n.d.), 'Burgess Park in the shade', http://www.friendsofburgesspark.org.uk/revitalisation/dont-put-burgess-in-the-shade/?utm_source=Friends+of+Burgess+Park+Newsletter&utm_campaign=ec8d7017e0-EMAIL_CAMPAIGN_2020_01_30_08_03&utm_medium=email&utm_term=0_c7314231e2-ec8d7017e0-152741513. Accessed 16 June 2020.

Friends of Burgess Park (2015), 'The making of a modern park', 23 May, http://www.bridgetonowhere.friendsofburgesspark.org.uk/podcast/the-making-of-a-modern-park/. Accessed 16 June 2020.

Fukuyama, F. (1992), *The End of History and the Last Man*, London: Hamish Hamilton.

Gann, T. (2014), 'I helped shut down the MIPIM housing show because cities should be for people, not profits', *The Independent*, 16 October, https://www.independent.co.uk/voices/comment/i-helped-shut-down-the-mipim-housing-show-because-cities-should-be-for-people-not-profits-9798297.html. Accessed 1 March 2020.

Gray, J. (1998), *False Dawn: The Delusions of Global Capitalism*, London: Granta.

Greenfield, A. (2017), *Radical Technologies*, London: Verso.

Han, B.-C. (2017), *Psychopolitcs: Neoliberalism and New Technologies of Power*, London: Verso.

Harman, G. (2005), 'Heidegger on objects and things', in B. Latour and P. Weibel (eds), *Making Things Public: Atmospheres of Democracy*, Cambridge, MA: MIT Press, pp. 268–71.

Hearn, A. (2008), 'Insecure: Narratives and economies of the branded self in transformation', Continuum: Journal of Media & Cultural Studies, 22: 4, pp. 495–504.

Holman, N. (2010), 'The changing nature of the London plan', in K. Scanlon and B. Kochan (eds), London: Coping with Austerity, London: LSE, pp. 29–40, http://eprints.lse.ac.uk/30790/. Accessed 1 March 2020.

Hopkins, D. (2004), Dada and Surrealism: A Very Short Introduction, Oxford: Oxford University Press.

Jenks, C. (1995), 'Watching your step: The history and practice of the flâneur', in C. Jenks (ed.), Visual Culture, London: Routledge, pp. 142–60.

Jenks, M., Burton, E. and Williams, K. (2005), 'Compact cities and sustainability: An introduction' in M. Jenks, E. Burton and K. Williams (eds), Compact Cities and Sustainability, Oxford: Spon Press, pp. 2–5.

Jordan, S. (2016), 'Hacking the streets: "Smart" writing in the city', First Monday, 21:1, https://firstmonday.org/ojs/index.php/fm/article/view/5529/5192. Accessed 15 June 2020.

Kollewe, J. (2019), 'High times: 76 tall buildings to join London's skyline in 2019', The Guardian, 5 March, https://www.theguardian.com/business/2019/mar/05/tall-buildings-london-skyline-2019. Accessed 15 June 2020.

Lang, F. (1927), Metropolis. Berlin: UFA GmbH.

LDA Design (2010), 'Burgess Park masterplan', http://moderngov.southwark.gov.uk/documents/s79358/Appendix%203%20Burgess%20Park%20Master%20Plan.pdf. Accessed 16 June 2020.

Lees, L. and White, H. (2019), 'The social cleansing of London council estates: everyday experiences of "accumulative dispossession"', Housing Studies, 35:10, pp. 1701–22.

McVicar, J. (2012), 'Charlie Richardson was evil, he should have been tortured like his victims', The Independent, 22 September, https://www.independent.co.uk/news/uk/crime/charlie-richardson-was-evil-he-should-have-been-tortured-like-his-victims-8163896.html. Accessed 17 June 2020.

Martin, N. (2015), Iain Sinclair: Noise, Neo-Liberalism and the Matter of London, London: Bloomsbury Academic.

Metzidakis, S. (1996), 'Breton's structuralism', L'Esprit Créateur, 36:4, pp. 32–42.

Neuman, M. (2005), 'The compact city fallacy', Journal of Planning Education and Research, 25, pp. 11–26.

Negus, K. and Pickering, M. (2004), Creativity, Communication and Cultural Value, New York: Sage.

Nietzsche, F. (2000), The Birth of Tragedy, Oxford: Oxford University Press.

Novara Media (2013), 'Regeneration, gentrification and social cleansing', 11 October, https://novaramedia.com/2013/10/11/regeneration-gentrification-and-social-cleansing/. Accessed 6 March 2020.

Novara Media (2014), 'Housing and gentrification: discussing the Heygate Estate', 8 March, https://novaramedia.com/2014/03/08/housing-and-gentrification-discussing-the-heygate-estate/. Accessed 16 June 2020.

Raban, J. (1974), *Soft City: What Cities Do To Us, and How They Change the Way We Live, Think and Feel*, London: Hamish Hamilton.

Raban, J. (2008), 'My own private metropolis', *Financial Times*, https://www.ft.com/content/247bc052-64dc-11dd-af61-0000779fd18c. Accessed 1 March 2020.

Richardson, T. (2017), 'Assembling the assemblage: Developing schizocartography in support of an urban semiology', *Humanities*, 6:47, pp. 1–14.

Rogers, R. (1997), *Cities for a Small Planet*, London: Faber and Faber.

Rorty, R. (2005), 'Heidegger and the atomic bomb', in B. Latour and P. Weibel (eds), *Making Things Public: Atmospheres of Democracy*, Cambridge, MA: MIT Press, pp. 274–75.

Shaw, K. (2018), *Hauntology: The Presence of the Past in Twenty-First-Century English Literature*, London: Palgrave Macmillan.

Sheldrake, R. (2009), *Morphic Resonance: The Nature of Formative Causation*, Canada: Park St Press.

Shortell, T. and Brown, E. (2014), 'Introduction: Walking in the European city', in T. Shortell and E. Brown (eds), *Walking in the European City: Quotidian Mobility and Urban Ethnography*, Farnham: Ashgate, pp. 1–20.

Sinclair, I. (2001), Interview by *Fortean Times*, http://www.classiccafes.co.uk/Psy.html. Accessed 1 March 2020.

Sinclair, I. (2003), *Lights Out for the Territory*, London: Penguin.

Sinclair, I. (2011), *Ghost Milk: Calling Time on the Grand Project*, London: Penguin.

Sinclair, I. (2012), *Lud Heat*, Cheltenham: Skylight Press.

Sinclair. I. (2013), Interview with the author, London, 23 August.

Sinclair. I. (2017), 'Iain Sinclair: the last London', *London Review of Books*, 28 March, www.youtube.com/watch?v=B05mdDG8k2s&t=315s. Accessed 1 February 2020).

Sinclair, I. (2018a), *The Last London*, London: Oneworld Publications.

Sinclair, I. (2018b), London Overground [documentary] (dir. J. Rogers), 13 July, https://www.youtube.com/watch?v=lJZ-BHAgslo&t=913s. Accessed 1 March 2020.

Sinclair, I. (2019), *Living with Buildings*, London: Profile Books.

Sinclair, I. (2020), E-mail to the author, 20 May.

Smith, N. (2005), *The New Urban Frontier Gentrification: Gentrification and the Revanchist City*, London: Taylor and Francis.

Solnit, R. (2001), *Wanderlust: A History of Walking*, London: Penguin Books

Southwark Council (2007) ,'Design and access statements: Supplementary planning document', September, https://www.southwark.gov.uk/assets/attach/1809/Design_and_access_statements-SPD.pdf. Accessed 1 March 2020.

Wilson, A. (2005), *London: A Short History*, London: Phoenix.

Wilson, E. (1991), *The Sphinx and the City*, London: Virago Press.

Young, D. (1995), 'Ethnographic surreality, possession and the unconscious', *Visual Anthropology*, 7:3, pp. 191–207. https://doi.org/10.1080/08949468.1995.9966648. Accessed 1 March 2020.

Wolfreys, J. (1998), *Deconstruction: Derrida*, New York: Macmillan Education.

Zuboff, S. (2019), *The Age of Surveillance Capitalism*, New York: Public Affairs.

Afterword
Decentring the Smart City

Rob Kitchin, National University of Ireland, Maynooth

At the core of this book has been the entwining of imaginaries and equality with respect to present and future cities, particularly their incarnation as smart cities. Collectively the authors have sought to imagine a different kind of smart city, both in terms of how we think about them and their realization. At the heart of this reimagining is equality and a belief that smart cities should serve the interests of all their residents in equal measure. Unsurprisingly, the concepts of power and capital, and the counterpoints of justice, citizenship and democracy, feature prominently in the discussion. Like much of the critical literature on smart cities, the chapters make the case that smart cities as presently conceived and realized predominantly serve the interests of companies and states, which often work in tandem within a neo-liberal framing.

Smart cities are the latest, technology-driven incarnation of entrepreneurial urbanism that recasts the entire urban realm as a market, rather than the urban being a place where markets function (Kitchin 2015; Shelton et al. 2015). Within neo-liberalism what were public infrastructures and services, run by the state for public good, are outsourced, privatized and deregulated, delivered through private, for-profit operators. The state facilitates this marketization of infrastructure and services, and their increasing technocratic nature, through its restructuring and neo-liberal re-orientation and state-sponsored innovation and market creation. Here, rather than act as the sole service provider, the public sector is cast as partner or broker, working in conjunction with or procuring services from the private sector. Bodies such as the EU's European Innovation Partnership on Smart Cities and Communities (EIP-SCC) promote public–private collaboration, actively seeding new marketplaces through funding mechanisms and encourage the creation of living laboratories for the trialling new technologies in order to facilitate adoption (Cardullo and Kitchin 2019b). At the same time, municipalities view the smart cities agenda and the creation of well-managed, forward facing and efficient

and optimized city infrastructures and services as a means to attract inward investment and talent and drive city-region economic development, competitiveness and
productivity (Shelton et al. 2015; Townsend 2013).

Smart city technologies also have consequences for the state's work, altering
governance practices and shifting the nature of governmentality and citizenship.
Through new technologies such as city operating systems, centralized controlled
rooms, coordinated emergency response systems, digital surveillance, predictive
policing and intelligent transport systems, how populations are managed, services
delivered and infrastructure controlled and regulated has become more technocratic, algorithmic, automated and anticipatory (predictive) (Kitchin 2014). In
turn, governmentality shifts from a disciplinary calculative regime in which people
self-regulate behaviour based on the fear of surveillance and sanction, to control
regimes in which people are corralled and compelled to act in certain ways, their
behaviour explicitly or implicitly steered or nudged through their embedding in or
use of systems (Vanolo 2014). The transformation in the organization and ethos
of government by neo-liberalism and the use of smart city technologies alters the
social contract between the state and citizens. Neo-liberal citizenship moves away
from inalienable rights and the common good towards individual autonomy,
freedom of choice and personal responsibilities and obligations defined largely by
market principles, with checks and balances that seek to limit excessive discrimination and exploitation (Ong 2006). In other words, citizens have choices and
freedoms as long as they have capital to afford them and they comply and behave
as states and markets dictate. Within the smart city then, citizens are largely cast as
consumers, although they can equally be positioned as data points to be exploited
or policed or subjects to be steered, nudged and controlled (Cardullo and Kitchin
2019a). If there is civic engagement, it is in the form of a participant, tester or
player who provides feedback or suggestions, rather than citizens being cast as
active, engaged participants (a proposer, co-creator, decision-maker or leader).

Unsurprisingly, those critiquing smart cities are concerned that their rationale
and deployment is being overly determined by the interests of companies (capital) and states (power) (Cardullo et al. 2019; Sadowski 2020; Söderström et al.
2014). For-profit systems are inherently underpinned by the logics of capitalism
in which inequalities and discrimination are a built-in design feature for accumulating capital. Smart cities are a key contemporary component of the second circuit of capitalism, core to property development and a spatial fix for capital. It is
no coincidence that new greenfield cities and large urban regeneration projects are
cast as smart city developments (Coletta et al. 2019; Datta 2015; Wiig 2017). The
technologies themselves enact the logics and practices of platform and surveillance
capitalism, extracting profit through service arrangements with states and the data
of citizens (Sadowski 2020). In the latter case, additional value is accrued through

'data colonialism', in which the process of accumulation is achieved by enclosing communal and personal resources, and data dispossession with no renumeration and monetization as a feature of a product or service, control of this exploitative relationship residing with the data extractor. Through the use of data-driven, algorithmic technologies, the surveillance gaze and levels of control are deepened with respect to managing populations, enhancing state power. Smart systems are often differentially focused on managing particular populations (along the lines of race, ethnicity, gender, disability, etc.), automating and deepening inequalities (Eubanks 2017). And in more authoritarian regimes, smart city technologies provide a means to target, track and corral the location, movement and activities of people in fine detail (Liang et al. 2018).

As such, while companies and states promote their technologies as being citizen-centric, there is significant scepticism concerning such rhetoric (Kitchin 2015). In general, what is meant by 'citizen-centric' is a weak form of stewardship (delivering on behalf of citizens) and civic paternalism (deciding what is best for citizens), rather than citizens being meaningfully involved in the vision and development of the smart city (Shelton and Lodato 2019). Instead, the underlying ethos remains steadfastly neo-liberal, with the notion of 'citizen-centric' being an empty signifier, giving the impression of participatory intent while the actual structural relations remain firm.

The chapters in this book provide a critique of the neo-liberal smart city and its framing and imaginary of the future city. They draw on the ideas and ideals of justice, citizenship and democracy to imagine a smart city that strives for equality and fairness. As with data activism and data justice, they divide into two approaches for realizing their vision – those that seek to recast the smart city, inverting the ethos and use of smart city technologies (e.g. Caldwell, Chapter 7; O'Shea, Chapter 5; Smith et al., Chapter 9), and those that are more oppositional to the notion of smartness and the deployment of smart city technologies (e.g. Dare, Chapter 1; Sledmere, Chapter 10; van Ditmar, Chapter 2).

Milan and van der Velden (2016) identify two main classes of data activism. The first, proactive data activism, uses open government data and creates its own datasets to seek political action and social change, co-opting the techniques of data science, states and companies to range back against them. The second, reactive data activism, seeks to challenge, undermine and dismantle present asymmetrical arrangements of data power and politics through political protest and legal challenge. Similarly, D'Ignazio and Klein (2020) chart the differences between data ethics and data justice. Data ethics aims to make data-driven systems fairer, accountable and transparent. However, it locates the source of ethical issues in individuals and technical systems, and pursues solutions that are procedural in nature (e.g. through data governance structures and legislation). D'Ignazio and

Klein (2020) contend that the focus on procedures and compliance works to secure power rather than challenging and transforming it as their components and solutions can be captured by vested interests to serve their own ends. Moreover, the solutions pursued deal with symptoms without tackling root causes, curtailing only the worst excesses of data capitalism and data power without fundamentally changing them. In contrast, data justice is organized around a different set of concepts – justice, oppression, equity, co-liberation and reflexivity. These concepts locate the source of ethical issues in unequal and uneven structural power and work towards dismantling them and putting in place alternative arrangements. In other words, they challenge data power rather than securing it and are more difficult to co-opt.

Most visions of the citizen-centric smart city follow the proactive data activism and data ethics approach. They seek to facilitate the co-option of smart city technologies by citizens and encourage the adoption of regulatory and compliance mechanisms for governing the smart city centred on notions of bias, fairness, accountability and transparency (Kitchin 2016; Townsend 2013). Rather than being oppositional to the smart city and the use of digital technologies to mediate urban life, such an approach is about re-envisioning and orientating the smart city so that they are fair and proportionate in their operations. For others, this approach of co-option and regulation reifies existing structural relations, rather than challenging and transforming them (see Cardullo et al. 2019). It places the emphasis on technical and procedural interventions, ignoring the wider neo-liberal political economy and capitalist relations that underpin smart city deployments and sustains inequalities. They posit that there will be no fundamental shift in the inequalities inherent in present visions of smart cities, which will continue to serve primarily the interests of companies and states, without wider political change, therefore the logics and realization of the smart city needs to be opposed and alternative urban visions forwarded.

What the latter suggests is the need to decentre the smart city, where decentring 'is to 'see through' technology and position it in relation to systems of oppression, whose norms and values are wired in' to smart city initiatives (Gangadharan and Niklas 2019: 895). In other words, we need to move away from the reification of technology and how it can be co-opted and regulated, instead situating smartness within the wider (re)production of social relations (Gangadharan and Niklas 2019). We need to stop casting 'smartness' and digital technologies in a privileged, significant independent role and recognize that they are the agents of wider structural forces. This requires us to focus on and imagine the future city in a more holistic sense, and how smartness might or might not be a means of realizing a fairer, more open and tolerant city. Rather than trying to work out how to insert equality into smartness, instead the focus is squarely on equality and reconfiguring structural relations and figuring out how smart technologies can be used to create equality and equity *in conjunction* with other kinds of interventions, such as social, economic and environmental policy, collaborative planning, community development, investment packages, multi-stakeholder engagement and so on.

The issues facing cities are not going to be fixed through technological solutionism, but a multifaceted approach in which technology is one just one component (Morozov and Bria 2018). Homelessness is not going to be fixed with an app; it requires a complex set of interventions of which technology might be one part, along with health care and welfare reform, tackling domestic abuse and a shift in the underlying logics of the political economy (Eubanks 2017). Congestion is not going to be fixed with intelligent transport systems that seek to optimize traffic flow, but by shifting people from car-based travel to public transit, cycling and walking. Similarly, institutionalized racism channelled and reproduced through predictive policing will not be fixed solely by tinkering with the data and algorithms to make them more robust, transparent and fairer, but by addressing institutionalized racism more generally and the conditions that enable it (Benjamin 2019). In such a decentred perspective, platform and surveillance capitalism are not framed as separate and distinct forms of capitalism, and racism expressed through smart urbanism is not cut adrift from the structural logics and operations of institutionalized racism (understood in purely technical and legal terms). Rather, smart city technologies and their operations are framed with respect to capitalism and racism per se, and the solutions are anti-capitalist alternatives and anti-racism in which smart city technologies might or might not play some part.

This is not to say that a proactive activism/ethics approach centred on smart city technologies has limited value. The efforts and ideals of civic media, citizen science and citizen-led projects to develop their own and co-opt smart city technologies, along with initiatives to tackle biases and seek fairness, transparency and accountability in corporate and state systems, inherently has utility. But as D'Ignazio and Klein (2020: 61) make clear, they are 'inadequate on their own' to address the injustices enacted and reproduced through smart city initiatives. Instead, they need to be approached in a decentred way, framed in relation to wider structural conditions and coupled with more radical ideas and interventions in order to create a more just and equal society. This requires a developing different imaginary for creating equitable cities in which smart technologies play some role rather than necessarily being front and centre. The chapters in this book provide some routes on to this path, but there is much work still to be done.

REFERENCES

Benjamin, R. (2019), *Race After Technology*, Cambridge, UK: Polity.

Cardullo, P., di Feliciantonio, C. and Kitchin, R. (eds) (2019), *The Right to the Smart City*, Bingley: Emerald.

Cardullo, P. and Kitchin, R. (2019a), 'Being a "citizen" in the smart city: Up and down the scaffold of smart citizen participation in Dublin, Ireland', *GeoJournal*, 84:1, pp. 1–13.

Cardullo, P. and Kitchin, R. (2019b), 'Smart urbanism and smart citizenship: The neoliberal logic of "citizen-focused" smart cities in Europe', *Environment and Planning C: Politics and Space*, 37:5, pp. 813–30.

Coletta, C., Heaphy, L. and Kitchin, R. (2019), 'From the accidental to articulated smart city: The creation and work of "Smart Dublin"', *European Urban and Regional Studies*, 26:4, pp. 349–64.

Datta, A. (2015), 'New urban utopias of postcolonial India: "Entrepreneurial urbanization" in Dholera smart city, Gujarat', *Dialogues in Human Geography*, 5:1, pp. 3–22.

D'Ignazio, C. and Klein, L. F. (2020), *Data Feminism*, Cambridge, MA: MIT Press.

Eubanks, V. (2017), *Automating Inequality: How High-Tech Tools Profile, Police, and Punish the Poor*, New York: St Martin's Press.

Gangadharan, S. P. and Niklas, J. (2019), 'Decentering technology in discourse on discrimination', *Information, Communication & Society*, 22:7, pp. 882–99.

Kitchin, R. (2014), 'The real-time city? Big data and smart urbanism', *GeoJournal*, 79:1, pp. 1–14.

Kitchin, R. (2015), 'Making sense of smart cities: Addressing present shortcomings', *Cambridge Journal of Regions, Economy and Society*, 8:1, pp. 131–36.

Kitchin, R. (2016), *Getting Smarter About Smart Cities: Improving Data Privacy and Data Security*, Dublin: Data Protection Unit, Department of the Taoiseach.

Liang, F., Das, V., Kostyuk, N. and Hussain, M. M. (2018), 'Constructing a data-driven society: China's social credit system as a state surveillance infrastructure', *Policy and Internet*, 10:4, pp. 415–53.

Milan, S. and van der Velden, L. (2016), 'The alternative epistemologies of data activism', *Digital Culture & Society*, 2:2, pp. 57–74.

Morozov, E. and Bria, F. (2018), *Rethinking Smart Cities: Democratizing Urban Technology*, New York: Rosa Luxemburg Stiftung, http://www.rosalux-nyc.org/rethinking-the-smart-city/. Accessed 30 March 2021.

Ong, A. (2006), 'Mutations in citizenship', *Theory, Culture & Society*, 23:2–3, pp. 499–505.

Sadowski, J. (2020), *Too Smart: How Digital Capitalism Is Extracting Data, Controlling Our Lives, and Taking Over the World*, Cambridge, MA: MIT Press.

Shelton, T. and Lodato, T. (2019), 'Actually existing smart citizens: Expertise and (non)participation in the making of the smart city', *City* 23:1, pp. 35–52.

Shelton, T., Zook, M. and Wiig, A. (2015), 'The "actually existing smart city"'. *Cambridge Journal of Regions, Economy and Society*, 8:1, pp. 13–25.

Söderström, O., Paasche, T. and Klauser, F. (2014), 'Smart cities as corporate storytelling', *City*, 18:3, pp. 307–20.

Thatcher, J., O'Sullivan, D. and Mahmoudi, D. (2016), 'Data colonialism through accumulation by dispossession: New metaphors for daily data', *Environment and Planning D*, 34:6, pp. 990–1006.

Townsend, A. (2013), *Smart Cities: Big Data, Civic Hackers, and the Quest for a New Utopia*, New York: W.W. Norton & Co.

Vanolo, A. (2014), 'Smartmentality: The smart city as disciplinary strategy', *Urban Studies*, 51:5, pp. 883–98.

Wiig, A. (2017), 'Secure the city, revitalize the zone: Smart urbanization in Camden, New Jersey', *Environment and Planning C: Politics and Space*, 36:3, pp. 403–22.

Contributors

Dr Glenda Amayo Caldwell is an associate professor in architecture, and the academic lead research in the School of Architecture and Built Environment, Faculty of Engineering at the Queensland University of Technology (QUT). She is an architecture and design scholar with internationally recognised expertise in physical, digital, and robotic fabrication, leading Industry 4.0 innovation through human-centred research in design robotics and media architecture. She is a design lead at the Advanced Robotics for Manufacturing (ARM) Hub. Glenda is the co-leader of the QUT Design Lab's Design Robotics and Digital Fabrication Research Program and the author of numerous publications in the areas of media architecture, urban informatics, and design robotics. Originally from Pittsburgh, PA, USA, Glenda lives in Brisbane, Australia with her husband, two sons, and giant labradoodle, Rubio. She is thankful to all her collaborators, participants, colleagues, supporters, friends, and family who have contributed to making her research meaningful and fulfilling.

Chris Chesher is senior lecturer in Digital Cultures in the Department of Media and Communications at the University of Sydney. His research interests in emerging media technologies are informed by media studies, cultural studies, science and technology studies and urban studies, and he has recently focussed on topics including smart city, smart home, mobile media and social robotics. In urban studies he has published on smart street furniture, comparisons between the mediation of space by satnavs and computer games, and an analysis of mobile phones at a U2 concert taking an actor-network theory approach.

Dr Alma Clavin is an urban geographer and social sciences researcher in the School of Geography UCD. Her research and practice deals with grassroots urban sustainability. Alma has worked for a number of public, private and non-governmental organisations in Ireland and the UK on community planning, energy and sustainability issues. Alma's research interests, although rooted in the discipline of geography, have been interdisciplinary in nature, merging the fields of geography, art, architecture, planning and design. She has published in academic journals and contributed to edited volumes on topics such the impacts of urban grassroots food growing initiatives on human agency and wellbeing. Currently her main research activity involves engaging with practitioners and theorists to enhance critical participative enquiry in everyday urban environments. Most recently she has coordinated an Environmental Protection Agency (EPA) funded collaborative action research project, creating a community-led greening strategy in Dublin city. Alma continues to research and work with inner city communities to explore local greening deficits and the particular health and wellbeing impacts of greening for residents living in high density housing complexes.

ELEANOR DARE has taught arts and technology related subjects since 2007, at Goldsmiths, UAL, the OU, RCA and UCL. Eleanor was formerly Reader in Digital Media and Head of Programme at the RCA and currently works at Cambridge, Faculty of Education and Central Saint Martins. Eleanor has published many papers and chapters addressing themes of critical computing, pedagogy and the neo liberalisation of Higher Education.

DR DELFINA FANTINI VAN DITMAR is a design researcher and lecturer at the Royal College of Art, Design Products + Futures Programme. Delfina is a transdisciplinary researcher, whose work focuses on the tensions between 'smartness', design, society, architecture and the environment. She has a BA in Biology and completed a year of an MFA at Konstfack University in Stockholm. She also holds a PhD from the RCA with a thesis entitled 'The IdIoT'. The thesis investigated the socio-political implications of technological 'smartness' and the algorithmic processes, characterised as the 'Algorithmic Paradigm', which are starting to permeate our bodies and the central infrastructure of our homes and cities. Specifically, her research questioned and critically analysed the embedded epistemology of Internet of Things (IoT) technology. She has been a crit and visiting lecturer in several institutions, including The Bartlett, Architectural Association, Goldsmiths, Brighton University, Manchester School of Art, University of Canterbury, Liverpool University, Critical Media Lab Basel and TU Berlin among others.

DR SUSAN FLYNN is a lecturer at the School of Education and Lifelong Learning at Waterford Institute of Technology. She is also a research associate of the Equality Studies Centre at University College Dublin, where she completed her PhD in Equality Studies, examining digital media, inclusion, and professionalism. Her current research focuses on the tensions and inequalities that digital technologies produce. Previous edited collections include *The Body Onscreen in the Digital Age* (2021); *Critical Pedagogy, Race, and Media: Diversity and Inclusion in Higher Education Teaching* (2021); *Surveillance, Architecture and Control: Discourses on Spatial Culture* (2019); *Surveillance, Race, Culture* (2018); *Spaces of Surveillance: States and Selves* (2017).

JUSTINE GANGNEUX is a research associate at the Urban Big Data Centre at the University of Glasgow. She has a background in Sociology, with her research interests sitting at the intersection of digital sociology, critical data studies, governance, and urban studies. Before joining UBDC, Justine worked on various research projects in areas such as digital media, data literacy, youth studies, smart cities, and governance. Her most recent research project examined Scottish local government's engagement with data in response to the Covid-19 pandemic, focusing in particular on arising data uses, needs, and capabilities, and emergent forms of (collaborative) governance. Justine has published in international journals including Big Data & Society; Information, Communication & Society, the Journal of Youth Studies; and Sociological Review.a

FRED GARNETT started teaching about the social impact of technology in 1984. When the web came along he started building web-based learning projects, and was part of the London Borough of Lewisham project "Citizens Connect" looking at how the Internet could develop active citizenship and building the TaLent Community Grid fir Learning. He became Head of Community Programmes at the UK Department of Education in 2000, helping build digital learning centres and online platforms, also advising DCMS, the British Library, Home Office, the Tate & Kew Gardens on early digital strategies. He was made a Royal Society of Arts Fellow for "innovative and creative work in community learning" In 2002 he helped build a social-network for learning which was rejected by the UK government. That team became the Learner-Generated Contexts Research Group looking at social-media models of learning, In 2011 he developed the Ambient Learning City project in Manchester. This work was subsequently developed as Participatory Smart Cities with Bristol and Lisboa. His Learning City 2.0 work was part of the Timisoara City of Culture 2021 bid. In 2020 he wrote Digital Learning: Architectures of Participation with Nigel Ecclesfield. He is currently advising an Academy Trust on post-pandemic strategies.

DR MATTHEW S. HANCHARD is a research associate at the University of Sheffield School of Sociological Studies (iHuman institute). He currently works on the Wellcome Trust funded 'Orphan drugs: high prices, access to medicines and the transformation of biopharmaceutical innovation' project (219875/Z/19/Z). Matthew's research interests include critical data studies, digital society and digital media, science and technology studies (STS), the sociology of medicine/

health and illness, and novel methodologies. He also has a strong commitment to promoting open science and open data practices in qualitative social research.

DR RICHARD HAYES is currently vice president for strategy at Waterford Institute of Technology. He is a graduate of Maynooth University and University College Dublin, Ireland, from which he received a PhD for a thesis on American theatre. He has lectured in a number of higher education institutions in Ireland and abroad and has published articles and essays on many aspects of Irish and American literature. He has in more recent years focused in his scholarly activity on aspects of urban and regional development and has a particular interest in the relationship between higher education institutions and the regions in which they are based.

JUSTINE HUMPHRY is a senior lecturer in digital cultures in the Department of Media and Communications at the University of Sydney. Justine researches the cultures and politics of digital media with a focus on digital inequalities and the social consequences of smart, mobile and data-driven platforms in everyday life. She has extensively researched mobile communication and homelessness and collaboratively researched mobile apps and antiracism, smart homes and voice assistants, and mobile robots in public space. She was the co-chief investigator of the 'Smart Publics' USyd/Glasgow partnership funded project (2019-2020) investigating the design, uses and governance of smart street furniture in Glasgow and London. Her book: *Homelessness and mobile communication – Precariously Connected* is contracted with Palgrave MacMillan for publication in 2022.

SIMON JOSS is professor of urban futures in the Department of Urban Studies at the University of Glasgow. His research interests encompass urban governance, 'smart' and 'sustainable' cities, and the use of data in policy and planning. Simon is associate director of the Urban Big Data Centre (University of Glasgow), a research hub and national data service co-funded by the UK's Economic and Social Research Council. He is member of the British Standards Institution's Smart and Sustainable Cities committee."

DR CARLA MARIA KAYANAN is a political-economic geographer with strong interests in the spatial organisation of work under a tech-economy and the resultant landscapes of urban inequality. Currently, she is a postdoctoral research fellow for the School of Geography at Ireland's University College Dublin where she is examining how Dublin's tech-sector development contributes to issues of housing affordability, accessibility and rising homelessness, as well as studying new emergent metropolitan governance structures resulting from Ireland's National Planning Framework. Carla has informed policy as a researcher for the Brookings Institution Metropolitan Policy Program and the Coalition for Smarter Growth, has contributed to policy formation on tax increment financing for the Michigan State Senate, and has liaised with UN Special Rapporteurs to protect human rights for indigenous peoples through Mexico City's *Centro de derechos humanos Miguel Agustin Pro Juárez*. Carla holds a PhD in urban and regional planning from the University of Michigan, an MA in social sciences from the University of Chicago and a BA in sociology and Spanish language and literature from the University of Maryland. Her work appears in scholarly journals, media outlets, and in policy papers.

ROB KITCHIN is a professor in Maynooth University Social Sciences Institute and Department of Geography. He was a European Research Council Advanced Investigator on the Programmable City project (2013–2018) and a principal investigator on the Building City Dashboards project (2016–2020) and for the Digital Repository of Ireland (2009–2017). He is the co-author or co-editor of 31 academic books, and co-author of over 200 articles and book chapters. He has been an editor of *Dialogues in Human Geography*, *Progress in Human Geography* and *Social and Cultural Geography*, and was the co-editor-in-chief of the *International Encyclopedia of Human Geography*. He was the 2013 recipient of the Royal Irish Academy's Gold Medal for the Social Sciences.

MANUEL LARANJA graduated in engineering from the Higher Institute of Technology, Universidade de Lisboa, with an MBA degree from the Warwick University, UK and a DPhil on technology and innovation policies from SPRU-Science Policy Research Unit at the University of Sussex, UK. He was director of the National Innovation Agency Portugal and currently occupies a full time teaching position at ISEG, Lisbon School of Economics and Management, Universidade de Lisboa as associate professor for management and policies of entrepreneurship and innovation. He also worked for more than 10 years as an advisor at the Prime Minister's Office, at the Ministry of Economy and at the Lisbon and Tagus Valley Regional Coordination Commission, in issues relating to the Technology and Innovation Policies and Management of Structural Funds. He currently teaches industrial strategy, innovation management and innovation policies and coordinates a masters on management and industrial strategy. He has published three books and many articles in high impact journals such as *Research Policy*. His main scientific interests are on entrepreneurial discovery, ecosystems, Smart Specialisation Policies for regional and national economic and social development.

He is founder of the ULab ISEG for transformative change in individuals, organisations and the society.

Sophia Maalsen is an ARC DECRA fellow and senior lecturer in the School of Architecture, Design and Planning at the University of Sydney. She is currently researching how the translation of computational logics and technologies is being applied to 'hack housing' and address issues of housing affordability and innovation. Her research is predominantly situated at the intersection of the digital and material across urban spaces and governance, housing, and feminism. She is interested with the way digital technologies mediate and reconfigure housing, the urban and the everyday.

Peter Merrington is a lecturer in the Business of the Creative and Cultural Industries at the University of York. Previously he was a Research Associate in the School of Social & Political Sciences at the University of Glasgow. His work is situated at the intersection of visual culture, media history and cultural studies, focusing on questions of film, art, place, labour, technology and creative practice. He was the Assistant Director of AV Festival, a leading international festival of contemporary art, film and music in North East England and he received a PhD in Fine Art from Newcastle University in 2016.

Niamh Moore-Cherry is an associate professor in urban governance and development at the School of Geography, University College Dublin and honorary professor at the Bartlett School of Planning, University College London. Her research is focused on understanding the governance of urban (re)development, metropolitanisation and its outcomes. She has a strong record in policy analysis and community engagement and her current work focuses on metropolitanisation in Ireland, urban governance, and the implications for spatial planning and quality of life in city-regions. Niamh leads a team in UCD School of Geography examining the relationship between *Cities, Governance and Sustainability* and has significant experience in working at the policy-practice-research nexus. She is the author of *Dublin Docklands Reinvented* (Four Courts Press, 2008), has co-edited three books and has papers published in leading international journals including among others: *Urban Studies, Land Use Policy, Regional Studies, European Planning Studies, Planning Practice and Research* and *European Urban and Regional Studies*. Niamh is a member of the Social Sciences Committee, Royal Irish Academy, and is a past president of the Geographical Society of Ireland.

DR EOGHAN CONOR O SHEA is an architect and lecturer who has practised in Kilkenny, Dublin, New Zealand and other exotic places in the world for almost 20 years. He currently lectures in the Department of the Built Environment in the Institute of Technology Carlow, and part-time on universal design at the Dublin School of Architecture at Technological University Dublin. His research interests have most recently focused on universal design evaluation methodologies at different scales within built environments.

ALAN REEVE is reader in planning and urban design at Oxford Brookes University. He has a background in English literature, with a BA from Leeds University, which he took in the late 1970s, and then taught, and in architecture and urban design, in which he has another first degree, a masters and a PhD. He ran the masters programme in urban design for a number of years, and has taught for three decades in this field. He has published book chapters as well as peer-reviewed journal articles, and undertaken research in urban theory, urban management, and regeneration and in topics related to place and identity. His current research interests continue to be around urban theory; and he is engaged in writing and research project on hauntology and design guidance at the urban scale; the application of phenomenological theory to the understanding of place atmosphere; and aesthetic justice in housing design.

ADRIAN SLEDMERE teaches at the London College of Communication (part of the University of the Arts). His main home is the advertising degree but he also contributes his expertise to a range of undergraduate and post-graduate courses in the school of media. For Adrian, research is largely an excuse to combine a passion for exploring London with a commitment to lifelong learning. Here, he is strongly focussed on the city with a particular emphasis upon the psychogeographic. In a previous life he worked as a musician and producer, collaborating with several major artists, before answering the call of academia. This continues to inform his research where he is also concerned with the political economy of the music industry, branding and how these areas figure within a neo-liberal context. He continues to dabble in music, contributing guitar and other elements to various projects.

CARL HAYDEN SMITH is the director of the Learning Technology Research Centre (LTRC) and principal research fellow at the Institute for Creativity & Technology, Ravensbourne University London. His research focuses on the relationship between technology and the human condition. He is developing a new form of Posthumanism called Hyperhumanism, which uses technology as a catalyst for developing our own innate human abilities. Carl has 20 years' experience conducting R+D into the application of hybrid technologies for perceptual, cognitive and creative transformation. Raising over £10 million in research funding, Carl has worked on numerous large-scale Leonardo LifeLong Learning, Erasmus+, FP7, XPRIZE and Horizon European projects including: Wearable Experience (WEKIT-ECS), REAP, AR4EU (Code Reality), Hobs Academy (LLDC), Hyperhumanism, Contextology (Context Engineering), Double Consciousness, Holotechnica. Academy, Technomancy.Club, Seventh Ray and the Museum of Consciousness. LTRC specialise in generating new forms of media including: Neuroadaptive Mixed Reality Training, Natural Media and Wearable experience (WE). Carl has given over 300 invited public lectures, conference presentations and keynotes in 40 countries and published more than 100 academic papers. His research interests include embodied cognition, spatial literacy, umwelt hacking, sensory augmentation, artificial senses and body hacking.

BRIDGETTE WESSELS is professor of social inequality in the digital age at the University of Glasgow. She has undertaken research in many areas of digital and social change, including digital and urban spaces, smart and connected homes, e-services, telehealth and data and digital literacies. Her most recent book is *Communicative Civic-ness: Social Media and Political Culture* (Routledge, 2018).